The Politics of Central Europe

Sage Politics Texts

Series Editor
IAN HOLLIDAY
University of Manchester

SAGE Politics Texts offer authoritative and accessible analyses of core issues in contemporary political science and international relations. Each text combines comprehensive overview of key debates and concepts with fresh and original insights. By extending across all main areas of discipline, SAGE Politics Texts constitute a comprehensive body of contemporary analysis. They are ideal for use on advanced courses and in research.

The Politics of
Central Europe

Attila Ágh

SAGE Publications
London · Thousand Oaks · New Delhi

SAGE Publications Ltd
6 Bonhill Street
London EC2A 4PU

SAGE Publications Inc.
2455 Teller Road
Thousand Oaks, California 91320

SAGE Publications India Pvt Ltd
32, M-Block Market
Greater Kailash – I
New Delhi 110 048

British Library Cataloguing in Publication data

A catalogue record for this book is available from the British
Library

ISBN 0 7619 5031 1
ISBN 0 7619 5032 X (pbk)

Library of Congress catalog card number 98-060274

Typeset by Type Study, Scarborough, North Yorkshire
Printed in Great Britain by Redwood Books, Trowbridge, Wiltshire

Summary of Contents

Contents

List of Tables

List of Appendices

List of Chronologies

PART ONE

AN INTRODUCTORY OVERVIEW

1

The Central European and Balkan Regions in Transition

CONTENTS

The concept of Central Europe

The collapse of state socialism in Central and Eastern Europe has changed European politics as a whole beyond recognition. The bipolar world system split Europe in two parts, 'Western' and 'Eastern'. Its disintegration, however, has re-unified Europe in the 1990s – at least in principle, since nowadays all European countries accept democracy and market economy as major organizing paradigms of social life, and a series of pan-European institutions have been formed to safeguard these paradigms in the new democracies. Whereas in the 1970s political scientists wrote books about Western Europe as a unit – and not simply and conventionally as a country-by-country analysis – by the second half of the 1990s the first books were being published about European Politics as such, books like *European Politics* (1996) written by Jan-Erik Lane and Svante Ersson, and *The Politics of the New Europe* (1997), edited by Ian

Budge and others. These books represent the new approach by considering Europe as a whole in its converging political systems and in its
specificities, which make it so different from the other continents. Of
course, this new approach presupposes a regionalization as well, that is,
it also takes a closer look at its smaller units. The question about the
Eastern borders of Europe remains somewhat open but there is no doubt
that the Eastern half of the continent is gradually being reintegrated into
the mainstream of European political development whilst retaining a
regional diversity, that is to say that 'unity in diversity' has re-emerged
as a guiding principle in the new Europe.

The greatest political change on the world scene in the past decade has
occurred in the eastern half of Europe, in what is usually called 'Eastern
Europe'. This Great Transformation has attracted and deserved the interest of world political opinion. The changes in the most advanced countries
of the former 'Eastern Europe' have seen the successful reintegration of a
region of relatively advanced former state socialist or 'communist' countries into a Europe of free nations. This is the region known as Central
Europe, stretching from the Baltic Sea to the Adriatic Sea, comprising six
countries and almost one hundred million people. The region nearby,
called the Balkans, and comprising six other countries and about 50
million people, also belongs to the zone of Great Transformation.
Although with mixed success and many difficulties and setbacks, these
countries too have followed the changes of Central Europe after some
delay.

This book discusses the political systems of the East Central European
(ECE) and Balkan regions using the terms and theories of comparative
politics. It does not deal with developments within the real East European
region of the former Soviet Republics. 'Eastern Europe' is a political
misnomer produced by the Cold War when Europe was split into two
parts. This divide cut organic contacts between both Western Europe and
Central Europe and among Central European countries themselves.
Although the vague and overgeneralized term of Eastern Europe (EE)
has gained wide currency and is still used in journalism and even in
some scholarly literature, the term 'Central Europe' has increasingly
regained its genuine meaning. Paul Lewis, in his book *Central Europe
since 1945*, rightly explains the liquidation of Central Europe by the effect
of Cold War and its aftermath: 'Until the very end of the 1980s Central
Europe had the appearance of an historical region still submerged by the
post-war flow of Cold War currents and which only with difficulty maintained a shadowy, if distinct, identity within a broader area of Sovietized
Europe' (Lewis, 1994a: 1).[1]

The most difficult question is how to define regions within Europe,
because here not only geography matters, but also history, cultural traditions and socio-political connections, and, above all, the particular traditional views of the various West European countries about the other
regions. For example, Central Europe as a region with borders and

constituent countries has always been seen in a very different way from typical British, German and French approaches, with their different historiographies and popular prejudices.

We all live in regions, and use regional terms in both everyday language and scholarly studies, although it is often very difficult to identify them precisely. This is the same with 'Western Europe', understood by many as a political entity that includes Greece, which is in fact situated very much to the south-east. It is equally rather difficult to describe the borders of Southern Europe (SE) or to give a good definition for South-Eastern Europe (the Balkan region) in every respect. Geographically and culturally, the regional border line is not so clear between the Balkans and Eastern Europe either, for example, between Romania and Ukraine (across Moldova). Otherwise, despite the changing borders between the Russian and Ottoman empires, both empires, having a common Byzantine tradition, left deep imprints upon these countries. The contrast is bigger between the regions of Central Europe and Eastern Europe proper, but there is again a long line of interaction, especially in the case of historical Poland, which has had drastically and frequently changing borders with its Eastern neighbour(s).

The geographical definition of Central Europe is at the same time both easy and difficult. Easy since it is a North–South belt of countries between the Baltic and the Adriatic Sea, sandwiched between East and West in Europe. Difficult since it is very complicated to demarcate its true borders, since historically they have changed a lot and, as a result, the cultural borders do not completely coincide with the political ones. Lewis points out correctly that the recent notion of Central Europe, as a group of middle-developed and small-sized countries, is much more politically and socio-economically oriented than simply geographically defined:

> That later conception of Central Europe was one developed by peoples, and, eventually, nations located between the greater powers and more extensive states of Germany and Russia. In this sense, the idea of Central Europe is one that is more political and cultural than geographic in origin. It is a region that does lie in the middle of Europe ..., but geographical form has not been its most important characteristic. (Lewis, 1994a: 8)

It is commonsensical that these three regions, Central Europe, the Balkans (South-Eastern Europe) and Eastern Europe proper (the former Soviet Union without the Baltic republics), have a lot in common compared to Western Europe. One can simply look at their missing Western features and 'Eastern' backwardness. But the view which places all territories between Prague and Vladivostok on a common denominator, as a 'Prague–Vladivostok hypothesis', would miss the point of their diverging historical developments and their basically different social structures across many centuries and, therefore, the opportunity of a meaningful socio-political analysis of the recent situation as well.

The features of Central Europe

Despite all the difficulties of defining regions in Europe, we use and need these comparative terms and theories, since the regions have common features and histories, and can and should be compared to each other on this common intra-regional base.

There are some strong arguments for the existence of a Central European region in contrast to the Balkans:

1 The geographical proximity of this North–South belt, from the Baltic Sea to the Adriatic Sea, to Western Europe. This is a zone of the 'lands in between', that is, between East and West, with everyday contacts to both. It is a region of relatively small countries and short distances; and with very intensive ties to each other and to the West nearby. It is a melting pot of cultures, peoples and cuisines, uniting these small countries into a bigger unit.

2 Central Europe has always had a historical advantage compared to the Balkans because of its closeness to the West. It has always belonged, so to speak, to the first wave of Europeanization, directly following the West European models. These Western contacts in Central Europe were formed first as cultural links and penetration by Western Christianity, which has been a common cultural tradition versus the rival tradition of Eastern Christianity. Central Europe has had a semi-peripheral status in the West European world system since the sixteenth century.

3 Historically, these waves of Europeanization–Westernization have been interrupted by the periods of 'Easternization', the last case of which was the period of Sovietization. Central European countries have also the common historical tradition of the Habsburg empire with its positive and negative imprints on their societies. Central Europe has developed a modern economy, society and polity earlier and better than the Balkan countries, and this closeness to Western development has been more marked recently.

4 Altogether the Central European countries can be defined in the concrete terms of economy, society and polity as a different region from both East and West. We can describe their belated industrialization, heterogeneous modern societies and mixed political traditions from the late nineteenth century on in precise modern social science terms. This description shows their historical backwardness compared to Western Europe as well as their historical progress compared to the Balkans and/or Eastern Europe proper. Thus, industrialization had begun in Central Europe already in the second half of the nineteenth century, with increasing middle and working classes, decreasing peasantry and a partly Westernized service sector, but came in the Balkans only much later.

5 The self-identification and collective identity of Central Europeans is equally important. The Central European identity in its diverse forms

has existed since the sixteenth century, first partially connected to the Habsburg empire, then as a residual consciousness after the collapse of the empire. This undercurrent of everyday thinking was revived and reinforced by the Cold War. The ECE countries, unlike the Balkan nations, had reform cycles of 10–12 years, ending up with revolutions against the Soviet rule, such as occurred in 1956 in Hungary, 1968 in Czechoslovakia and 1980–81 in Poland. The Central European identity was reinvigorated even more in the 1980s and became a kind of popular fashion as a definite resistance against Sovietization.

6   The idea of Central Europe played a great role in ensuring the peaceful and negotiated transition in all the countries concerned. At present, this common identity is the most important form of cultural contact among these nations, first of all for the intellectuals but also for a large part of the populations. This common identity has been recently expressed in several attempts to form regional organizations (Visegrád Group, CEFTA), which have increasingly become very important also for European integration. The regional differences appear in the fact that these Central European countries have a *re-democratization* process, that is they have revived their democratic traditions and institutions, versus the *democratization* process in the Balkan countries, which has actually been the first serious attempt at building democratic institutions.

Although Central Europe is a relatively well defined historical region, its borders have historically been somewhat changing, as indeed with all other European regions. The latest chapter in this story of historical border changes is the disintegration of Yugoslavia, which has split into its Western and Eastern parts. That is, Central Europe and the Balkans have clearly separated again. Moreover, the cultural, economic and political borders are not fully overlapping in Central Europe. In this respect, Austria is a particular case. It belongs historically to Central Europe, but after the Second World War was allowed to join the West and, therefore, it now has a consolidated Western political model which necessitates the introduction of the rather complicated term East Central Europe for the other countries of the region. The Baltic countries are an even more complicated case. They belong historically to Central Europe but they have been more distorted through their brutal integration into the internal empire of the Soviet Union than the other ECE countries, being part of the external empire only for a shorter period. Hence, the Baltic countries need more time for recovery, for turning back to the general trend-line of Central European developments (see Linz and Stepan, 1996). In the Balkans the main exception is Greece, attached to the West militarily and politically in the early post-war period, but having been part of Balkan developments as far as long-term historical tendencies are concerned.

In the spirit of long-term historical development and fundamental socio-economic differences, most of the comparative literature focuses on the regional specificities of Central Europe and considers the Balkans as a separate region: 'Names change over time in response to the political situation.... During the Cold War, there was no "middle" and the term Central Europe fell into disuse.... With the end of Communist regimes in East Europe, the term Central Europe quickly revived, and Hungarians, Czechs, and Poles started calling themselves Central Europeans' (Roskin, 1994: 11). As Roskin explains, we will also find it useful to split the region into Central Europe (from Hungary north) and the Balkans (land to the south of Hungary). Central Europe was largely dominated by the Habsburg empire, the Balkans by the Ottoman Empire. Each empire left behind different traditions, tastes and political styles. To this day, the Balkans are backward compared with Central Europe. The changes that led to the ouster of communist regimes in Central Europe came slower and later in the Balkans.

This is a very characteristic view, becoming more and more dominant in Western scholarship, represented clearly by the work of Adrian Hyde-Price: 'Before the war it was frequently described simply as "Central Europe". Since the end of Cold War, some writers have used the term "East Central Europe" to cover all countries between Germany and Russia' (Hyde-Price, 1996: 6–7). Hyde-Price notes, however, that this definition is so broad that it obscures the complex processes of change and differentiation at work in the former Soviet bloc. This term denotes a common regional identity which distinguishes them from their many neighbours: from West Central European states such as Germany and Austria; from the Soviet successor states to their east such as Russia, Ukraine, Belorus and the Baltic Republics; and from the states of South-Eastern Europe and the Balkans. It is true that the new democracies of East Central Europe share many characteristics and problems with other post-communist states. None the less, according to Hyde-Price they form a distinct group by virtue of their unique culture and history; their relatively advanced economic and political reforms; their particularly close relations with the West; and the degree of regional cooperation they have forged within the Visegrád framework.

There is also, however, a larger historical-geographical view, which unites these two regions into a bigger one. The series editors of the *Historical Atlas of East Central Europe*, for example, have defined East Central Europe as 'the lands between the linguistic frontier of the German- and Italian-speaking peoples on the west and the political boundaries of the former Soviet Union on the east. The north–south parameters are the Baltic and Mediterranean seas.... At present, this area comprises the countries of Poland, the Czech Republic, Slovakia, Hungary, Romania, Slovenia, Croatia, Bosnia–Herzegovina, Yugoslavia, Macedonia, Albania, Bulgaria and Greece' (Magocsi, 1995: XI). For the editors in describing these two regions the term East Central Europe is 'slightly more correct' than Eastern Europe. For them this time the emphasis is put on the distinction between East Central Europe so defined and Eastern Europe as the zone of post-Soviet republics, that is, on the separation of this region of small states from the former Soviet Union. This is also a good point, but geographically still needs some correction, since a small part of the Soviet Union was within the historically and geographically defined Central Europe (the three Baltic states and the Subcarpathian region), and beyond this, Western Ukraine culturally belongs to Central Europe. Furthermore, it is also not without contradiction that in this geographical approach Austria is left out from this wider Central Europe and Greece is taken in.

We have to accept the fact that the European regions are very complex and historically changing phenomena, yet we need a relatively stable definition. Therefore, for the purposes of this text we use the term **Central Europe** for Poland, the Czech Republic, Slovakia, Hungary, Slovenia, Croatia and Austria. Since Austria has had a different development in the post-war period we have to introduce the term **East Central Europe**, which we use for these countries without Austria, that is, only for the former state socialist countries. We employ the term **Balkans** in this book for Bulgaria, Romania, Albania and the Eastern republics of the former Yugoslavia (Serbia, Macedonia and Bosnia–Hercegovina).

The rediscovery of Central Europe

Since 1989, the public mood in East Central European (ECE) countries has changed from euphoria to disillusionment. At the time of the 1989 revolutions the whole region was full of enthusiasm. After a year or so the mood had turned, from overoptimism to deep pessimism. If the first year (1989) was described as 'annus mirabilis' or 'the year of the century', then the next year (1990) was 'annus miserabilis' and the third (1991), 'annus horribilis'. The collapse of state socialism and the external empire of the Soviet Union was followed with great interest in the West, but year by year this interest rapidly declined. The populations as well as the politicians of the ECE countries felt increasingly abandoned. They perceived the Western approach more and more as a benign neglect, as a 'business as usual' kind of passivity regarding the pan-European transformations. In the early 1990s indeed, Western Europe felt a necessity to turn inwards and concentrate on problems of EU architecture. It elaborated no vision for the new Europe as a whole and did not present a package programme to implement it in the ECE region and the Balkans.[2]

There was a vacuum situation in and around East Central Europe, and in the entire Eastern part of Europe in general. The newly democratized countries, unlike the Southern European ones in the 1970s, found themselves in the middle of nowhere. With the new crisis region in the Persian Gulf area, Western attention quickly turned away even from the ECE region. Initially, the Western powers wanted and supported the changes in the 'East', but when this process later on turned out to be slower and longer, dirtier and more difficult, then they escaped from taking action into an elegant and distance-keeping criticism. This was a period of relative vacuum in which mutual expectations diverged; the West expected quicker and cleaner transformations and the 'East' (first of all, ECE) expected more empathy and assistance.

This mutual misunderstanding came both from the socio-economic processes and from different perceptions. The EU had, in fact, very great problems of its own, but the ECE transformations after the collapse of the former system also proved to be more difficult and more complex than anyone would have previously thought. In subjective or theoretical respects, it was equally important that the ECE and Balkan revolutionary transformations came as a surprise and that their nature was not properly understood for a long time. There was a 'black hole' in the theory of the ECE and Balkan democratic transitions on the road between comparative communism and comparative democratization. Together with 'communism', the theory of comparative communism had also collapsed as a separate discipline dealing with 'Marxist' governments from Albania to Vietnam. For some years there was no proper conceptual framework to deal with the actual transition process and this situation produced some substitutes. The worst legacy of comparative communism was – and, to great extent, is – the overgeneralization as to the full 'Sovietization' of the entire Eastern part of Europe, that is, the conceptualization of all changes in the spirit of a totalitarian theory based mostly or exclusively on Soviet developments.

In the early 1990s, mainstream Western journalism presented a rather simplified triumphalism, with reports about the world-wide victory of liberalism, which demonstrated both the poverty and affluence of theory at the same time. The poverty was in the sweeping generalizations and simplifications; and the affluence appeared in the overproduction of partial theories and terminologies, creating a jungle of various theories and a chaos of misnomers and misinterpretations. The common reason for both phenomena was the transfer of theories and models from other regions and their direct application to fill the theoretical vacuum. This transfer came also from immediate Western perceptions and descriptions of events in the ECE and Balkan regions, coloured with prejudices and arrogance. It was a 'forgivable sin' temporarily, but it distorted the picture of the actual transformations to a great extent and did not allow for a proper 'theoretization' of systemic change.

By the mid-1990s, however, the dust has settled concerning the ECE transformations and a solid theory of comparative democratization has emerged as a new field of comparative politics. This makes it possible to give a general comparative theory of the ECE, and partially also of Balkan politics, and to produce a book within a general framework of comparative politics. It is still sometimes difficult to collect reliable comparative data on these regions, especially about the Balkan countries. None the less, parallel with the democratizations, political science as a science of democracy has also developed a great deal in these countries and they have produced more and more comparative data about their own transformations.

This book tries to summarize the results of the advance of comparative politics concerning East Central Europe and the Balkans and to present a common conceptual framework for all these changes. Actually, the fundamental changes in the Soviet external empire in 1989 led to the collapse of the whole bipolar world order, to the transition from the post-war Old World Order (OWO) to the New World Order (NWO) in the early 1990s. They have produced a 'comparative revolution' as well, that is, a change of paradigm in comparative politics (see Ágh, 1995b). The bipolar world until 1989 appeared also as a 'bipolar' concept in democratic theories: according to the former concepts of comparative politics, the democratic systems were on one remote pole and the authoritarian (and/or totalitarian) systems on the other, that is, in this theory the two systems were completely separated from each other. Nowadays, comparative politics sees the relationship between democracy and authoritarianism in a completely different way, much more as a continuum of different political systems between the two poles. The systemic change in the 'East' has produced three major conclusions for democratic theory which were already foreshadowed by the changes in Southern Europe and Latin America.

First, democracy is not a fixed stage of development or a static situation; that is, there are no 'final' democracies, only processes of democratization. Even the mature democracies have to renew, further develop and restructure their polities when challenged by new socio-economic developments. The myth of 'perfect' Western democracies has to be given up with the idealization of the present situation, since the West has recently undergone its own crisis of democracy and a systemic change different from that in the East. The bipolar model of democracy and authoritarianism no longer adequately reflects the global situation, since most of the countries are, or are still moving, between the two 'ideal' poles of democracy and authoritarianism, that is, in a process of democratization. Thus, the forms, degrees and directions of democratization are vitally important for comparative politics. Therefore, a typology of mixed and/or distorted forms of democracy follows, with an effort to describe and systematize them.

Secondly, democracy and democratization can only be described using a world system approach. Democracies have appeared in global waves, since these waves of democratization (like the reverse waves) presuppose certain preconditions or are connected with some structural prerequisites of the world system. Democracies may survive or develop, democratizations may succeed or fail for two kinds of reasons. First, the weakness or strength of domestic preconditions (like, for example, some Asian and African democracies which collapsed in the 1960s) affects their survival. Second, favourable or unfavourable environmental factors (like, for example, the ECE countries attached to the Soviet empire in the late 1940s) affect their success or failure. Given the fact that these environmental factors keep changing, neither the consolidation nor the 'breakdown' of democracies can be considered as final. Consolidated democracies continually face new crisis situations and oppressed democracies can restart their democratization process if international factors turn favourable in the ever-changing world system (Huntington, 1991).

Thirdly, democracy is possible even in 'fragmented' societies with many societal cleavages. This was first pointed out in relation to the small West European countries like the Benelux states and Austria by Arend Lijphart. His analysis has highlighted the distinction between formalist–minimalist democracies (with free and fair elections as the only requirement) and substantial democracies (with a strong economic and societal base). Substantial democracies may be achieved and stabilized through particular 'poli-technologies', or political devices and mechanisms, like consensual and 'corporative' processes, that is, through particular constitutional provisions and political institutions which help to solve conflicts and create compromises. This approach is extraordinarily important for the practice as well as the theory of the new ECE and Balkan democracies with different kinds of minorities.[3]

Theorizing global democracy

We can identify globally four major types of distorted democracies, or mixed regimes. Historical experience shows that these types can exist for decades, or either develop into full democracies or degenerate into pseudo-democracies. Robert Dahl has given a classical typology of political systems, based on two fundamental democratic values (competitiveness and inclusiveness), which can be very helpful as a point of departure here. First, we have to examine the recent political systems from the point of view of these traditional 'mixed' or 'hybrid' regimes. Dahl has described four types of political systems, namely:

1 **closed hegemonies**, with low degrees of both political competition and participation;
2 **inclusive hegemonies**, with a low degree of competition but a high degree of participation;
3 **competitive oligarchies**, with a high degree of competition and a low degree of participation; and
4 **polyarchies**, full democracies with high levels of both political competition and participation (Dahl, 1971: 7).

Even Dahl has suggested in the series of his works that the characterization of present democracies in the industrially advanced countries as polyarchies may not be 'perfect' and 'final' (see Dix, 1994). The issue of 'imperfect' democracies was raised forcefully in the 1980s by Arend Lijphart. Lijphart has distinguished between majoritarian and consensual democracies, clearly opting for the latter and pointing out the deficiencies of the traditional majoritarian varieties (Lijphart, 1984: 1–9, 21–32). Dahl, in his more recent works, has relied on this distinction made by Lijphart about the two major types of modern democracies, and he has analysed the 'prospect for democracy in nondemocratic countries' (Dahl, 1989: 313). Consequently, as a result of the Latin American and later South European democratic transitions, even prior to 1989, the complex set of issues surrounding the ongoing democratization process in the West and the chances of democracy in the South were raised quite clearly. By now, the bipolar thinking of 'democracy versus authoritarian rule' has almost disappeared in comparative politics and the search to identify mixed versions – both the in-between situations in the democratization process and the mixed regimes in the already structurally fixed, stable countries – has come to the fore.

In Dahl's typology, among the four types closed hegemonies classified as non-democratic systems are actually on one pole and polyarchies as real democracies are on the opposite pole. So he has classified only *two* basic or classical forms of mixed regimes, namely inclusive hegemonies and competitive oligarchies. In my understanding, however, nowadays there are altogether *four* major types of mixed, hybrid or distorted democracies which may be distinguished at the global level but which are particularly important for developments in the ECE and Balkan regions. My typology is as follows.

1 **Formalist** democracies (inclusive hegemonies in Dahl's terminology), in which *there is no actual counter-elite* as an organized and institutionalized opposition that could offer a fundamentally different political alternative. In this type the misinformed or often intimidated electorate re-elects 'freely' all the time the same ruling elite, maybe even with a large pseudo-participation. In this variant the *competition* principle is completely or largely missing or limited, but *participation* has been secured by mobilization mechanisms, which are at the same time manipulation schemes for the population. The classic example may be Mexico, but this model is also close to the mild totalitarian versions, including the post-totalitarian national-communist facade democracies of the Balkans (Serbia) and Eastern Europe (Russia), where democracy has been reduced to a series of 'rituals'.

2 **Elitist** democracies (competitive oligarchies in Dahl's terminology), in which there are some competitive elites but these groups share all power among themselves in an alternating fashion and *exclude the mass of the population from real political activities and decision-making processes, i.e. from meaningful political participation.* Consequently, politics becomes a remote world for the common man, as in the early British polity before the full franchise and/or in the post-colonial world (India and some Latin

American states, etc.). In elitist democracies the socio-economic elites are very strong compared to the political ones, but there are no real political parties, only the personal followings of some leading personalities in loosely organized forms. These organizations, however, try to mobilize the population in their personalized competitions. The forms of such regimes can be, for example, either populist dictatorships or delegative democracies (in the early 1990s Romania and Albania moved in this direction and also Bulgaria kept some features of an elitist democracy).

Beyond these classic versions, in my view, there have been two modern types as well.

3 **Partyist** (or 'partilitarian') democracies (*partitocrazia* in Italian), where parties are the only actors and they try to exclude all the other political and social actors from the policy-making process, monopolizing all decisions in macro-politics at the parliamentary level. Macro-politics or high politics thus becomes a *conflict of the party oligarchies*, like in Italy or Japan, with their clientura in the economic elite or vice versa. Strong party rule has been a characteristic feature of the less developed West European democracies. Nowadays, all ECE countries are at this stage or in this form of distorted democracy – namely, where participation is the lowest and political apathy is rampant; but party elite competition is both strong on the political stage through verbal wars and limited to the 'cartel parties', sharing state resources in common.

The party state (*Parteienstaat*) flourishes in the Western democracies as well, but to a lesser extent, particularly in the post-fascist democracies of (West) Germany, Austria and Italy, and also among the latecomers, in Spain and Greece. These are parliamentary systems with a high level of proportional representation, where the political class embraces also the highest ranks of central and public administration. The emergence of the modern party state and partyist regimes has coincided with the extension of the bureaucratic social and welfare state, that is to say, with the mechanisms of corporatist concertation, and with modern communications technology. The privileges and services of the party state go to all significant parties, including the opposition. It means, first of all, financing up to 80 per cent of the parties' budgets from public funds. These 'state parties' represent and communicate the interest of the state, that is, of the political class, to society. In such a way, sometimes, the parties can have a degree of independence from the political market, that is, from the elections, by using and abusing the patronage system widely. The partyist version of democracy can function relatively smoothly in a newly democratizing country, but it can also lead to rampant corruption and breakdown. Its existence explains to a great extent the emergence of anti-political movements in the West. Most probably, the ECE states will move in this direction towards milder partyist democracies along the German and the Austrian models, in the spirit of the saying, 'We need parties, and we know that we need them. But we do not like them' (concerning Southern Europe, see Gunther et al., 1995).

4 **Tyrannical majorities** as democracies are characteristic distortions of majoritarian democracies in particular historical circumstances. The temptation to abuse majority power is especially large in young democracies, in both parliamentary and presidential systems – but given their common character we use the term here for both varieties. The problem of tyrannical majorities became a most debated question in the late nineteenth century, when it was identified as an inherent tendency of the 'majoritarian' democracies. After the Second World War a system of Constitutional Courts was introduced in the advanced European democracies to counter the arbitrary parliamentary majorities on behalf of the long-term tendencies and vital democratic rights of minorities. The transitory systems of tyrannical majorities appeared with the second wave of democratization (Germany and Italy), and then, in a very manifest way, have become widespread with the third wave of democratization in East Central Europe, most strikingly in Croatia and Slovakia.

In these controversial systems of early democratization the random parliamentary majorities exploit their electoral successes using them under the guise of democratic legitimacy to act as 'tyrants'. Thus, they force majority decisions upon the whole polity and *refuse to make the necessary compromises with the opposition in the parliaments in particular and with the minorities in socio-political life in general.* They do not make any effort to establish a consensual democracy in this period of fundamental changes – that is, constitution-making and preparations for the consolidation of democracy. On the contrary, they would like to dictate the changes on their own terms and with their own directives. This type of distortion may occur to some extent in all contemporary democracies where simple parliamentary majorities or governments transcend their mandates. However, in various ways, this is the very characteristic of all young democracies. It appears as an 'infantile disorder', since the new politicians feel themselves to have a historical or moral mission to 'establish' their countries and, in extreme cases, against even the manifest will of the population (as for example the national-conservative government tried in Hungary between 1990 and 1994). In Croatia and Slovakia, however, tyrannical majorities have had a long run as a dominant and constant feature of the political system.

My typology shows clearly that both formal democracy and tyrannical majority violate the principle of *competition*, while elitist and partyist forms do more damage to *participation*. In this process of the distortion or degeneration of a young democracy, elite–mass linkages play a decisive role. This is true, above all, in the first stage of democratization – after the power transfer between the old and the new elites – when the new rulers try to demobilize the population and the resistance of civil society turns very quickly against the new rulers. In order to consolidate their powers, the new elites make efforts to limit both competition and participation, and usually a mixed solution is produced in which one or another of the principles become more damaged. Which distortion will prevail and to what extent depends on the character of the new elite and the resistance of the population. This is, of course, only a theoretical analysis, following neither the particular political histories of individual countries, nor their idiosyncrasies; thus, it tries to describe in broad outlines only the mainstream developments which are common to all young democracies. In the third wave, after 1974, more than 40 countries in Europe, Latin America and East Asia have shifted from authoritarian rule to democratic systems, but – as Huntington himself has emphasized – most of them are still 'something other than fully democratic societies' (see Vuylsteke, 1995: 38).

Historically, all four types have existed globally and there has even been a historical evolution from formalist democracies to partyist ones through elitist varieties, but the elitist and partyist versions can be alternatives as well, depending upon the degree of political articulation and/or social structure of the countries or continents concerned. These types, as minor tendencies or deviations, still exist in the advanced democracies as well, although they represent a major danger only for the young, unconsolidated democracies. Certainly, the formalist type represents the zero-level democracies typical in the Balkans and Eastern Europe proper as facade or quasi-democracies. The elitist type is most characteristic in Latin America, where low levels of political articulation produce weak parties and strong, unbalanced presidential systems. The partyist distortion is more common in the European countries where political life has been much more articulated and organized along party lines, with these parties playing a dominant role in parliaments. Partyist distortions are evident, but they appear to a lesser degree in most West European countries and to a much greater degree in the most advanced ECE countries. Finally, the tyrannical majorities as built-in tendencies in all 'majoritarian' systems can easily dominate in the ECE developments at an early stage of democratization or in those particular ECE cases which, as latecomers, have the heavy burden of nation-building for a longer time.

No doubt one has to distinguish first of all between:

1 the genuine, advanced and consolidated democracies of the West;
2 the young, immature but stabilizing democracies of the ECE countries and some Balkan countries; and
3 the facade or quasi-democracies of Eastern Europe proper and most of the Balkan countries.

Although these distinctions, and the intermediary forms between the different levels of development, are very important, the same typical deficiencies and distortions of democracies still permeate all levels and all forms. Simply said, there is but one comparative theory of democracy and democratization with common underlying problems. The recent 'systemic change' in the West shows that this region is not exempt from the diseases threatening democracy either, but the West is simply more resistant to them, given its more consolidated polity and stable economy.

Democratization in comparative perspective

In the mid-1970s a new wave of democratizations began in Southern Europe and Latin America, following the period of 'the breakdown of democracies' in the 1960s and early 1970s. This wave reached the Central European and Balkan countries in the late 1980s and the East European region in the early 1990s. Samuel Huntington has identified this tendency as the third wave of global democratization, considering the Anglo-Saxon democratizations in the late nineteenth century as the first wave and the democratizations in Western Europe as the second wave. The democratizations in Southern Europe, Latin America and Central and Eastern Europe have changed the global balance very much in favour of democratic regimes. The number of formally democratic states in the world rose from 25 per cent in 1973 to 45 per cent in 1990; while by 1993, 126 (or 68 per cent) of the 183 states of the world were democratic or being democratized. Therefore, these democratizations have initiated a global change, going beyond the above-mentioned regions and involving many countries from other regions as well, for example from South Asia or the Far East. At the same time, one has to caution against an overoptimism. There is no 'iron law' of democratization, leading inevitably to success once the democratization process is begun. It is conceivable that a great number of these new democracies will sooner or later fail (see Pridham, 1995: XII).

It is clear that the consolidation of new democracies is a very long and troublesome process, that is, it has a lot of obstacles to overcome and, in such a way, some new democracies will fail. Huntington warns us that the first two waves were also followed by 'reverse waves', and the same can also be expected in some countries of the third wave. Nevertheless, democracy will be consolidated at a much higher level worldwide, since these democratization processes have already basically changed both the structures of global institutions and the norms of international behaviour for states and organizations.

As a result of this global democratization, the general theory of democracy, as concerning the periodization and preconditions of democratization, has been rewritten in comparative politics. The new democratic theory originates from the seminal work *Transitions from Authoritarian Rule* (1986). This book was edited and co-authored by three leading Western scholars – Guillermo O'Donnell, Philippe Schmitter and Laurence Whitehead – comparing and generalizing the experiences of South European and Latin American democratic transitions. Whereas the worldwide debate has centred upon the minimal-procedural or extended-substantial meaning of democracy, these authors have already concretized their fundamental ideas on the emergence of a substantial democracy in Southern Europe within a solid conceptual framework. The impact of this new theory has reached all political science disciplines from political philosophy as theory of democracy to political sociology as the study of democratic political behaviour. After *Transitions*, democratic theory has been renewed, systematized and globalized; that is, it has become the common language of 'transitology'. This tradition of democratic theory is very valuable for Central European and Balkan democratization research as well, though it is manifestly Latin-America-centric and speaks with a 'Latin' accent. It is the task of the scholars in the ECE region to develop further, domesticate and regionalize this innovative theory. The global approach to democracy has taken a step ahead with the publication of *Transitions to Democracy* (1995), edited by Geoffrey Pridham, which gathers the harvest of the comparative democratization literature from the first half of the 1990s and documents its great progress.

A transitions model?

The impact of the democracy debates, of course, has been greatest upon the growing body of comparative politics regarding regional developments. As we have already indicated, the new democratizations have produced a 'comparative revolution', that is, a real scientific turning point in comparative politics as a discipline. Indeed, no theory, not even the simplest descriptions, of democratization in Southern Europe, East Central Europe and Latin America can escape the comparative efforts if it wants to give a correct picture of the transformations of the countries concerned, from Brazil to Hungary. These comparative efforts need a common base or a common denominator in order to be able to compare these regions meaningfully, and the countries within them. The common theoretical base for comparative democratization was outlined first by Dankwart Rustow in the early 1970s in his paper, 'Transitions to democracy: toward a dynamic model' (1970), through the periodization of systemic change. Since then, this periodization, with slight changes, has become the dynamic conceptual framework for democratic theory as a whole.

The three stages of democratization suggested by Rustow are the following.

1 Pre-transition or initial crisis – the preparatory phase of systemic change, from the final destruction of the old system, until the first free elections and the establishment of new constitutional regulations.

2 Democratic transition – the mixture of two systems in a creative chaos, with a complicated and painful process of democratic institutionaliz- ation and socio-economic transformation.
3 Consolidation – the coherent emergence of the new system in all social sub-systems, with the establishment of a democratic political culture – 'the invention of democratic traditions'.

Pridham specifies the period of transition as a stage of regime change that is decisive for systemic change. It commences at the point when the previous totalitarian or authoritarian system begins to collapse or disin- tegrate. During democratic transition, with a new constitution in place, the democratic structures become routinized and the political elites adjust their behaviour to liberal democratic norms. Transition tasks involve, above all, negotiating the constitutional settlement and finalizing the rules of procedure for political competition, but also dismantling authori- tarian agencies and abolishing laws unsuitable for democratic politics. In comparison, Pridham argues, 'democratic consolidation' is usually a lengthier process, but also one with wider and possibly deeper effects. Consolidation involves, in the first instance, the gradual removal of the uncertainties that invariably surround transition, followed by the full institutionalization of the new democracy, the internalization of its rules and institutional procedures and the dissemination of democratic values (see Pridham, 1995: XII).

In the South European literature of the 1980s the focus of investigation shifted from transition to consolidation. In this retrospective view, tran- sition was 'easy' and consolidation, as a long process, much more diffi- cult, consisting of a number of successive stages. In the ECE countries, the general impression is still the opposite one: the transition period, as the current historical task, is the most difficult and vulnerable, with the ex- pectation that the consolidation period will be relatively short and easy. Transition and consolidation, in my view, are complex processes in which the basic elements of systemic change may be composed for regions and countries in different ways, but always with the major focus on the *insti- tutionalization* of a political system during transition and on the social integration, participation and democratization of *political culture* during consolidation. First institutions have to be created and then the proper political culture to behave in; the former is the great task of the democratic transition period and the latter is that of the democratic consolidation period, with mutual overlaps of course. In the same way, parties are the main or dominant actors of transition and other socio-political actors, such as interest organizations and civil society associations, become de- cisive under consolidation. The partial consolidation of partial systems, or social sub-systems, may begin even in the transition period, but on the other hand, the consolidation of some institutions may be lagging behind until the end of systemic change.

In Southern Europe the whole process took 10–15 years. Eastern Europe, and to some extent the Balkans, is still in the pre-transition crisis with a strong continuity of ruling elites, parties and institutions, although Bulgaria is already beyond the point of no return in democratic transition. The ECE countries are already in the decisive period of democratic transition, demonstrating all the signs of the 'creative crisis'. The South European countries have come to the end of consolidation (Portugal and Greece), and in Spain the consolidation period is completely over.

For the process of democratization, however, not only the timing and the periodization are important, but also the regional specificities. These are kept by the countries even when they are already mature democracies, albeit these regional specificities are much more marked while these countries are still in the genuine democratization process. A regional approach to comparative democratizations, and to comparative politics in general, seems to be more fruitful than legal formalism, based on the comparison of the abstract, formal-legal features of political institutions like parliamentary or presidential systems and electoral laws across the globe.

Latin America was the first and Southern Europe the second stage of the third wave of global democratizations, and the research team of the *Transitions* made a distinction and a comparison between the two. Latin America was the interregional trendsetter, pioneering between the regions in democratization and also becoming the first base for its theoretization. Because of historical ties and the interdependence of geographical closeness, US political and research interest has focused upon Latin America. Some particular concepts of democratization emerged, like the 'possibilist' theories, elitist approaches etc., which have become very influential in comparative politics because they have been advocated by leading American scholars, and often mechanically transferred to other regions, although they reflected some very peculiar Latin American features.

Democratization in Southern Europe, however, has offered a quite new model. In these countries a European type of parliamentary democracy has emerged, and the external conditions provided by the EU have made the regions experience strikingly different from the Latin American cases. The EU created a very favourable environment for these countries, which, democratizing themselves in a still bipolar world, had to be 'saved' for the West. The experiences of the South European countries have greatly enriched democratic theory, which can be summarized in the statement that *parliaments have been the central sites and parties the major actors of the entire democratization process* (see Liebert and Cotta, 1990), which is the biggest lesson for the ECE countries from the South European democratization process.

Politicians and scholars of the ECE region have used both Latin American (LA) and South European (SE) theories, and slowly have developed their own model of a region-specific conceptual framework and terminology, mirroring ECE regional specificities. There are many parallels between the SE and ECE regions and some of their common features, by and large, can also be extended to the Balkans. But the developments in Eastern Europe, or those Balkan transformations having an East European character, have shown a big contrast to the ECE experience, with their violent changes and strong continuity of political elites. Usually the relatively strong new democracies in the Eastern half of Europe have a parliamentary system, the weak or pseudo-democracies, in turn, have presidential systems which are of an authoritarian nature, without being 'checked and balanced' by other power centres, since the parties and parliaments are very weak.

In general terms, LA democratizations can be described as undergoing cyclical developments or recurring crisis cycles between democratization and authoritarian renewal or frequent reverse waves, through which social and national populism leads to the breakdown of democracy. Hence, the future of fragile LA democracies is rather uncertain. The SE democratizations have already been consolidated through a positive spiral between economy and politics, due to the favourable external conditions created by the EU's 'promotion of democracy'. Thus, both the stages of full democratic institutionalization and the invention of democratic traditions have already been reached. ECE democratizations through negotiated transitions (close to the Spanish model) generated relatively balanced multiparty parliamentary democracies. Their evolutionary development, with many setbacks in some fields, is still going ahead. In the second half of the decade, they have also reached the start of the positive or virtuous circle between economic growth and socio-political stabilization.

The Balkan states have always been markedly different, and in the latest historical period are even more divergent from ECE developments. They have produced an open war or civil war, or at least violent actions during transition, with protracted pre-transition crisis and only a slow, partial and contradictory crossing to the period of democratic transition. Eastern Europe proper, that is, the former Soviet republics (except for the Baltic states), have been lagging behind Balkan developments with their 'red-brown' parties and elites, that is, with the various combinations of nationalism and communism, producing fake or dubious democracies. These three regions can only be connected as one model through sweeping generalizations, by referring back to the previous common totalitarianism, although they had already fundamentally diverged under the period of state socialism and continue to diverge essentially in their democratization processes. For this model which lumps all three regions together, everything is grey, since there are no specific, meaningful explanations for the regions and countries. This model sees no difference between the three regions and, therefore, it may be called the 'Prague–Vladivostok hypothesis', which increasingly confronts all the facts and events of the past decade of historical changes.[4]

The recent work of Collier and Levitsky (1996) on comparative democratizations summarizes the results of democracy research within the past decades. The authors classify the definitions of democracy and describe four types:

1 the electoralist (free and fair elections);
2 procedural minimum (basic civil liberties added);
3 expanded procedural minimum (elected governments have effective power to govern);
4 established industrial democracy (additional political, economic and social rights);
5 maximalist definition (some efforts for socio-economic equality and popular participation in political institutions).

This theoretical classification has, however, very practical functions, too. Some countries in the Balkans correspond only, and not always, to the minimalist–electoralist definition; some ECE countries (Slovenia, for example), in turn, go rather close to the maximalist definitions. It is therefore a good base for practical differentiation among the new democracies and also shows their chances for consolidation, since the latter is possible only in the case of rather 'maximalist' new democracies. Based on these definitions, the authors identify six sub-types according to the missing features along the minimalist–maximalist continuum which are very instrumental for the differentation among countries or between their phases of democratization, for example the sub-types of facade or formal democracy for the Balkans.[5]

The comparative adventure of drawing a positive parallel between the SE and ECE regions, and a negative one between the latter and the Balkans, however, needs deep further elaboration and specification. It can only be provided through the analysis of international relations, focusing on the Europeanization process which is an emerging conceptual base for interregional comparison of the new democracies in Europe; and through the detailed country studies. We will return here at the end of this book in drawing up our final conclusions about the ECE and Balkan democratizations.

Notes and further reading

1 I deal in this book only with the latest literature on the recent changes in the ECE and Balkan regions, although there has also been a considerable literature on their historical developments (see, for example, Held, 1992). I note here only

that Jenô Szücs, an eminent Hungarian historian, has elaborated a theory about *The Three Historical Regions of Europe*, as the title of his work indicates, meaning Western, Central and Eastern Europe (published first in English in *Acta Historica Academiae Scienciarum Hungariae*, vol. 29, Nos. 2–4, 1983). History matters a lot in these countries, of course, but I can give here only a brief historical overview of the ECE and Balkan regions. In this book I refer to the major publications of wider interest and access in the reference section, and to some shorter articles and smaller documents only in the notes.

2 It is easy to object that the Western perception of the 'Eastern' democratization was more complex even in the early 1990s; still, the most important thing here is to indicate the 'Eastern' perception of the Western behaviour as an important political factor influencing their developments. As one marked case of Western oversimplification put it, lumping together the ECE region and the Balkans on one side and forgetting about the democratic traditions and institutions on the other: 'They were, moreover, relatively poor, uneducated, unsophisticated peasant countries, ill-equipped as peoples to sustain effective democratic institutions.' (Hill, 1994: 276). This is a nice illustration of 'the Prague–Vladivostok hypothesis'.

3 There has been a huge literature on the recent democratizations and the new democracy theory (see, for example, Pridham, ed., 1995). I have tried to present them and to elaborate their criticism in my current writings, but here I summarize only the basic ideas of the theoretical debate and I do not engage in detailed discussions.

4 The Baltic development is an open question – whether they catch up with the ECE developments or not. The positive perspective is more likely. This optimism has been formulated by Gray (1996), summarizing the recent political science literature on the Baltic democratizations.

5 The work of David Collier and Steven Levitsky (1996) is very rich in theoretical analysis and references to the democratization literature, although it still focuses on the Latin American case and rarely mentions the Central and East European democratizations. Yet it is a very important point of departure for a theoretical analysis and a practical classification.

Chronologies

Historical chronology of East Central Europe and the Balkans

330–1453	Byzantine empire
8th–9th centuries	Bulgarian and Serbian kingdoms emerge, they accept Orthodox Christianity and fight for their independence against the Byzantine empire

9th–10th centuries	Polish, Czech-Moravian and Hungarian kingdoms emerge, convert to Western Christianity and fight for their independence against the German empire
1054	The Great Schism between Western and Eastern Christianity
1361	Muslim Ottomans beat Bulgarians at Adrianople
1389	Ottomans beat Serbs at Kosovo
1526	Ottomans beat Hungarians at Mohács
1529, 1683	The Turkish sieges of Vienna
16th–17th centuries	Hungary is incorporated into the Habsburg empire
1620	Bohemia becomes part of the Habsburg empire
1699	Treaty of Karlowicz, Turks forced to leave Hungary
1772–1815	The Partitions of Poland between Russia, Prussia and Austria
1878	Berlin Congress, the independence of Bulgaria, Serbia and Romania
1913	Turks leave the Balkans; the end of war between the successor states
1914–18	First World War
1918–19	End of empires and emergence of independent nation-states
1939–45	Second World War
February 1945	Yalta Treaty, Europe is split into two parts
1944–47	Early transitions to state socialism in the Balkans
1945–47	Post-war redemocratizations in East Central Europe
1947	Cold War begins, with a bipolar world
1947–49	Forced transitions to state socialism in East Central Europe
1949–89	State socialist regimes as the Soviet external empire

Democratizations in Southern Europe, East Central Europe and the Balkans

25 April 1974	Revolution in Lisbon, start of the third wave of global democratizations
20 November 1975	Franco dies
9 June 1976	Act on Parties in Spain
15 June 1977	The first free elections in Spain; Adolfo Suarez government
27 October 1977	The Moncloa Pact in Spain
28 October 1982	PSOE wins elections in Spain; Felipe González first government
1 January 1986	Spain becomes full member of the EU
6 February 1989	The first national roundtable negotiation in East Central Europe begins between the Polish government and Solidarity

11 February 1989	The ruling party in Hungary (HSWP) issues a declaration which allows for the multi-party system
5 April 1989	The Polish government and Solidarity sign a pact about the peaceful transition
4 June 1989	The first (semi-)free elections in Poland
13 June 1989	The national roundtable negotiations start in Hungary
11 September 1989	Hungary parts the Iron Curtain for East German citizens
12 September 1989	The Mazowiecki government in Poland; the first non-communist government in the ECE region
18 September 1989	The participants of national roundtable negotiations sign an agreement in Hungary
9 October 1989	The HSWP dissolves itself and the HSP as a social democratic party emerges
12 October 1989	The shock therapy of Leszek Balcerowicz in Poland initiated
9 November 1989	The Berlin Wall falls
10 November 1989	Todor Zhivkov resigns in Bulgaria
17 November 1989	The Czechoslovak regime falls after a Prague mass demonstration
25 December 1989	The execution of Nicolae Ceausescu in Romania
11 January 1990	The first mass demonstration in Albania

PART TWO

TRANSFORMATION IN EAST CENTRAL EUROPE AND THE BALKANS

2

The Europeanization of Central and Eastern Europe

CONTENTS

External dependence and linkage politics

In the early 1990s, the questions 'Why did state socialism fail?' or 'Why did it collapse ?' and 'Why did it do so quickly and unexpectedly?' were raised many times. The answers are very important for us, since the consequences of this collapse were decisive for the formation of the new political system. In general terms, the whole process of collapse shows the extreme degree of international conditionality and the dependency of the small ECE and Balkan states. The ECE states made their transition to state socialism in the late 1940s mostly for external reasons. The new system was imposed upon them from outside as a result of the Old World Order, the post-war arrangement which gave these states to the Soviet Union in the Yalta system as part of its sphere of influence or external empire. This annexation took extreme and brutal forms in East Central Europe, with the Cold War bipolarization. In the Balkan states, the new socio-political system of state socialism was much more indigenous, and therefore the transition to state socialism took place much earlier and even without the presence of the Red Army, as in Yugoslavia and Albania.

The state socialism produced in East Central Europe by the Yalta system collapsed after almost 50 years because of the globalization of the world system. The first blow came in the 1970s with the *globalization* of the world economy, when the state socialist countries were unable to manage their transition from extensive to intensive industrialization. They had to open up more and more to the world economy but were increasingly unable to compete in the world market, so their reaction was either a new isolationism with technological decay (Czechoslovakia and Romania) or a running ahead with loan-based modernization projects which produced heavy indebtedness (Poland and Hungary). In both ways, during the 1970s the ECE countries became dependent on the Western economy and its demonstration effect delegitimized them. The future-oriented state socialist model of legitimacy failed, since it argued that these countries would successfully catch up with the West, which obviously did not materialize and, as a result, the whole project of over-taking the West completely lost its credibility.

In the 1980s, globalization appeared via penetration of global communi-cations as well. State socialist regimes were based not only on economic isolation but first and foremost on a cultural and communication isolation. When they began to feel the impact of the demonstration effect of the advanced Western countries, they were inevitably 'softened up' step by step. The erosion of credibility, relating to catching up with the West through a state socialist model of power concentration with the postpone-ment of democracy and consumption in favour of accelerated economic development under the guidance of the ruling party, was complete by the late 1980s. This erosion was accelerated and pushed to the critical point of collapse through the demonstration effect of Western developments, as displayed in the global media. Finally, in the late 1980s, when the legiti-macy of the state socialist regimes had been completely eroded, their ailing economies also came close to a deep crisis. This negative spiral of external and internal processes, and subjective and objective factors produced the final collapse. In this process the pressure of the international environment played a decisive role, although some pioneering reform countries, like Hungary and Poland, did much to foster their own self-liberation.

The conventional wisdom in the West identified the 'Gorbachev factor' as the main reason for the collapse of state socialism at that time (see, for example, Dawisha, 1990 and Holmes, 1997). It focused only upon Soviet perestroika, whereas Soviet developments were to a great extent only reactions to the self-liberation efforts of the ECE countries. What was the major cause for the dissolution of the Soviet external empire? Gorbachev's 'revolution from above' or the fight of the ECE nations for their independence? The usual Western simplification underlines only the sig-nificance of the Gorbachev factor and neglects the actions of smaller nations as mere 'pawns on the historical chessboard'. However, this point of view is historically false and misleading in the explanation of the pre-transition crisis.

In his famous 'long telegram', written with very deep insight and fore-shadowing history, George Kennan sent a very important message from Moscow in 1947

> It is unlikely that approximately 100 million Russians will succeed in holding down permanently, in addition to their own minorities, some ninety million Europeans with a higher cultural level and a long experience of resistance to foreign rule. One of the most dangerous moments to world stability will come when, some day, Russian rule begins to crumble in the East European area. (Kennan, quoted from Rupnik, 1989: 107)

This dangerous moment came in the late 1980s, when, after a long period of erosion, the whole external empire was liquidated by the resistance of Central Europeans. It is enough to mention 1956 in Hungary, 1968 in Czechoslovakia and 1980–81 in Poland to understand why the Soviet Union became necessarily a garrison state and a militarized society. Realizing the failure, Gorbachev himself more recently admitted that the Soviet economy was the most militarized economy in the world, with the largest percentage of military expenditures. Without a huge army, the Soviet Union would have not been able to 'hold down' the ECE states, the nations most actively against Soviet rule. But the Soviet Union had to pay a high price for it, with a militarized society and a backward economy. This model of military oppression blew up in the late 1980s under the double pressure of the increasing resistance of the ECE states on one hand and the new arms race and restructuring of the world economy on the other.

The warning issued by Kennan was very insightful, but it was still not unprecedented. Alexander Yanov explains its original form as the Leont'ev Dilemma:

> In the 1880s Konstati Leont'ev, the most incisive of the Russian conservatives of the past century, insistently advised the dictator Alexander III not to be swayed by pan-Slavic sentiments, but to leave Eastern Europe in peace. The Leont'ev Dilemma can be summed up as follows: we haven't been able to integrate Poland into our imperial, 'Byzantine' culture over the course of nearly a century; what would happen to us if we had to handle another half-dozen Polands? (1987)

Yanov extends this dilemma to the Soviet external empire and underlines the role of Hungary, with the demonstration effect of its middle classes, in ruining the Soviet empire

> This tragic history has a corollary, however. Just as Leont'ev predicted, 'half a dozen Polands' are indeed constantly working away at the empire's

destruction.... Hungary began its process of liberalization not with an upris-ing, not with a revolutionary attempt at national democracy, but rather with the elevation of its own 'bourgeois Philistines'. Naturally, to achieve this, it first of all had to breach the empire's economic model which, as always, had been set up to block the upward movement of the middle class. (Yanov, 1987: 284–5)

Creating its external empire and extending it to East Central Europe, the Soviet Union committed political and economic suicide by raising an insurmountable obstacle to its own development. The ECE countries could only be kept within the empire through a system of strong military rule, not just through a potential – but from time to time, actual – military oppression and intervention. It necessitated a vast army which diverted huge resources from the Soviet Union's economic development and modernization. It made the Soviet economy increasingly non-competitive in the world market, fatally condemned and structurally determined the entire Soviet society to underconsumption and the Soviet state to the oppression of its own civil society. Thus, the final failure of this empire was pre-programmed. The time-bomb was ticking and this self-destruct-ing model reached its final limits in the second half of the 1980s.

Gorbachev did not initiate an opening at all. He merely realized that Soviet power was declining terribly. His merit was not in creating this new situation, but in recognizing it and reacting to it. The waves of national liberation movements in the ECE countries shook the Soviet empire, deprived it of its global ideological legitimacy and also weakened its socio-economic base domestically. The resistance to absorption into the Soviet empire was strong in the ECE countries, recurring in crises every 10–12 years which then needed a repeated effort to effect a violent 'nor-malization'. This tough and permanent resistance manifestly separated East Central Europe from the Balkan and East European regions where there was no active resistance to the Soviet rule in the form of uprisings or mass demonstrations. The Brezhnev doctrine was formulated in Novem-ber 1968 to determine the elbow room for the ECE countries within the external empire. It defined 'socialism' as a double pledge of loyalty to the Soviet Union externally and to the ruling party internally. The garrison state underlying the Brezhnev doctrine had become totally bankrupt by the mid-1980s, and then Gorbachev came as a crisis manager. So the Gorbachev factor was not the cause of transformation in East Central Europe but its result, since it was the resistance of the ECE nations that undermined the empire. By the late 1980s, the Gorbachev factor was not the solution either. It became more and more part of the problem and an obstacle to the real solution of the last crisis of the external empire.

International and domestic factors: the Gorbachev doctrines

Gorbachev elaborated a series of doctrines about the ECE region which followed, rather belatedly, world developments as well as the rapid transformations of the ECE countries themselves. A short overview of the Gorbachev doctrines allows us to analyse the different patterns of break-through in the ECE and Balkan states from Poland to Romania.

Gorbachev doctrine No. 1 came as a denunciation of the Brezhnev doctrine, which could not be kept up in its original form by the late 1980s. First, Gorbachev denounced the Brezhnev doctrine in a very cautious way in his Prague and Belgrade speeches in 1988, but finally and officially only at the Bucharest meeting of the Warsaw Pact leaders (7 July 1989). Nevertheless, the big question mark above the Polish and Hungarian changes in the late 1980s was whether the Brezhnev doctrine and the Yalta system still existed, or to put it in another way, where were the 'walls' of the ECE countries' relative independence in the efforts to reform their political systems? It is true that a fatal blow was already given to the Brezhnev doctrine by Soviet inaction in Poland in 1981, since the Soviet Union was too weak both externally and internally to intervene. (Even bullets were in short supply, a joke said at that time.) But when the military regime in Poland failed to contain Solidarity in the late 1980s, Soviet leaders were forced to make a second compromise: more elbow room for the Polish elite and counter-elite in exchange for more voluntary self-limitation.

The essence of doctrine No. 1 was that the twin, interconnected taboos of the ECE developments, fixed by the Brezhnev doctrine, namely the leading role of the party and membership in the Warsaw Pact, could not be touched upon, but were softened up. Greater elbow room was offered if guarantees were given voluntarily to keep the former rule in a liberalized way. Soviet pressure for this compromise solution was not communicated publicly; it was part of the voluntary acceptance of the countries concerned that by doing it, they did not admit this Soviet pressure manifestly. Actually, this first stage of the 'moving walls' – when it could not be foreseen at all that after some time these walls would be removed completely – was a return to the situation before the transition to state socialism, to the year 1947, when the Communist Parties in the ECE countries already had hegemony but not yet a monopoly of power, so they coopted certain other political forces by offering them marginal power positions. The Polish developments forced the Soviet leadership to rethink its ECE strategy. At the same time, Poland, with the recurring political crisis in 1988–89, was the experimental ground for Gorbachev doctrine No. 1. It led to the national roundtable negotiations and the first (semi-)free elections, creating a new balance between government and opposition under the dominance of a Communist president, prime minister and leading ministers in foreign affairs, home affairs and defence. This mixed political system had its own 'moving walls', in that it was corrected several times under the pressure of changing international circumstances. Still, the basic features of this early compromise shaped the Polish scenario for a long time, until the first free elections in October 1991, and even afterwards in the form of the strong presidential role, meant originally to secure Communist hegemony in the new situation. Poland has paid a high price for being first in the political breakthrough towards democratization and in the application of doctrine No. 1, with its long-lasting half-solutions.

In general, the Gorbachev doctrine was designed to meet the challenge of the Polish and Hungarian changes. Poland opened the way to democratization and became the trendsetter for the other countries. The Soviet leadership found itself having to react to the accelerating changes in East Central Europe. Taken always by surprise, it had no coherent policy and simply reacted to events belatedly through improvisations. Yet Gorbachev wanted to orchestrate all changes in the 'camp' from Moscow by restricting the vanguard states and pushing ahead the conservative ones in terms of political modernization. Actually, the quickly changing situation meant that he increasingly lost all his coordinating power. It is certain that in the reform countries Gorbachev did not initiate anything, as many Western analysts presupposed, overgeneralizing as usual from the East European situation or from Neo-Stalinist Czechoslovakia, the German Democratic Republic (GDR) and Romania. Obsessed by the Gorbachev factor, they did not realize that Gorbachev had simply been lagging behind the events.

Gorbachev doctrine No. 1 was itself a belated reaction, an external copy of internal perestroika, meaning a reform process initiated, regulated and controlled from above, by one power centre, and ultimately, by one personality. This approach might have worked for some time in the Soviet Union, but its extension basically did not work in Poland and Hungary, where the period of the reforms initiated and controlled from above was irreversibly over. The doctrine, as a power bargain, was too little for the reform countries, even for their reform-minded ruling elites, and too much for the conservative ones in the Neo-Stalinist countries, who formed a 'Holy Alliance' against the reform countries in Summer 1989.

Gorbachev, as we have seen, came to realize in 1985–7 the utterly dysfunctional nature and workings of the Soviet system and the erosion of external empire. He set out to reform it in order to preserve it, at least in its general framework. He did not understand that the dissolution process of the empire had already reached a point of no return and that the whole system could not be reformed at all. Gorbachev did not foresee, as nobody else did, that his actions and measures would unleash fundamental socio-economic forces beyond his control and that these spontaneous movements could not be contained through either conservative-violent or reformist-compromising actions. Thus, Gorbachev doctrine No. 1 was doomed to failure in advance, like gorbachevism as such, but at that time nobody could foresee this failure either. The doctrine failed directly in Hungary in 1989, however, since both government and opposition leaders refused it, as a principle leading to a Polish way of incomplete transition. The Hungarian roundtable negotiations in June 1989 began with a mutual understanding of the necessity for fully free, competitive elections. Thus,

Hungarian developments from the very beginning had a momentum going beyond Gorbachev doctrine No. 1, which has, however, left its imprint on Polish experience.

Gorbachev doctrine No. 2 rose, again belatedly, in late 1989 as a sharp reaction to the collapse of the ECE state socialist regimes. At the end of the year, the Soviet leadership had to accept grudgingly the disintegration of the external empire in Central Europe, while the Soviet hardliner generals blamed their leadership's 'capitulation policy'. The Soviets gave up East Central Europe, and partly the Balkan region as well. This was more or less manifestly admitted by Gorbachev in the early December 'Malta–Yalta' summit meeting with US President Bush. This meeting redrew the map of Europe between the superpowers, since the Yalta system, ossifying the lives and determining the fates of the ECE and Balkan countries for more than 40 years, was liquidated. But there was a new agreement to stop the domino or snowball effects at the borders of the internal empire. The Soviet Union implemented it immediately by taking harsh measures against the internal decomposition process, which culminated in the massacres in the Baltic states in January 1990. The Western powers tacitly accepted Gorbachev doctrine No. 2 as a project to give up the external empire in order to save the internal empire by any means, since they also had fears of further instability in the region. They preferred Gorbachev as a crisis manager at home instead of the chaos resulting from the decomposition of the Soviet internal empire. Although the Western powers accepted and supported doctrine No. 2, it led once again to failure because the collapse of the internal empire could not be prevented either.

Unlike Gorbachev doctrine No. 1, associated only with acceptance of some vague reform measures step by step, the gradually emerging Gorbachev doctrine No. 2 meant complete freedom from Soviet influence for the ECE countries with a new strategy of drastic systemic change. This stage of international development is best illustrated by the Czechoslovak case, where the Husak–Jakesh regime simply collapsed under international pressure and its full capitulation came very shortly after the Prague mass demonstration on 17 November 1989. The events in November moved at incredible speed, above all in the GDR, Czechoslovakia and Bulgaria. These ruling elites realized that they had no other chance except to negotiate, or even capitulate, since they could not expect any Soviet assistance for another violent 'normalization'. Czechoslovakia enjoyed the advantages of the latecomers, but the drastic changes also produced some counter-productive effects, since the Velvet Revolution was soon to be followed by the 'Velvet Divorce' between the Czech Republic and Slovakia.

Gorbachev doctrine No. 3 emerged in 1991, given the fact that in Eastern Europe there was no real systemic change yet but the old regime had already disintegrated. Some features of the nineteenth century type of violent revolutions swept through the Balkan and East European regions, with the changes being stuck in a pre-transition crisis and forming unstable facade democracies. These countries were dangerous and destabilizing neighbours for the ECE states, and this negative effect was very forcefully felt in the early 1990s when these states had their own most difficult period of democratic transition. One response to these cumulated difficulties occurred in 1991, and may be called Gorbachev doctrine No. 3. This latest doctrine was a direct reaction to the internal disintegration of the Soviet Union and a desperate effort to maintain its unity under the new circumstances. Both internally and internationally this doctrine, when it emerged, was defensive and not offensive. Domestically, it allowed for the reorganization of the Soviet Union's republics in the form of a confederation, with much more autonomy for the republics from the central state. Whereas Gorbachev's effort in August 1991 failed to create this confederation, since the Russian hardliners organized a *coup d'état* immediately before the signing of this treaty regarding the 'new' Soviet Union, nevertheless this new organization later still emerged in the form of the Commonwealth of Independent States (CIS). The new Russian leadership has step by step regained control over the former republics, first militarily, as indicated by the Grachev doctrine (named after the minister of defence in the first half of the 1990s), about the Russian sphere of interest in the 'close neighbourhood', and then economically, through the 'rouble zone' (keeping the Russian currency etc.).

Internationally, Gorbachev doctrine No. 3 meant a big turnaround from a 'Threat by Force' to a 'Threat by Weakness', that is, by threatening the West with the dangerous consequences of political disorder in a country with a huge nuclear arsenal, or, in more general terms, threatening the West with those conflicts that might emerge in a disintegrated Soviet Union, such as a series of local wars without a patron power or a domestic crisis manager. This doctrine was by and large accepted by the Western powers at the London G7 summit meeting in July 1991 because they (1) feared the 'imperia absentia' (missing or decomposing empire) and thought that the empire could be kept together by Gorbachev; (2) considered that a domestic crisis manager could be more effective in preventing local wars or in securing a damage limitation effect; and (3) the key issue for them was the nuclear arms limitation treaty and for this they needed a reliable and stable partner. But even with Western assistance, Gorbachev failed to keep together the Soviet 'Dis-Union' and the republics became legally independent. Nevertheless, Gorbachev doctrine No. 3 has in some ways still worked, since Yeltsin has succedeed in re-establishing Russian dominance over most of the internal empire in the form of an informal empire. This Russian dominance in terms of a crisis manager role has not been against the will of the Western powers, overburdened as they are with the same role in the other parts of Europe (Yugoslavia) or of the world.

However, for the ECE states there has been a dangerous continuity of Russian regional dominance embodied in the Gorbachev, then in the

Yeltsin–Grachev doctrine. The Russians have never given up the idea that they must play a dominant role in the ECE and Balkan regions, at least in the areas of foreign and security policy. They lost momentum in the early 1990s, but reformulated their strategy after 1992. Russian efforts to regain influence have meant a permanent threat for both the domestic stabilization and European integration of the ECE and Balkan states. The ECE states feared for some years that the West would conclude some kind of a new Yalta agreement with the Russians to please and stabilize them. The Russians, for their part, have withdrawn their troops but have left an ecological disaster and huge debt behind. This debt, resulting from the former unbalanced bilateral trade, was acknowledged, but it has not yet been fully paid back, and remains a serious obstacle to resumption of normal trade.

Furthermore, it was still the Soviet Union that concluded a bilateral treaty with Romania in 1991, embodying again the principle of limited sovereignty, that is, not allowing Bucharest to establish contacts with other security organizations. In 1991 the Soviet Union also wanted to force such Bucharest-type treaties of limited sovereignty upon the other countries, such as Czechoslovakia and Hungary, but it failed to achieve this. Russia has continued the same strategy, in declaring its special right to veto the NATO integration of these countries. The West has hesitated too much in its efforts to integrate the ECE countries in order not to disturb the Yeltsin leadership in consolidating their power. The West has been seeking stability in Russia at any price, but a solution to the security problems of the young ECE democracies is feasible only through their integration into NATO. The Eastern Europe (EE) factor has remained destabilizing for the ECE region, although this effect has become much less dangerous by the second half of the 1990s. It can only be completely eliminated, however, through the full integration of the ECE region into the Euro-Atlantic community.

Perspectives for Europeanization

The East Central European countries, with their 1989 revolutions, contributed significantly to the global changes, but they still have remained captives of the international system and external factors in their later democratization process. The change in the ECE and Balkan regions was self-generated, through a domino or snowball effect in which some pioneering countries mobilized the others for change by demonstrating their own revolutionary changes. The term 'domino effect' suggests only a mechanical sequence and repetition, but the events of the year displayed a cumulative change from country to country; therefore, 'snowball effect' captures the essence of the accelerated transformation better. The ECE countries fought for their self-liberation, yet the welcome and long expected changes appeared to them as the collapse and capitulation of their societies and economies, in some ways like the result of a lost war. They were, in fact, 'forced to be free'. This result is not a new situation in political history. The same happened to some countries (Germany, Italy and Japan) in the early post-war period when this term was used for the model of 'democratization-through-defeat'. What is paradoxical, however, is that although some ECE countries (Poland and Hungary) mostly 'liberated' themselves from the Soviet rule, actually and finally, they were still 'defeated'.

Since the sixteenth century, the Central European countries have been the semi-periphery of the modern world system, 'shuttling' between long periods of Europeanization and de-Europeanization, the last period of which was the Sovietization. This shows that they have always conducted a 'forced-course development', that is, were extremely dependent on the international environment and vulnerable to the brutal interventions of the great powers, which several times even included the drawing of artificial borders in the eastern part of Europe. This type of dependency, currently also called 'path dependent development', was also very characteristic of the inter-war period, and presented in its most absurd form in the establishment of the Soviet external empire which diverted the ECE countries from their domestic structures, meeting all revolutions with violence, like 1956 in Hungary. This feature of external dependency has returned in a specific way in the recent democratization. There is no doubt that Huntington (1991) considers the waves of democratization a function of the world system as such and not only the result of internal developments. This is why and how the countries of the second and third waves have been 'forced to be free'.

The forced democratizations in the early post-war period took place in an emerging bipolar world system, in the Old World Order. The United States had a very strong vested interest in supporting the new democracies through the Marshall Plan for a simultaneous transformation of the economy and polity, that is, for the creation of both a modern market economy and a multi-party democracy. The 1989 revolutions, in turn, meant not only the collapse of the external Soviet empire but the whole bipolar world, with the emergence of the New World Order. The first paradox of this second generation of forced democracies is that the Western powers were very much interested in the defeat of state socialism but, because of the lack of the enemy image in the abruptly changed situation, they did not show any substantial engagement in supporting the new ECE democracies. These countries tried to be free on their own, yet they were forced to be free in an imposed way; then they were abandoned to a great extent. This leads us to the second paradox: the ECE countries have been forced to play a role expected from outside which has not always been the optimal way of democratization seen from the inside.

The paradoxes of democratic transition had appeared already, but were solved in the circumstances of the Cold War confrontations by massive

US political and economic assistance. That is, in this wave of democratizations, these West European countries were 'forced to be free', but the ways
and means for the political and economic consolidation were provided for
them by the 'patron powers'. Claus Offe formulates this paradox, as the
principle of the necessity of simultaneous transition in politics and
economy, quite clearly:

> The only circumstance under which the market economy and democracy can
> be simultaneously implanted and prosper is that one in which both are
> forced upon a society from outside and guaranteed by international relations
> of dependency and supervision for a long period of time. This, at least, is
> arguably the lesson offered by the war ruined postwar democracies of Japan,
> and, with qualification, of the Federal Republic of Germany. (Offe, 1991: 874)

Therefore, Offe is very pessimistic about the fate of the ECE developments, since 'there is no obvious "patron power" that would be a
natural candidate for the task of supervising and enforcing the peaceful
nature of the transition process' (1991: 889).

In my understanding, the failure of the ECE democratizations has not
been predetermined at all, although the paradoxical nature of the transition appears in a much more marked way than in the post-war democracies. This forced democratization has been negative for developments in
the ECE countries in many respects by imposing alien standards upon
them which are based on the overgeneralizations and oversimplifications
of international organizations like the IMF and the World Bank. At the
same time, it has been overwhelmingly positive because it has created a
new 'forced-course development' for democratization which has protected against the 'authoritarian renewal', that is, against the national–
conservative anti-democratic forces and influences coming from inside.
This positive aspect of forced democratization has dominated so far, but
with many disturbing 'side effects'. The problem remained open for some
time of whether the ECE countries would follow the success story of the
South European forced democratizations or they would face the reverse
wave, that is, the breakdown of democracy after this short period of recent
re-democratization. This question, however, was finally and favourably
decided by the mid-1990s when economic consolidation began in ECE
countries. The first signs of the ensuing social and political consolidation
can also be observed, the vicious circle has now been changed into a
'virtuous', positive circle.

Even the United States failed in the post-war period in most cases of
promoting forced democratization throughout the world – in Europe, first
of all in Greece and Turkey. The special compromise, the *facade* or *formalist*
democracy, which took place there has a relevance also for recent developments in the Eastern half of Europe. Where the internal political and
economic circumstances did not exist for a substantial democratization,
the forced democratizations were derailed and produced a minimum

democracy of constitutional formalities, as a facade for an actually authoritarian regime. This is clearly the Greek case in its 'ally phase', when the United States accepted Greece as an *ally* in the bipolar European security order and did not impose democracy upon it as a *model*.

The turning point for Greek democratization came in the mid-1970s. The 'transition trigger' resulted from a concerted effect of the external–internal linkages, including the global and domestic economic crisis. In this respect the Greek transformation is the closest to ECE developments, with one major exception: the engagement of the European Union countries in promoting democratization was extremely strong in Greece and it has been surprisingly weak in the ECE countries. In the mid-1970s the Greek political elite suffered defeat from outside (the Cyprus conflict) as well as from inside (the crisis of the Colonels' regime). It was simply forced to change the political system dramatically by adjusting it radically to West European standards, that is, to give up the formal or facade democracy and to change it into a substantial one. The forced or imposed character of systemic change was not at all new in Greek political history and the crisis was solved by a shift from US dependency ('ally') to the EU substantial democracy 'model'.

The forced democratization in Greece was the first EU 'promotion of democracy' in the third wave, followed by the cases of Spain and Portugal, but it has remained also the most difficult one. Greece was a very special case of 'democratization-through-defeat'. This time, however, the EU forced the Greek partner to be democratic not by military, but mainly by economic means. The 'capitulation' of Greece to a forced democratization was mostly based on the Greek perception of, and accommodation with, their own 'penetrated society' and external dependence:

> The Greeks themselves, however, take for granted an explicit connection between the political regime and its external links ... it often seems as if a considerable proportion of the population views the polity as an only partially autonomous sub-unit of its broader international environment. Long before political scientists recognized the importance of linkages between national and international systems, the Greeks believed that the nature of their regime was largely determined by the 'foreign factor'. (Verney, 1990: 205)

The experiences and perceptions of the ECE populations have been historically very similar, yet the present situation is fundamentally different. Many alien and artificial elements were imposed upon the countries of the forced democratizations, but these inorganic elements became after some time mostly organic, producing or triggering a real democratization effect. The forced democratization by the EU in ECE countries at present still lacks both the means and resources of triggering successful democratizations, but this can drastically change during negotiations about full membership in the late 1990s. This contrast of high expectations and lack of support places an external overload on ECE democratizations, while the crisis of the Balkan and East European facade democracies also means a special additional burden for the ECE countries. The forced democratization can only be successful if either the external pressure (Japan) or the internal socio-economic potential (Germany) is big enough to trigger the positive spiral of simultaneous changes, that is, the political and economic systemic changes reinforce each other in democratization and marketization. Despite the lukewarn assistance of the EU, in the ECE region both have been sufficient so far, and since 1994 both factors have been strengthening each other, such that a backslide to facade democracy in the ECE countries seems to be avoidable. As we know from post-war history, facade democracies can result either from the failures of forced democracies or from situations where, if they are stable enough domestically, the external patron or 'winner' accepts a pseudo- or superficial democratization with an external facade that looks 'democratic' from outside. This is the case with the Balkan and East European countries nowadays, and this dubious situation of their Eastern neighbours is a significant danger for the new ECE democracies which are at a historical crossroads.

Consequently, it is very important to emphasize the fundamental differences between the 'successful' forced and the 'failed' facade democracies, but at the same time also the differences between facade democracies and authoritarian regimes, because even limited and formalist human rights matter a lot compared to the former authoritarian regimes. Still, our main concern here is to point out that facade democracies represent a blind alley in the democratization process. Therefore, the earlier divergence between a forced, substantial democratization (Italy) and a facade, superficial one (Greece before the mid-1970s) is crucial for our argument here. Nowadays, the Western powers have offered an easy compromise for the Balkan and East European region; if they build up a thin democratic facade and provide some domestic political stability, they are considered democratic countries and eligible for Western assistance. In this case the crucial issue is whether these facade democracies can be consolidated despite their deep economic crisis and with minimal Western assistance, or whether the breakdown of democracy is unavoidable because of their fragile economies, as has been so in many countries of the same type in the post-war period. International organizations treat the East European countries in the same way as underdeveloped countries, but this treatment may not be beneficial nor sufficient for their stabilization. Actually these basically unstable countries now embody a big danger both for the new European order and for their neighbours, the whole ECE region. Yugoslavia and Russia alike represent a failure of EU crisis management, although in different ways, for Yugoslavia may indicate the future of the former Soviet Union, since the Serbian and the Russian empires had much in common.

If we change the comparative focus, the difference between Southern Europe and East Central Europe is as great as that between East Central

Europe and Eastern Europe. In my opinion, between the SE and ECE regions it is not so much the internal points of departure which are different, as has been mentioned, but first of all the external conditions. As I have discussed earlier, the EU engagement was clear in the SE case with a 'model' approach (the mandatory acceptance of the EU model of democracy and market economy) and it was dubious for some time in the ECE case. More importantly, however, democratic transition in Southern Europe took place in a stable region and in the balanced international system of the Old World Order. In the early 1990s, however, the ECE democratization tried to succeed in stabilizing itself in the troubled waters of a not-yet-emerging New World Order, but the external conditions in the neighbouring East European and Balkan regions were even more detrimental in both socio-economic and politico-military aspects for the ECE countries, although some improvement since then can be noticed.

The whole analysis proves that the ECE and Balkan regions can be properly treated in a conceptual and theoretical framework of linkage politics, that is, through the organic connection between the international and domestic factors with the dominance of the former, as appears also in the Europeanization process. There have been various scenarios of linkage politics (and the so-called penetrated societies) in international public opinion and scholarship about the revolutionary changes in the ECE and Balkan regions, the analysis of which introduces us to Europeanization and to country studies in these regions. The political science literature about East Central Europe and the Balkans may be outlined in four basic scenarios, although their conceptual framework is completely different, as are their 'predictions' and consequences. The first two are, in fact, repetition scenarios, that is, polarized images of the past projected into the future. The second two, in turn, are real transition scenarios, containing genuine social change and conceptualizing the future in completely different directions. Finally, the first and fourth scenarios are, indeed, about East Central Europe, the second and third are embracing the Balkan region, or all of 'Eastern' Europe, as well. All the scenarios characterized below are coherent theoretically but appear very rarely in pure forms in the present jungle of theories and interpretations. The overwhelming majority of the analyses about the ECE countries and the Balkans combine the divergent features of these competitive scenarios into one contradictory, narrative-descriptive and/or theoretical-analytical framework.

Four scenarios for the future

Sleeping Beauty (the Raped West)

The first scenario states that the Western-style modernization process was brutally broken by the Soviet conquest in Central Europe after the Second

World War. The Soviet external empire imposed alien roles and rules upon these nations, yet it was unable to change the fundamentally Western nature of their (civil) societies. This amounts to a definition of Central Europe as always having been part of the West, but suffering from time to time from Eastern aggression. After its 'Easternization' with a new effort at 'Westernization' this region is maintaining and restoring its character. Obviously, nowadays, the latest Eastern invasion is over, and Central Europe once again is 'automatically' returning to the West. It is the story of the Sleeping Beauty being woken by the Young Prince. Politicians as well as the peoples of Central European countries thought in late 1989 that the return to democracy and a free market society could be resolved quickly and easily, 'overnight', by the pluralization and privatization programmes without major pain and conflict but with significant Western assistance. The Western character of Central Europe will, therefore, almost completely be restored, and the ECE countries will soon join the community of free European nations.

This is the great utopia of an easy transition and it was a common wisdom and belief everywhere, but most vehemently formulated and preached among the Czechs who considered themselves as the only real Western nation in Central Europe. With the initial euphoria over by the summer of 1990, disappointment became widespread and a counter-utopia came to the fore. The euphoria of 1989 gave way to the gloom of 1991. Nothing proceeded as smoothly as had been forecast. This more sober view of the transition has recently been confirmed by the only application of this absorption scenario, namely the case of East Germany, which has indeed been quickly Westernized, but this has not been an easy and painless transition either.

Deep-freeze (the Eternal East)

The second scenario reflects the mentality of the Great Uncertainty after the collapse of the previous regime and prior to the consolidation of something completely new but as yet unknown. When the initial euphoria ended, everything became uncertain, not only the present and the future, but also the past. The new regimes glorified the past, that is the inter-war period before 'communism' and even earlier historical times, without too much careful selection among historical traditions. At the same time, the contradictions of a backward 'Eastern' Europe from the pre-war period seemed to return. Apparently, these countries were simply deeply-frozen by the 'communist' regime and their problems were not created by the external empire, since they proved to be too well-known from previous historical periods. The past was glorious and shameful; glorious for the national-conservative leaders attempting an 'authoritarian renewal', and shameful for the liberal intelligentsia and press, and also for the West. It was even suggested by the Western press that the Soviet oppression came from the same 'eternal' East Europeari soil. Consequently, it was not really alien at all for the ECE and Balkan regions, as stated before, to be in a revolutionary mood. Quite the contrary, these negative features expressed the real nature of these 'East European' nations: the century-old contradictions of state-led modernizations, hopeless emotional nationalisms, lack of democratic culture and free market behaviour.

Thus, instead of the programme 'Return to Europe', the opposite, 'Return to the Past', came to the fore, that is, all the demons of the past returned. *The Economist* formulated this verdict about East Central Europe with real Western arrogance in its headline: 'The East is East, West is West'. The Deep-freeze scenario, in fact, was not really 'home-made' in the ECE region itself. It reflected more the disillusionment of the West in its own unfounded expectations of an easy transition, although the natives shared the pessimism of this scenario without greatly advocating its qualification, that is they did not accept the identification of Central Europe with Eastern Europe. The Westerners seemingly were disappointed because of the slow pace of change and the newly emerging contradictions. Above all, it provided them with a good excuse to turn away from the ECE region to more burning issues in other parts of the world. (On 2 August 1990 Iraq invaded Kuwait and Operation Desert Storm started on 16 January 1991.) This scenario was very popular in the USA, focusing mostly, if not exclusively, on superpower relations and on issues of global crisis management, and being less interested in the small ECE nations with their idiosyncrasies. Consequently, they have a preoccupation with stability in the 'marginal' zones and, by withdrawing their former commitments for assistance, have adopted an approach of damage limitation or a stand of benign neglect.

The greater part of the new Western pessimism might have been connected with the fear caused by the decline and disintegration of the Soviet Union, parallel with the Yugoslav crisis in 1990–91. The Soviet 'Dis-Union' had, indeed, a destabilizing effect for the whole world and not just for its neighbours with a delicate transition to democracy. The Western leaders were nervous that the behaviour of the nuclear-armed paranoid Russia would become unpredictable and focused even more on Russia than before. For them it seemed best to create out of the entire Central and Eastern Europe some 'quarantine' or buffer zones to protect the West from any spillover effect across borders. The Western powers and institutions began to think about the whole 'East European' region as a European extension of the Third World. It is Yugoslavia which offers the best illustration of this second scenario, as an excellent display of the 'Return to the Past' with the revival of its 'demons'. Yugoslavia has been a summary of the contradictions of the former 'Eastern' Europe, and a real test case for the West in crisis management. However, Yugoslavia has manifestly proved the separation of Central Europe from the Balkans, as Comisso notes: 'the forces pulling Yugoslavia apart are but local manifestations of traditional divisions that mark the entire region' (Comisso, 1991: 4).

Latin Americanization (the Extended South)

It is this third scenario which is the real worst-case scenario. As the second scenario concentrates upon the fighting nationalisms, the third focuses on the socio-economic crisis. This scenario of Latin Americanization came into being around 1991 as a combination of a feeling of being abandoned by the West with the shock of the domestic economic crisis in the context of the larger world system. Latin America is, of course, a huge continent. Latin Americanization as a tendency has been introduced into political science by the authors of *Transition from Authoritarian Rule*, based on some large countries of South America (Brazil, Argentina, etc.) as a pattern of recurring crisis: moving not only from authoritarian rule to democracy but also, after a time, from democracy back to the authoritarian rule. The tendency towards Latin Americanization for the whole of 'Eastern' Europe, however, appeared long before 1989 as a result of erroneous Soviet-type modernization. This threat was mentioned both in the Western press and in public opinion of the countries concerned. This idea has returned with a vengeance only in the 1990s in terms of a new scenario and gained currency in wide circles of the population and with opinion-makers when the socio-economic situation began to deteriorate tragically.

Historically, it is true that Central Europe (with parts of Southern Europe), since the sixteenth century, has always been the semi-periphery of the West European core, in this respect showing some parallel with the Latin American countries as well. The semi-peripheral status, however, provides the possibility for joining the core as well, not only of falling back to the real periphery. The genuine danger for East Central Europe of becoming 'Southernized' came in the 1980s with the growing foreign debt, increasing poverty and unemployment, and, as a result, with a marginalization among the European nations in per capita terms. After decades of 'cannibalistic' modernization (the eating up of resources by old-fashioned heavy industries from the real development, that is, human investments, etc.) some characteristic features of underdevelopment appeared in ECE post-war history and these negative features began to dominate in the 1980s (again, more in Eastern than in East Central Europe, but even the latter could not escape).

In the actual socio-economic processes, Soviet-type modernization meant a craze to create a late nineteenth century model of heavy industry, in which all the resources of a nation were sacrificed for this kind of industrial development. Its results are now much worse than those of a lost war, since these pseudo-investments mostly devoured the material and intellectual resources required for a possible take-off of real

development. Even for Hungary, with its long evolutionary modernization period under state socialism, the 'moment of truth' came in the late
1980s with declining real incomes and the erosion of the previously relatively strong middle strata. For Poland, this Soviet-type modernization
was even more disastrous, making Poland into a showcase of Latin
Americanization and the best illustration of this third scenario, with a
huge foreign debt and social crisis during the 1980s. The real danger of
Latin Americanization has arisen from the growing pauperization of the
lower middle strata which may split the whole society into two parts, as
two nations in one, namely into a Europeanized-modernized society and
a provincialized-traditionalized one, according to the classical Latin
American dual society model.

In politics, Latin Americanization means that mass dissatisfaction due
to economic hardships will prevail over democratization tendencies, and
some right-wing populist movements will pave the way back to the
authoritarian rule. This populist upheaval can generate support for a
'strong man', a president like the Latin American-type *caudillo* (and his
junta), against weak parliamentary regimes. The end of the story is well
known, with the men in uniform seizing power, but this 'solution' only
leads to a deeper crisis. The particular pressure facing the populations of
the ECE countries, suffering from the socio-economic crisis, could have
led to a Latin Americanization in the early 1990s, but this danger has
already been avoided. This is not so clear in the Balkans, where the
socio-economic crisis is much deeper and the presidential systems with
the special role of the army are stronger, like Romania, for example.
Finally, the features of Latin Americanization have been quite marked in
the East European countries, with their uncontrolled presidential systems
and facade democracies.

Fair Weather (the Promising North)

The fourth scenario is, again, optimistic, but this time very cautiously. It
offers a historical argumentation for the European integration of East
Central Europe, presenting it as a long and tedious process. The ECE
region is different from the West, indeed, but so were the Nordic
countries many decades ago when they began their long march towards
the core, and finally, in the early post-war period they succeeded in
catching up with the most developed countries. The Nordic countries
have not only overcome their relative backwardness but have invented a
new social model in their welfare democracies which may be more
favourable compared with that of the West. This story has been repeated,
mutatis mutandis, by Southern Europe, although in a very different way.
These countries have been involved in the European integration process
as a 'promotion of democracy' by the EU. The Nordic way of development has always given some aspiration to Central European politicians

and political scientists with its social democracy and basic community approach, and with its active small states' foreign policy. Nowadays, however, South European developments are more encouraging, and the Mediterranean way of catching up to the European core from the recent past has provided even more aspiration for the ECE countries, first of all by the so-called Spanish model of negotiated transition. The democratiz-ation and marketization models of East Central Europe now revolve around the idea of this historical sequence: after such a long period of Bad Weather, that is, unfavourable external circumstances historically, there is at last a Fair Weather period, when international factors seem to be encouraging and facilitating the full European integration of the ECE region.

All four scenarios contain some elements of reality; they are true and valid, however, to greater or lesser extents. As I have tried to indicate, the first two scenarios have mostly an analytical value, since there is no real possibility of a Great Leap to the future or a Return to the Past. The second two scenarios are real open historical opportunities; one for most of the Balkan countries and the other for the ECE countries. The most decisive factor would be the international one, and more precisely, the readiness of the EU in the 'promotion of democracy' programme in East Central Europe and in the Balkans which seems to have materialized in a modest way in the second half of the 1990s. On the other hand, the Fair Weather scenario presupposes a 'help for self-help' strategy, that is, a very active structural accommodation and adjustment programme of the ECE countries, and partly also the Balkans, to the EU in terms of an intensive learning process. When we focus on the fourth scenario in East Central Europe, we have to be aware of the necessity of fundamental domestic transformations instead of only passively waiting for Western assistance.

These four scenarios have undergone some changes in the 1990s, and they may be given more concrete – economic or security – content, facili-tating the description of the particularly complex process of Europeaniz-ation.

1 **Germanization** as the partial integration of East Central Europe into the EU through a semi-formalized German sphere of influence. This partial integration can materialize in an intensive economic relationship of currency, trade and investment issues, bordering on dependency. The EU's relative passivity towards the ECE countries invigorates their efforts to join the dynamic German economy and Germany may take this oppor-tunity to extend seriously its activity to this region after having fully absorbed its eastern provinces. This backdoor entrance to the EU's econ-omic system, however, also has some negative consequences in terms of the relationships to the other EU countries and as a unilateral economic connection it leaves open the questions of the political and military inte-gration of this turbulent region into the EU. But this scenario may be

helpful in economic stabilization and can lead to a genuine democratic transition in the case of a more marked German effort for ECE forced democratization.

2 **Turkization** means just the opposite option; the formal integration of of the ECE region into Western military organizations (NATO and WEU or both) providing military security for the EU against the permanent Eastern European crisis zone on its ECE borders, but being also unilateral, with all the other issues of integration remaining unsolved. The Turkish case shows, in fact, that some countries can be kept in this half-way situation for decades, and they are not eligible for the other aspects of integration, although they may even have an association treaty with the EU. The ECE countries are in many ways different from Turkey, most evidently in their geographical and cultural proximity to the EU, but this can also be the major reason to turn them into a fortress, a buffer zone between the island of calmness and the sea of turbulence. This scenario in the long run would reduce the ECE democracies to the Eastern European type of facade democracies with some formal rules of democratic behaviour in the spirit of 'electoralism'.

3 **Yugoslavization** is obviously the worst case scenario for the ECE region. It is very unlikely, but it cannot be completely excluded. This low-probability scenario presupposes the full abandonment of the ECE region by the EU and the re-intensification of low-intensity conflicts by Serbia into high-intensity ones with the whole region. However, this escalation of regional conflicts may threaten everywhere in the Western part of the former Soviet Union from Moldova to the Baltic States. This is, above all, true in Russia where fragmentation as 'bantustanization' can turn into a desperate re-centralization effort by which Russia may make attempts to reconquer its previous sphere of influence. In the rimlands of the ECE region, there have been so many unpredictable events that this 'absurd' scenario cannot be excluded either. Also, the EU has not fared too well in its role of crisis management in the Balkan and East European regions at all. This collapse would mean the breakdown of democracy in the ECE countries also, with little hope that in the next re-democratization wave the EU would have better prepared neighbourhood policies and crisis management strategies.

4 **Europeanization** is the optimal scenario for the ECE region, in which all the aspects of European integration will be treated in a coherent way. This would presuppose a strategic vision or 'grand design' on the EU side and a concentrated effort by the ECE countries to overcome their 'post-communist' crisis. The victory over short-termism and narrow-mindedness on both sides could lead to the full accomplishment of forced democratization in the coming 10–15 years. This is a high-probability scenario because the Europeanization process has already begun in many fields, albeit very controversially and with long delays.

The major decision concerning the Eastern enlargement was taken at the EU Copenhagen summit in June 1993. The Conclusions of the

Presidency has notified that 'the associated countries in Central and Eastern Europe that so desire shall become members of the European Union' and specified the preconditions of the entry:

> Membership requires that the candidate country has achieved stability of institutions guaranteeing democracy, the rule of law, human rights and respect for and protection of minorities, the existence of a functioning market economy as well as the capacity to cope with competitive pressure and market forces within the Union. Membership presupposes the candidate's ability to take on the obligations of membership including adherence to the aims of political, economic and monetary union. (quoted from Luif, 1995: 177–8, see the list of enlargements, p. 170)

There are two major requirements for this positive turn in the ECE region towards Europeanization. First, the elaboration of a Grand Design by the EU of ECE integration after the Intergovernmental Conference (from March 1996). This process led to the Amsterdam EU summit in June 1997 which indicated the start of negotiations in early 1998. The second major requirement has been, domestically, the start of a positive spiral or virtuous circle between socio-economic and political consolidation, with the emergence of a new professional political elite in the ECE countries having a firm commitment to Europeanization. By the late 1990s both seem to be given. The Europeanization has both a general historical meaning and a particular one as a set of special requirements for full membership into the EU. To meet these requirements in the second half of the 1990s, the ECE states have to overcome their former vague and ideological approach of the 'Return to Europe' through a pragmatic approach and a process of structural accommodation. The consolidation of young democracies of necessity runs parallel with their full European integration, that is, there can be no consolidation without European integration and there can be no European integration without a socio-economic and political consolidation, either.

We have seen so far a series of pragmatic steps in the Euro-Atlantic integration. First, a new set of all-European institutions have been organized in the 1990s as a European architecture in the New World Order, replacing the Old World Order of the post-war period. Second, most of the countries of Central and Eastern Europe have been included in the Council of Europe as basic means of regulation of their democratic behaviour. Third, the EU integration began with the associate membership of ten Central and East European states and five of these started negotiations about full membership in early 1998. Fourth, there have also been some steps taken in the area of security integration; as a result of this process, in July 1997 Hungary, Poland and the Czech Republic were invited to join NATO and there will be a second round as well. Fifth, several regional organizations have been formed in Central and Eastern Europe which have served both to aid preparations for EU membership and to formulate long-term arrangements with the neighbouring countries. And finally, the micro-regions connecting different countries across states boundaries – EU members, associate members and non-members – have an extra significance, since they organize ties at the level of civil society and public administration and they have been the best preparation of the common people for EU citizenship.

Chronologies

International chronology of pan-European institutions

1 August 1975	Helsinki Final Act, establishment of CSCE (Conference on Security and Co-operation in Europe)
11 March 1985	Mikhail Gorbachev elected First Secretary
2 May 1989	Hungary lifts the Iron Curtain on the Austrian border
6 June 1989	Gorbachev renounces the Brezhnev doctrine at the Assembly of the Council of Europe in Strasbourg
8 June 1989	Four state socialist countries receive special guest status in the Council of Europe
1 August 1989	EU launching of the Phare programme (Poland and Hungary: aid for economic reconstruction)
2–3 December 1989	The Malta meeting between Bush and Gorbachev
10 April 1990	The Bonn CSCE summit accepts the principles of free market economy for the whole of Europe
29 May 1990	The European Bank for Reconstruction and Development (EBRD) is created for the assistance of Central and Eastern Europe
15 July 1990	Kohl and Gorbachev agree upon German reunification in Stavropol
3 October 1990	German reunification
21 November 1990	CSCE summit in Paris, The Paris Charter
17 January 1991	The Gulf war begins, the importance of the Central and Eastern European region for the Western powers drastically reduced
19 June 1991	Albania joins CSCE
28 June 1991	Liquidation of Comecon (CMEA)
18 August 1991	*Coup d'état* in Moscow against Gorbachev
8 December 1991	The Soviet Union ceases to exist
21 December 1991	The Commonwealth of Independent States (CIS) formed
5–6 December 1994	Budapest summit, from CSCE to O(Organization)SCE
5–6 December 1996	Lisbon summit of OSCE (55 members)

European integration in the Council of Europe

[Special guest status (SGS) and membership (M)]

Hungary	8 June 1989 (SGS); 6 November 1990 (M)
Poland	8 June 1989 (SGS); 26 November 1991 (M)
Czecho-Slovakia	7 May 1990 (SGS); 21 February 1991 (M)

  [The Czech and Slovak republics separate 29 June 1993 (M)]

Bulgaria	2 July 1990 (SGS); 7 May 1992 (M)
Romania	1 February 1991 (SGS); 7 October 1993 (M)
Albania	25 November 1991 (SGS); 13 July 1995 (M)
Slovenia	3 February 1992 (SGS); 14 May 1993 (M)
Macedonia	4 May 1992 (SGS); 9 November 1995 (M)
Croatia	4 May 1992 (SGS); 6 November 1996 (M)

  [Croatia is the 40th member of the Council of Europe]

European integration of East Central Europe and the Balkans in the EU

16 December 1991	Association treaties with Poland, Hungary and Czecho-Slovakia

  (with the Czech and Slovak republics renewed later on)

17 November 1992	Association treaty with Romania
22 December 1992	Association treaty with Bulgaria
12–14 December 1992	The Edinburgh EU summit issues the document 'Towards a Closer Association with the Countries of Central and Eastern Europe'
22 June 1993	The Copenhagen EU summit approves the Eastern enlargement
3–5 June 1994	The Corfu EU summit on pre-accession strategy
5–10 December 1994	Essen EU summit (decision about criteria)
16–20 December 1995	Madrid EU summit (decision about timing)
29 March 1996	Intergovernmental Conference starts in Torino
16–17 June 1997	Amsterdam summit decides about the start of negotiations

European integration in security organizations

19 November 1990	Conventional Armed Forces in Europe (CFE) Treaty signed in Vienna; NATO and WTO still divided
21 February 1991	WTO ceases to exist as a military organization
27 May and 19 June 1991	Soviet withdrawal from Czecho-Slovakia and Hungary

1 July 1991	WTO dissolved as a political organization
20 December 1991	North Atlantic Cooperation Council
9 January 1994	Partnership for Peace (PfP) project launched
End 1995	Nine countries of the ECE and Balkan regions join PfP
9 July 1997	NATO invites Hungary, Poland and Czech Republic to become members

European integration in regional organizations

Pentagonale – Hexagonale – CEI

11 November 1989	Talks in Budapest about Pentagonale
31 July 1990	The first Pentagonale meeting in Venice (Czecho-Slovakia joins the organization after Austria, Hungary, Italy and Yugoslavia)
27 July 1991	Hexagonale meeting in Dubrovnik, Poland enters
18 July 1992	Hexagonale turned to Central European Initiative (CEI) in Vienna
15 July 1993	Budapest summit of CEI (ten members with Macedonia)
16 July 1994	Trieste summit of CEI
8-9 November 1996	Graz (Austria) summit of CEI (16 members with Moldova)

The members of CEI in 1996 (with the year of the entry):
Albania (1996), Austria (1989), Belorus (1996), Bosnia (1992), Bulgaria (1996), Croatia (1992), Czech Republic (1990), Hungary (1989), Italy (1989), Macedonia (1993), Moldova (1996), Poland (1990), Romania (1996), Slovakia (1990), Slovenia (1992), Ukraine (1992); (small) Yugoslavia was suspended in 1992

Visegrád – CEFTA

15 February 1991	Visegrád Three (Czecho-Slovakia, Hungary and Poland) formed in a small city near Budapest; later, Visegrád Four
5 October 1991	Central European Free Trade Area (CEFTA) formed (Visegrád Four and Slovenia joins later) by the Cracow Declaration
7 May 1992	Summit in Prague
1 March 1993	CEFTA enters into force
25 November 1994	Poznan summit of CEFTA
1 January 1996	Slovenia enters CEFTA
13 September 1996	Jasna (Slovakia) summit

Black Sea region

11 July 1991	Black Sea regional organization formed between Turkey, Romania, Soviet Union (with Greece and Yugoslavia as observers)
22 June 1992	Black Sea cooperation agreement signed in Istambul

South-East European Cooperation Initiative (SECI)

9 December 1996	SECI organized in Geneva from the post-Yugoslav states and their neighbours

European integration in micro-regions

1978	Alps-Adria Region formed between the counties of Austria, Hungary, Germany, Italy and Slovenia
December 1991	The Polish-German Neisse Euro-region
14 February 1993	Carpathian Euro-region formed by some counties, or provinces, of Hungary, Poland, Romania, Slovakia and Ukraine
March 1993	The Polish-German Oder Euro-region
28 February 1996	Tisza-Maros Euro-region (Hungarian, Romanian and Serbian border region)

3

The Triple Transition and Nation-Building

Interrelationships in a fourfold process

There has been a debate whether the term *transition* can be used in the analysis of the ECE and Balkan regions because it indicates a direction and goal for changes, or whether the term *transformation* has to be used because it is free of this 'teleological' meaning. Of course, there are also many transformations in these regions, but in my view the term transition has to be kept, since there is, indeed, a general direction of change. This is the Europeanization process which offers a general conceptual frame-work because it is not simply about democratization and marketization in abstract terms, but about a particular type of political, economic and social systemic change which fits within the EU and meets the quite concrete EU requirements.

Systemic change has to be considered at least as a threefold process. It cannot be reduced simply to *political* transition, and even less to the power transition between the old and new elites after the first free elections. Systemic change is a very complex process, embracing *economic* and *social* transitions as well, but later on we have to deal very briefly also with *nation-building*, a fourth parallel process. The most vexing problem for the whole complex of systemic change is the interrelationship – correspondence and/or disharmony – of these four partial processes. There is no doubt that the political transition has a relative priority at the very beginning, necessarily creating some overpoliticization of the whole process temporarily, but later on the political transition has to proceed much more in harmony with socio-economic changes, or rather the political transition has to facilitate the efficient accomplishment of economic and social transitions.

What we experienced in the first years, however, was just the opposite. Politics dominated, even 'ran amok', so that overpoliticization for some time created more problems than it solved. This basic contradiction – which we analyse in more depth later in terms of 'overparliamentarization' and 'overparticization' – seems to be unavoidable, since it is so difficult to establish a democratic polity after so many decades of authoritarian rule. But if this process of genuine and full-scale democratization is delayed too long then it can derail the whole process of systemic change by neglecting the management of the socio-economic crisis and, as a result, the fatally deepening social crisis can lead to the breakdown of democracy. We already know from the political history of East Central Europe that this has been avoided, yet, we have to analyse this short period of authoritarian renewal carefully. We must look also at the crisis management efforts of the recent ECE governments which have already produced relative economic growth and a lessening of social conflicts. The period of 'selfish' politics, when macro-politics concentrated only on its own internal transformation and relatively neglected the socio-economic dimension, is more or less over in East Central Europe. None the less, the emerging partyist democracies have also produced a new alienation from politics and political elites which may become a serious obstacle to further democratization.

To assess the general situation of systemic change we need a conceptual framework which takes all factors into account. According to Huntington, the young democracies have to face three major problems. First, the *contextual* (or structural) problems come from the nature of the whole society in its long-term development; it is obvious that the relative underdevelopment of Central Europe compared to Western Europe has been a product of earlier centuries and not only of recent decades. Second, the *transitional* problems are temporary, originating from the nature of the recent 'Great Transformation' between two social systems. Finally, the *systemic* problems are characteristic of the given social system prevalent in a given country. This means that one set of systemic contradictions has disappeared for good (those connected only with state socialism) but a new set of contradictions has emerged in the new system, as Huntington argues with justification (Huntington, 1991: 209–10). The separation of long-term structural problems (the historical traditions on one side and the emerging systemic problems on the other) from the short-term transitional ones is very important. Namely, somewhat modifying Huntington's theory, we can say that the long-term structural problems and the specific systemic problems of the former state socialist regimes have a legacy in common: that is, a continuity in the form of *structural* problems in the fields of the economy, politics and culture alike in contrast to the genuine *transitional* problems and the new *systemic* problems.

We deal with political transition in this book, but now we have to extend this analysis briefly to the economic transition in order to be able to analyse the impact of the latter on the political changes. This is even more so in the case of social transition, which we have to look at in a somewhat more detailed way because it influences the political transition quite directly.

Political transition

Structural problems   Historically, the Central European countries developed a particular mixture of authoritarian and democratic traditions with long authoritarian periods and short recurring reform-cycles of democratization. State socialism was not a completely alien element: but it reinforced and Easternized the long-term authoritarian traditions which were weaker in East Central Europe and stronger in the Balkans. The recent democratization has to break with these authoritarian traditions and the tendencies towards de-Europeanization. The negative legacy is the *relative lack of democratic institutions and political culture* as an institutional and cultural deficit.

Transitional problems   The short period of democratic transition has been overburdened by too many political transformations going on at the same time, partly strengthening, partly weakening each other. The deep socioeconomic crisis certainly makes the political transition even more difficult. The necessary structural changes in the economy lead unavoidably to more social problems (unemployment for example), which worsen the political conditions and may even threaten the democratization process through a rising mass dissatisfaction and extreme right-wing populism. The major transitional problem is, however, the *lack of political experience, skill of governance and a clear European orientation*. The new transitional problems can be described with the terms 'authoritarian renewal' and 'politics running amok'. The transitional political elites have been superseded in East Central Europe but the new ones have not yet become professional, and the change has been minimal in most Balkan countries. This delays the fundamental transformation of both economy and society.

Systemic problems   The new system has established democratic political institutions, but it so far has created only a half-made, 'partyist' democracy, that is, a democracy mostly for the party elites. The basic democratic values of competition and participation have not yet been fully developed for the entire population; democratization and re-institutionalization have hardly reached the sphere of organized interests and civil society. The macro-political actors, and mainly the governments as the leading institutions, tried to organize a political monopoly over other political and socio-economic actors and to establish a new order in which the ruling parties of the countries concerned have a socio-economic clientura in an 'Italian' way. The real participatory democracy of the West European type is thus still missing, although in different countries in various ways. The consolidation of democracy is still ahead that would produce not only a stable and coherent, but also a fully fledged or all-embracing democratization.

Economic transition

The economic transition at first belied the high expectations of the late 1980s but has turned to a new kind of development by the mid-1990s in East Central Europe and to some stabilization in the Balkans. This transition has become a 'transformational recession', combined with a profound and unique qualitative change as a long-term transformation on one side, but the economy has suffered from several grave problems at once as an accumulation of many short-term effects on the other (see Kornai, 1993). The economic transition, therefore, has to be analysed from the above-mentioned dimensions.

Structural problems   State intervention in the economy has been a long-term tradition in the relatively backward ECE region, and even more in the very backward Balkans. Along these lines, the command economy under state socialism created industrial giants, first of all in heavy industry, based on state subsidies. The structural transformation of the whole economy was already unavoidable in the late 1980s, with a major shift from industry to the service economy. Yet, for some time in this 'creative destruction', destruction dominated and creation was minimal. After 1989 the GDP of the ECE countries decreased for several years, usually by 20–25 per cent in East Central Europe and even more drastically (in some cases up to the half of GDP) in the Balkan countries. This was most apparent in agricultural production, but it was also quite stark in industrial output. Industry began a slight recovery only around 1993 in the ECE countries, and agriculture since then has been stabilized (Table 3.1 and Table 3.2). In the first half of the 1990s, annual inflation was usually at a two-digit figure in the ECE countries and a three-digit figure in the Balkan

TABLE 3.1   *Annual percentage change of GDP, 1989–1995*

	1989	1990	1991	1992	1993	1994	1995
Albania	+9.8	−10.0	−27.7	−9.7	+11.0	+8.0	+6.0
Bulgaria	+0.5	−9.1	−11.7	−7.3	−2.4	+1.4	+2.5
Croatia	−1.6	−8.6	−14.4	−9.0	−3.2	+0.8	+2.0
Czech Rep.	+1.4	−0.4	−14.2	−6.4	−0.9	+2.6	+4.0
Hungary	+0.7	−3.5	−11.9	−3.0	−0.9	+2.9	+2.0
Poland	+0.2	−11.6	−7.6	+2.6	+3.8	+5.2	+6.5
Romania	−5.8	−5.6	−12.9	−8.7	+1.4	+4.0	+6.0
Slovakia	+1.4	−0.4	−14.5	−7.0	−4.7	+4.8	+5.0
Slovenia	−1.8	−4.7	−8.1	−5.4	+1.3	+5.5	+6.0

Source: EBRD Transition Report, 1995

TABLE 3.2   *Change of GDP, 1989–1995 (1988 = 100)*

	1989	1990	1991	1992	1993	1994	1995	(1996)
Albania	109	99	71	64	72	77	81	78
Bulgaria	100	91	80	74	72	74	75	78
Croatia	98	89	76	70	67	68	69	74
Czech Rep.	101	101	86	81	80	82	85	90
Hungary	100	97	86	83	82	84	86	88
(Macedonia								55)
Poland	100	88	82	83	87	91	97	105
Romania	94	88	77	70	71	74	79	88
Slovakia	101	109	86	80	77	80	84	90
Slovenia	98	93	86	81	82	86	92	98

Source: EBRD Transition Report, 1995

ones (Table 3.3). In Hungary, for example, over the past three decades up to 1989, there was a cumulative inflation of 300 per cent. Since 1989, there has been another 300 per cent inflation. Despite these big figures, however, cumulative inflation in Hungary has been relatively the lowest in the regions concerned.

Transitional problems   The transition period really needed a policy of efficient crisis management right from the start, with the first governments concentrating on the socio-economic aspects. Instead, this legislative agenda was neglected to a great extent, and in contrast legislation focused on historical justification, 'decommunization' and ideological issues. The 'transition costs' from the command economy to a market economy, and from an industrial stage to a post-industrial stage, have been high for the ECE and Balkan countries, but better crisis management could and should have decreased these high economic and social costs. The transition cost for the whole economy has been the negative balance of payments, which has to be corrected in the coming years (Table 3.4).

TABLE 3.3   *Annual rate of inflation (per cent), 1990–1995*

	1990	*1991*	*1992*	*1993*	*1994*	*1995*
Albania	n.a.	104.0	237.0	31.0	16.0	n.a.
Bulgaria	26.0	338.5	91.3	72.9	96.2	62.0
Croatia	n.a.	123.0	665.0	517.0	97.6	n.a.
Czech Rep.	n.a.	56.7	11.1	20.8	9.8	9.5
Hungary	28.9	35.0	23.0	22.5	18.8	28.2
Poland	550.0	70.3	43.0	35.3	32.2	27.8
Romania	4.0	223.0	199.0	296.0	62.0	30.0
Slovakia	n.a.	61.2	10.0	23.2	19.8	9.9
Slovenia	n.a.	117.7	201.3	32.3	19.8	12.6

Source: EBRD Transition Report, 1995

TABLE 3.4   *Balance of national budget as percentage of GDP, 1990–1995*

	1990	*1991*	*1992*	*1993*	*1994*	*1995*
Bulgaria	–8.5	–3.0	–12.0	–11.0	–9.0	–6.0
Czech Rep.	n.a.	n.a.	0.0	1.0	1.0	0.0
Hungary	–0.3	–3.2	–6.9	–5.5	–8.3	–6.5
Poland	–1.0	–4.0	–8.0	–3.0	–3.6	–3.5
Romania	–1.0	1.0	–3.6	–1.8	–2.5	–2.5
Slovakia	n.a.	n.a.	n.a.	–6.8	–4.0	–4.0
Slovenia	n.a.	n.a.	n.a.	0.5	–1.0	0.0

Source: EBRD Transition Report, 1995

Privatization has been the first priority for all the new governments, although they have maintained some political control over the economy. The transformation from a state to a market economy has meant a transitory decline of labour productivity (Table 3.5). The biggest problem of privatization is that governments have established a clientura not only with the new appointments in state firms but also by the special favours they have granted through privatization.

Systemic problems   Once the market economy has fully emerged, it will end the 'birth pangs' and eliminate these 'genetic diseases' of privatization. In the ECE countries the large majority of the active population already works in the private sector, which produces about three-quarters of the GDP. In the Balkans it may be around one-third of the active population and the GDP. Eastern markets have collapsed and with the EU commercial contacts have become predominant and vital for both regions.

TABLE 3.5   *Annual percentage change in labour productivity, 1991–1994*

	1991	*1992*	*1993*	*1994*
Bulgaria	–5.6	–1.9	0.0	+12.2
Czech Rep.	–14.4	–2.3	–1.2	+5.1
Hungary	–6.2	+3.8	+13.4	+10.0
Poland	–3.0	+14.3	+12.6	+15.5
Romania	–15.5	–13.4	+9.0	+14.7
Slovakia	n.a.	+2.2	+2.4	+7.0
Slovenia	–1.4	–3.3	+6.4	+13.2

Source: EBRD Transition Report, 1995

Social transition

So far we have looked at the political and economic aspects of systemic change. It can be argued that the third aspect, social systemic change, is even more important than the other two. All political transitions begin with *social tensions,* and the last period of systemic change, the consolidation of democracy, can be accomplished only by a radical transformation of the *social structure* and the rise of a new one. In the new system the broad middle classes give a solid base for a well-established democracy. It suffices to say here that political systemic change dominated in the first period; now, in the second period of democratic transition, it is the socioeconomic transformation which comes to the fore. The cultural and ideological transformation forms the final stage: the whole democratization process should come to an end with the mass emergence of democrats or the democratic political culture of civil society.[1]

Social systemic change has, in my understanding, three major elements which to a certain extent can also be put into chronological order as they emerge and dominate during the change process. The deep *social crisis* appears first, leading, as a second stage, to both political changes and *social structure transformations* and, finally, the radically changed social structure mobilizes new *social actors.* These last might have been on the scene from the very beginning, but they can act in full vigour only when they get the support of the newly emerged strata, whom they will serve by articulating and aggregating social demands and channelling them into politics. The emergence of the new social actors as organized interests is, at the same time, the 'end' of the transformation of politics as well, as organized interests are incorporated into institutionalized policy-making.

The social crisis   The social crisis had already manifested itself in the late 1980s, through the lack of social mobility, declining real wages, housing shortages and a labour force that was overworked with its harmful health consequences. This growing social crisis was a prime instigator of the social movements, re-organized trade unions and, in general, mass political pressures in general. However, it only became a great problem when the new regimes and their governments did not take management of the socio-economic crisis seriously. Since the social crisis was initially neglected or mishandled by the new transitional political elite, who focused attention on ideological and political fights, the crisis turned into one of credibility for the new governments. This grew into a crisis of the new democratic order, which for some time threatened to become uncontrollable.

The recent social crisis has three main aspects. First, there has been a drastic worsening in material living conditions: between 1989 and 1994 real wages fell by 15–20 per cent in the ECE region and by 30–50 per cent in the Balkans. When real wages began to decline, for some years this was compensated for by the second or shadow economy at the expense of overwork on a huge scale (which produced a dramatic decrease in the average life expectancy for the male population between 40 and 60 years). Despite these extra efforts, however, from the late 1980s real income began to decline for a large part of the population, because they had no further means to stop or balance it. The income structure has been significantly transformed, indicated by the growing percentage of the black economy, non-reported economic activities and tax evasion. In general, the period between 1989 and 1994 was critical for the social transformation, as well as drastically strengthening the social crisis. This critical period of social systemic change appeared across the whole region, albeit less drastically in Hungary and in the Czech Republic. It ruined the expectation that democracy automatically means welfare, and produced a desperate situation for a large part of the population. The collapse of the former economic system with its international trade connections produced in the first half of 1990s a general misery akin to following a devastating war, with the phenomenon of abject poverty in the Balkans.

TABLE 3.6   *Actual percentage unemployment, 1990–1995*

	1990	*1991*	*1992*	*1993*	*1994*	*1995*
Albania	7.6	8.6	26.9	29.0	19.5	n.a.
Bulgaria	1.5	11.5	15.6	16.4	12.8	11.0
Croatia	n.a.	n.a.	12.9	16.9	17.0	17.0
Czech Rep.	0.8	4.1	2.6	3.5	3.2	2.9
Hungary	2.5	8.5	12.3	12.1	10.4	10.4
Poland	6.1	11.8	13.6	16.4	16.0	14.9
Romania	n.a.	3.0	8.4	10.2	10.9	12.0
Slovakia	1.5	7.9	11.0	14.4	14.8	13.0
Slovenia	4.7	8.2	11.1	15.4	14.2	14.5

Source: EBRD Transition Report, 1995

The greatest social price for the political and economic transformations has been paid by pensioners, who have been victims of the high inflation rate and who have not been compensated by the state. Of course, the social price has also been particularly high for the unemployed. In the ECE countries the number of unemployed seemed to peak in 1993 around 12 per cent and then declined slowly. However, in some Balkan countries like Serbia and Macedonia it reached 30 per cent and there is no sign of decline so far (Table 3.6). However, the hard core of chronically unemployed, even in ECE countries, has been untouched by the small recovery. The social strata mostly hit by unemployment are the skilled and unskilled workers of the huge state factories on one side and the low level clerical workers on the other. In both groups those that are worst hit are primarily those who are in their fifties and resist retraining. Shock therapy was used in the economy of some countries and a more evolutionary treatment was applied elsewhere, but the whole population was drastically shaken everywhere by a sudden drop in the standard of living and mass unemployment in the early 1990s. Again, the situation has been more tragic in the Balkan countries, with no recovery so far.

The second aspect is social polarization – the growing distance between winners and losers of the political and economic transformations. Although mass poverty (in the extreme case, homeless people) has manifested itself, with some millions under the social minimum line (elderly people, unemployed, big families and the Roma or Gipsy population etc.), the real losers are not to be found among the poorest strata, whose position has deteriorated only slightly, but among the lower strata of the middle classes. The socio-economic position and prestige of the latter have declined drastically. Thus, instead of building a middle-class society with large middle income strata in between (the state socialist society with its relative egalitarianism was a pseudo-model of middle-class society), the social systemic change has so far brought about the phenomenon of the 'missing middle' in the social structure. One-third of society is usually growing richer, sitting on the islands of modernity, but two-thirds are still growing poorer and the 'old' middle strata (clerical employees, teachers, skilled workers) have lost a large part of their incomes. Their social position or status has become critical and this was an invitation for the large-scale nationalist-populist extremisms in East Central Europe and still is in the Balkans. However, in the mid-1990s the standard of living began to increase in the ECE countries and the major restructuring of society also came to an end. As a result, a marked decrease of social crisis can be noticed in the second half of the decade.

Finally, the social crisis has been accompanied by a psychological crisis: people feel abandoned, cheated and frustrated; families and friendships fall apart; many people sell their political loyalties for better and more secure jobs, and change ideological colours shamelessly, for instance, becoming devoted Christians from devoted communists overnight. In the early 1990s, in the midst of so many drastic changes, the social security system was fatally weakened, family and kinship relations became unstable, the national health system was crumbling and most people could not afford the necessary medical treatment. The compensation they usually got from the new governments was 'success' propaganda and long talks about the re-establishment of the glorious past of the nation and promises about its bright future. The masses, however, made their own subjective evaluations about the systemic change: many people did not see it as a change for the better, as a success – some saw it as just the opposite, and perceived it as a humiliation and defeat. Even after some consolidation of social services, in both regions most people perceive themselves as being losers from social systemic change. The peoples of the ECE countries already have become rather tired of so many changes, and although the situation has improved a great deal, they have noticed the economic recovery only to some extent and with some doubts.

The social structure transformations   The systemic change has brought about a fundamental transformation of social structure, but the new social structure is only *in statu nascendi*; therefore it has to be analysed with special care. The new social structure should obviously serve as a base for the new political and party system as well, with the new entrepreneurial middle classes being the focus of these social developments. The former classes and strata of the lopsided and overextended industrial society have begun to erode and diminish, but their decline has been much quicker than the formation of new strata. In recent years a dual society has emerged, a *state society* and a *market society*, and most people have participated in both. Although state redistribution and market incomes have had markedly different characteristics, they have been in most cases complementary. The two contradictory systems still coexist and compete with each other, even though the decline of state society and the rise of the market society can be clearly seen. The dominance of the market society has been reached in East Central Europe, in both employment and GDP terms, but it is still only around one-third in the Balkans with the huge burden of the bankrupt state sectors.

Altogether, kinds of 'fragmented societies' have emerged and the separate strata live in the same social framework without organic contacts with each other. In the most acute case, the marginalization of some social strata and micro-regions leads to structural unemployment. The remainder of the 'overdimensioned' industrial society is left in unhappy 'cohabitation' with dynamic new industries and service sectors. Modern agricultural society, still paralysed by legal insecurity, is in bitter cooperation with the re-emerging, ailing neo-traditionalist peasant society. It is a sad victory for the prophets of archaic 'private property'. The stratum of public employees, from education to public administration, also constitutes a large segment of losers, as they are victims of a shrinking budget. This is in contrast with the political-administrative elite (about fifteen to thirty thousand people in the ECE and Balkan countries) who enjoy new privileges and happily share the benefits of government-directed privatization.

The social actors   The first freely elected governments usually began with an argument based on the absolute priority of national interests. The national interests were, supposedly, exclusively represented by the governments, since after the free elections they claimed that they had democratic legitimation to represent these general interests directly. In this new–old paternalistic state model, there has been no significant place for autonomous organized interests, including the business interest associations that allegedly expressed 'dirty, materialistic-particularistic interests' against the sacrosanct national interests represented by the government. Furthermore, under the state socialist regimes most of the former interest organizations were given scope to be only transmission belts. In the new regimes, therefore, they were thought to be unnecessary and were delegitimized. This logic is false in many ways. First, interest organizations can be delegitimized only by their members. If their members abandon them, they disappear; if they get support *en masse*, then they remain powerful social actors. Second, the whole logic of the direct and exclusive representation of national interests by governments is also false. The governments usually disliked not only the 'old', but also the newly emerging interest organizations, although some of them had manifestly anti-communist ideological profiles.

Against all the efforts of the governments, interest organizations have emerged and/or re-emerged as influential social and political actors. Governments have been forced to conclude some kind of a social pact and/or establish national Interest Reconciliation Council-type organizations, involving the peak organizations of the employers and employees. In the Central European countries, compared to the West, there has always been an organizational or institutional deficit in the meso-politics of organized interests, also called in this case the 'missing middle'. In the Balkans the organized interests have been even weaker. The process of institutionalization in the meso-politics, however, has accelerated in the past years, with the growing support of newly emerging social strata. Among the interest organizations the trade unions arrived at the crisis point earlier, but they also achieved consolidation and institutionalization earlier. The major trade union confederations are competitive, of course, but they are cooperative as well within the national Interest Reconciliation Councils. The trade union structure of the ECE countries at present shows both the 'Nordic' tendency of organizational unification and the 'Southern' tendency of political diversification. The confederations are very active domestically – representing both the 'old' industrial and the 'new' dynamic strata – and also internationally in the pan-European organizations. Compared to trade unions, the employers organized themselves belatedly, first into some kind of Economic Chambers, as they had much weaker, if any, former organizations in the state socialist regimes.

The employers' organizations are still overfragmented and overcompeti-tive. These various organizations are based on property size and field of production as an organizing principle, but the infighting is still domi-nated by the bifurcation of chamber and interest organization functions, by the inherited rivalry between state managers and big private owners, and also by the divergence of interests between large and small entrepre-neurs. These provide many opportunities for dispute. Nevertheless, in these troubled conditions of the 'creatively chaotic' transitions, the employers' organizations have lately developed significantly. Since their institutional deficit is bigger, they are even more critical of the govern-ments' economic policy than the trade unions (see Ágh and Ilonszki, 1996).

We can now summarize the social systemic change in the following way, and this prepares the general assessment as well.

Structural problems   As an overreaction to the belated industrialization, the state socialist regime extensively 'overindustrialized' the ECE and Balkan countries; thus, a mixture of two different – urban and rural – archaic structures coexisted until the late 1980s as a division of labour between overindustrialized and backward agrarian regions. In these regions, the masses of unskilled workers were regularly commuting to the former from the latter. The traditional institutional deficit, the 'missing middle', the lack of interest organizations and of structures of political representation for the social actors were characteristic of soft authoritarian regimes of both right and left, that is both in the inter-war and post-war periods continuously. Thus, the modernization of the social structure as the mobilization-institutionalization of social actors has to overcome this common negative historical heritage.

Transitional problems   The deepening social crisis and the widespread appearance of crime (to a great extent 'imported' from the Eastern neigh-bouring countries) have to be managed in paradoxical circumstances, i.e. in conditions of a shrinking GDP yet with a growing demand for social security provisions. It results in increasing inflationary pressures and a soaring state budget deficit; this threatens the economic recovery, which is the only way to solve the social crisis. First, the governments were unable to cope with this aggregation of problems (similar to the catch-22 situation) and their neglect and/or low performance even caused some extra problems. The lack of social sensitivity of the first, rapidly changing, governments only deepened the social crisis during the first phase of democratic transition. The worst of the social crisis is over in the ECE countries, and the consolidation of the new social structure has begun, but the Balkan states are still in a deep social crisis.

Systemic problems   The old social structure has almost collapsed but the new one has not yet emerged. The governments have had two means to promote social transformations. The first is through privatization, which so far has produced more of a quasi state-dependent bourgeoisie than a broader stratum of smaller independent owners. That is, there is some kind of new dependency instead of a growing domestic bourgeoisie and broad middle classes. The second is through agricultural transformation, where modernization has been accelerated in order to meet the EU requirements, but the traditional features of agriculture have not been fully eliminated even in the ECE states, as privatization actually has created too many small owners.

There have been a lot of disturbing external factors in the social transformation, but it is enough to mention the most important one: the mass migration to East Central Europe by its Eastern neighbours. The Yugoslav war caused a forced mass migration, with many official and unofficial refugees. However, the pressure of migration has been much greater than the effects of the Yugoslav war; it has come from several neighbouring – even from some very remote – countries, as economic refugees going westwards. Because of the deep socio-economic crisis in the Balkan countries, hundreds of thousands have left their homelands as economic migrants, about 5–10 per cent of the active population. The population of Bulgaria, for example, has decreased in the past few years by half a million. The Western nations have considered the ECE countries as a 'filter' to stop these refugees. This mass migration has meant an extra economic and social burden for the ECE region. Cost and crime have come together with the economic refugees who are usually 'black economy' workers and traders. International agencies have provided some assistance, but the interregional, Central and East European social transformation in general has also caused an extra problem and burden for East Central Europe, worsening its own social crisis.

Summing up the results of the political, the economic and the social systemic change, in terms of a general assessment in the spirit of cautious optimism, one can state that the economic performance of the ECE region was quite good in 1996 and the Balkan countries had also some results in efforts at economic stabilization (see Appendix). On that basis, one can return briefly to the situation of the major social actors. If we look for a more precise sociological identity of the 'masses' active in the democratic transition, then we can see that the educated urban masses have been the most characteristic and decisive participants of systemic change in the ECE and Balkan regions. The same process can be observed at the global level in the third wave of democratization. The educated urban masses – and those in the modernized, entrepreneurial agricultural sector – have been very large, conscious and politically well-organized actors. They have done this through parties, organized interests and the media, but they have also been direct political actors, as the prime movers behind the political transformations. These 'socio-liberal' minded strata were very small and politically weak in the inter-war period in Central Europe and even more so in the Balkans, to which the traditionalist-conservative governments and politicians in the early 1990s have wanted to return for a political model. But that traditional society has disappeared for good, and the first freely elected governments, in their efforts to go 'back to the past as a future', faced resistance from new educated urban stratum. The clash between traditionalist and modernizing political and social actors resulted in a negative-sum game in the early 1990s, in which to some extent everyone was a loser. Historically and politically, however, the real losers in East Central Europe – and to a lesser extent also in the Balkans – are by now the traditionalist-conservative, anti-European and populist forces who have lost ground over recent years against the democratic offensive of the new, educated and urbanized masses, who are committed to Europeanization.

Neo-traditionalism versus national-populism

In the early 1990s, the above-mentioned 'authoritarian renewal' produced the twin phenomena of neo-traditionalism and national-populism in East Central Europe as two different but intertwined political and ideological tendencies. Two kinds of parties and ideologies have risen: the moderate and the radical. These have appeared in the forms of *centre-right national-conservatism* and *extreme right national-populism*. These two tendencies also differ sociologically, since moderate neo-traditionalism represents the historical political class in general, whereas national-populism is indicative of the lowest – poorest and least educated – social stratum specifically. Actually, most members of the former political class, or their families as successors, have maintained their convertible skills over the past decades, managing to get back to the leading positions of political and/or economic life. So, they have been successful in the recent reintegration process. Large lower groups of the same class, however, have failed to reintegrate into politics and the economy because of their lack of convertible skills. In the former system, they were only the lowest or the marginal group of the ruling class or nomenklatura. This can even be said for their situation in the inter-war period when they were 'the poor provincial relatives of the political class'. They have always been less educated and 'civilized', but closer to the 'people', and it is in the representation of the latter that they have specialized against the 'elite'.

The moderate conservatives focus on the representation of the whole 'nation', by which they mean the national state in a paternalistic-etatist approach; this goes with an arrogance towards common people, since these 'good families' assume they have been born to rule over them. The radicals of the same traditional ruling class or political class claim always to have their 'oppositional' role by representing the 'people', since, allegedly, they originate from, and are deeply interwoven with, the people themselves. The clash between the moderates and the radicals on the right is, in fact, the usual, centuries-old fight or competition for power between the two layers of the same political class. In Central, and even more in Eastern Europe, the nobility constituted the political nation (the *corpus politicum*) for many centuries, in some cases and to some extent until the end of the First World War. It did not allow mass participation in political life, that is, it monopolized all political activities for itself, even in the nineteenth century as infighting between the two major groups of the same political class. Formalist and/or elitist democracies (inclusive hegemonies and competitive oligarchies), as forms of a milder authoritarian rule, were nothing other than conversion mechanisms from the traditional to the modern way of power concentration and perpetuation. This restoration of power by the former ruling class through a conversion process was quite manifest after the First World War when an international demand emerged for a democratic facade to the political system. The elections, however, were usually neither fully free nor general in Central Europe, and much less so in the Balkans, in the interwar period.[2]

The moderates and radicals, centre–right conservatives and extremist-populists have maintained something in common throughout all the periods of distorted democracy or authoritarian rule of the past century. Namely, their basic value orientation is common: the central values of 'nation' and 'people' are shared by both tendencies; only the emphasis and priority are different. Neo-traditionalist conservatives see the nation from the angle of the strong national state as a politico-technical problem of governance, and nation is combined for them with religious values and state–church traditions as a 'national-Christian' regime. Nation for populists is not an 'institution' (state) first of all, but an emotional-cultural community or 'destiny' embodied in the masses of true 'nationalists' as a more or less spontaneous 'movement'. The term 'people' also has a special meaning for each, in two counter-positions. First, it has an ethnic connotation – our people versus other 'peoples'. In this respect, 'our people' are considered to be homogeneous and undivided, having the same origin and coming from the same 'blood'. Second, it has a social connotation, refering to an archaic peasant society which is obedient and loyal in the eyes of the conservative ruling class, but rebellious and resistant towards the elite, as the national-populists see it. The definitions of nation and people are, in fact, self-definitions, for these two political tendencies ascribe or attribute such a role to themselves. The centre–right conservatives think that only they have traditionally the legal-intellectual capacity to govern the national state, preserve the continuity of the national existence in its institutions and beliefs, and rule over the obedient population. The populists argue that the nation exists in and through the 'people', which only they can represent and mobilize against internal and external enemies, since they have the credibility, having been the only followers of the centuries-old tradition of the popular fight against the elite.

Behind these social and political positions – the 'well-established' versus the 'relatively deprived' strata – there are also different politico-cultural styles: intellectual elitism and rulers' arrogance versus anti-intellectual populism and popular hatred towards elites. In addition, there is the cult of constitutionalism and institutions versus the cult of spontaneity and socio-cultural movements. However, the more we describe their differences, the better we can see their common background in terms of the pre-modern mentality as to society and politics. Both are state-dependent social strata; for them politics is first of all a 'job', not so much a 'profession'. Thus, they have a 'cult of state' – the almighty, strong, omnipotent national state which has to be staffed (so it offers good careers and promotions for them). People and nation are the battle cries as a cover-up for the strong state. The latter is their 'market', which has to be competed for in order to gain greater power and influence; by using this power it is possible to enter into the fortunes of the clientura system.

The particular reason for the re-emergence of this duality and the sharpening contradictions is that systemic change has produced both winners and losers, and those people who are on the winners' side are moderates and those on the losers' side are radicals. The former argue that systemic change has not yet been completed, according to the scenario of 'our past is our future'; the latter claim that there has been no systemic change at all, just a compromise between the old nomenklatura and new capitalist elites. Thus, radicals demand a radical redistribution of power and wealth for the losers, that is to say, for themselves, if necessary also by violent political means. The moderates and radicals in most cases have formed separate parties, but sometimes they have been united under umbrella organizations which are similar in ECE countries; however, these organizations have turned out to have more and more internal contradictions and they have gone against themselves from within. A new turning point could be clearly observed in their relationship soon after the takeover by new political elites; this began the period of open mutual animosities between them. First they rushed to power more or less together, but later on their roads became separated by different power positions. As Michnik (1994) notes, in the early 1990s: 'The politicians of the victorious parties say, finally we have won the elections in order to have "our own" county leaders, chief administrators, directors and ambassadors.' The 'insiders' have been satisfied and have disciplined themselves as moderates, but the 'outsiders' have turned against the new elites and demanded a 'second revolution'. As Michnik puts it: 'In the first period the fight was for the freedom, in the second one it is for power. In the first period the slogans of pluralism and reform dominated. In the second one those of the revenge and vengeance, of the fight for all pieces of state power and for all kinds of privileges have prevailed' (Michnik, 1994: 25, 29).

This second period is the age of 'false prophets' and 'masquerade democrats', in Michnik's terms, indicating very well the new front line and the transitory distortion of the young democracy. Yet the twin forces have not been fatally separated even in this second period, with the fierce fight for power between 'haves' and 'have nots', that is, moderates and radicals. At the time of the collapse of state socialism, in the period of the total crisis of values – that is, in a historical period of vacuum between two social systems – the old, traditional political sub-cultures offered themselves as the only points of departure or orientation in this complete chaos. *Communism in East Central Europe has been followed by traditionalism* in the twin forms of elite nationalism and national-populism. This is even more so in the Balkans, where traditional mass populism and national-communism are still very high on the political agenda.

The major difference between the Central European and Balkan development has been in the nation-building process. The Central European countries have had some historical continuity of their states and institutions with their own constitutions and ruling classes. The Balkan countries, in turn, established their own state institutions and ruling classes only hurriedly before the First World War but, in fact, their real 'strong' states appeared only after the Second World War. Conservativism and traditionalism, therefore, have different meanings in the ECE and Balkan states nowadays. It means a nostalgia for the post-medieval and half-modern estates-like state in the ECE countries, with restricted participation and dominance of the historical political class. In the Balkans, however, the stateless national tradition – dating back to the period of the Ottoman empire as an emotional tradition of kinship community – has merged with the current mass national populism which has only 'charismatic' leaders but no genuine participatory institutions and no democratic patterns of political culture. The new institutional order in the Balkans has been based on the continuity with the quasi totalitarian or communist authoritarian systems which has been 'weak' in its own institutional development but 'strong' in respect to the population by excluding them from meaningful political activity.

At this point, we have to make a further distinction in the ECE developments between the manifest anti-Europeanism of the national-populists and the outdated, traditionalist-Christian Europeanism of the moderate conservatives. The traditionalist centre–right parties have been Europeanized from outside, in their European contacts and demonstrative actions, but they have failed to Europeanize themselves from inside, in their mentality and institutions. Still, they maintain a facade of Europeanization, reducing their Europeanism to simplicities such as: 'We have always been Europeans historically, since we have defended Western Christianity against Eastern barbarism.' The moderate conservatives usually have no idea of the late twentieth century Europe, with its post-modern/post-industrial reality, and therefore they have not been able to manage a turn towards real European integration in their own countries. The national-populists are more or less openly against 'Europe'. They create myths about national idiosyncrasies, such as true 'Hungarianness' or 'Polishness'. They turn their sense of inferiority into an aggression against 'traitors' at home and 'exploiters' abroad: for them, the two enemies are obviously connected by a world-wide chain of conspiracy against the peoples of East Central Europe. Their political programmes have been based on a paranoid philosophy of 'everybody is against us'. Therefore, they demand a strong nation-state to defeat all enemies. This conspiracy against the nation, in their view, has been directed by an alliance of 'old bolsheviks' and 'new–old rulers' : that is, a cosmopolitan 'judeo-bolshi-liberal' bloc against the common people, and in their arguments and theories the well-known versions of fascist propaganda have returned from the period of the Second World War.

In the ECE countries the moderates, the neo-traditionalist conservatives, were not prepared for a long time to distinguish themselves from the radicals – the extreme right-wing national-populists. The latter had the political support and the timid, indirect legitimation of the moderates – sometimes even giving government positions to the radicals – with the former trying to widen their constituency through extremist 'movements'. The real challenge and confrontation with them has come not from inside but from outside, although domestically the Europeanizing political forces have also strongly resisted any kind of anti-European traditionalism. This is because the extreme right-wing parties have been re-activated in Western Europe, and the ECE moderates have turned against their own extremists to the extent that they have witnessed opposition to them from abroad. International pressure, in the form of direct warnings by Western governments to the ECE national-conservative moderates forced them by the mid-1990s to change their course and effect, reluctantly, a half-hearted divorce with the national-populists. The borderline between the two major tendencies of this traditional political class has not become clear as yet, but the manifestly anti-European and anti-liberal national-populism has proved to be a burden domestically and internationally for the moderates. The neo-traditionalist conservatives have made some spectacular steps towards divorce, which has been facilitated and necessitated by attacks against them by the radicals with the deepening social crisis – as the history of the disintegration of the Hungarian Democratic Forum shows. However, their basic common features do not allow them really to separate themselves. These social processes have been behind party formation in the ECE countries, and to some extent in the Balkan states, which we discuss later.

National-populism and social-populism

Populism has become known as 'social-populism' in the world through its earlier American and Russian versions and, more recently, mostly Latin American forms. In most parts of the world, the nationalist (or ethnic-religious) colouring has only tainted social populism, or – if this nationalist orientation has deeply penetrated it – the social dissatisfaction has remained dominant in the populist movements. However, because of their belated nation-building process, in Central Europe and the Balkans the nationalist content has always dominated, as was indicated early on by the German '*Volk*' populism of the nineteenth century. In Central Europe the relationship between the two roots or sources of populism is the opposite; namely, *national* demands have integrated *social* ones and dominated over them. This traditional national-populism has been reborn in the process of systemic change as well, since national grievances have also returned, that is to say, national identities and minorities have remained an unsettled issue. National-populism has become one of the minor political trends in East Central Europe but it has been the dominant characteristic of the new political system in most Balkan states, like Serbia and Romania. The great divide between moderates and radicals is that conservatives are state (or politics) enthusiasts and followers of the paternalistic etatism; populists, in turn, are typical representatives of the anti-establishment, 'anti-politics' and try to replace politics with the 'operating principles of other societal spheres of action', namely with the 'movement' of common people or 'little man'. The national-populists are, however, not in opposition against the (conservative) elite but to a great extent they are within the elite and integrated to it. They use their anti-political stance as a means of gaining more power for themselves, or in the extreme Balkan cases with the charismatic leaders of masses, the national-populists are the political elite itself, as in Serbia and Albania and, mostly in the first half of the 1990s, in Romania and Bulgaria. Even Slovakia, as Carpenter states in the title of his paper, indicates 'the triumph of nationalist populism' (Carpenter, 1997).

Populism in general is the most typical 'anti-political' actor. It has a 'childish' political discourse based on commonplaces; it preaches a kind of anti-elitism, follows a set of traditional values, and bemoans the 'lost community' and the 'cheated' small man in a crisis-stricken society. Pro-action national-populism had a powerful appeal, indeed, for some years in ECE countries, and still has in the Balkans. To some extent, it goes beyond sheer demagoguery, and it does try to offer a comprehensive and coherent 'nationalist' political economy. Still, national-populism is an emotional and overdriven version of a backward-looking economic nationalism, predominant nowadays with its extreme right direction; nevertheless, it can also take the opposite, extreme left direction – they meet and partially overlap, however, according to the 'horseshoe model' of the left-right continuum which characterizes the political crisis periods (see the governing coalitions in Slovakia and, until 1996, in Romania). Pre-modern political values – nation, family and religion – figure high on the agenda (the official slogan of the Hungarian Independent Smallholders Party is 'God, Homeland, Family' and its popular saying is 'Wine, Wheat, Peace'). They reject the values of individualism and free market which are advocated by Western conservatives. The re-emerging populism relies largely on the constituency of emotions rather than on theories or arguments, and therefore, as a spontaneous 'movement', it is inappropriate for rational governance unless its rule becomes very authoritarian.

These national-populist political forces were an undercurrent during the 40 years of state socialism; however, with their covert but never forgotten ideas emerging as a traditional reflex to national problems and social crisis they have come back with a vengeance. I call this political tendency and mentality an elitist populism or 'populism from above' because this is a peculiar political behaviour of the lowest strata of the traditional ruling class or reborn political class. This tendency nowadays has no popular mass support in East Central Europe, unlike social-populism in Latin America, although the teasing problems of national issues and ethnic minorities are of major concern to a large part of the population. Nevertheless, the region's masses (with the exception of Slovakia and Croatia) have refused all nationalist extremisms so far, so national-populism emanates only from above and its bearers and followers have to try to find a constituency for themselves, a followership for the leadership. We witness the opposite situation in the Balkans, where the liberal-democratic, Europeanizer movements and parties have no mass support and national-populism has become the dominant mass movement and a social base for the whole political system.

The story of these twin political phenomena in East Central Europe, the neo-traditionalist conservatives and national-populists, has shown that these traditional-nostalgic parties and movements have remained mostly elitist efforts and have not received large popular support in the region, unlike in the pre-war period (Slovakia and Croatia may be exceptions temporarily). It is not only that the masses have been much more democratic than the first new elites, but it also seems that the still somewhat vague but increasing democratic culture has prevailed against the authoritarian efforts of transitory elites. After the collapse of the state socialist regimes, there was a swing historically to the other extreme, and the traditional political classes took this opportunity to seize power – fully or partly, for the longer or shorter run – or to determine the political agenda. In this sense, communism was indeed followed by traditionalism, that is, by paternalistic etatism and romantic nationalism. The populations of the ECE countries realized this emerging new front line somewhat belatedly and reacted to it angrily, since for them the new rulers as traditionalists were not so different from the old ones, the communists.

The authoritarian renewal was the major reason why the initial euphoria within East Central Europe turned to disillusionment, that is, from the 'annus mirabilis' in 1989 to the 'annus horribilis' in 1992. The responsibility of the new transitional, national-conservative political elites is quite clear domestically; they made national-populism into a real political force, not fighting against it, but more or less legitimizing it and incorporating it into normal political life. This was a self-defeating strategy for the new conservative elites, as the reaction of the respective populations was to vote this tendency out of power, even if only gradually. Slowly but surely new, professional political elites have risen in the ECE countries and with a strong European commitment turning against both neo-traditionalism and national-populism. The West, particularly the European Union, also has some responsibility for these distortions of democracy and the emergence of 'traditionalism' in the ECE states, primarily because of benign neglect. As far as the Balkans are concerned, it has been in fact a series of failures by the EU in crisis management against the victorious and agressive national-populisms. We hope that the doomsday scenario in the historical fiction of 'Looking back from 2992' is just a warning; it is certainly true that the Western powers have been much too preoccupied with their post-Maastricht problems and they have 'failed to picture the consequences of excluding the eastern, ex-communist part of the continent. The West Europeans shut their doors to many of Eastern Europe's exports, thereby condemning countries like Poland, Hungary and Bohemia – which with help might have managed to leap to democratic capitalism – to a long period of economic and political disorder' (*The Economist*, 1993: 18).

The authoritarian renewal produced a crisis in East Central Europe in the early 1990s but it did not prove to be a signal for a new reverse wave, which may have begun, by the way, in some Balkan and East European countries – the most obvious extreme case is Belorus. In the ECE region the major threat caused by the authoritarian renewal is over, but it has left damage in its wake through lost opportunities and distortions because of decelerated development. The major detour towards traditionalist conservatism, with its formalist democracy and hegemonic party, however, has been avoided. The long-lasting effect of these distortions is still with us and the political culture is also still burdened with some vestiges of traditionalist conservatism and nationalism. In the Balkans there is a serious danger that this new–old national-communism becomes a new tradition as an invitation for authoritarian rule.

The transitional political elites

The transition of power between ruling elites in 1989–90 was seen by many in East Central Europe as an absolute turning point in systemic change and was advertised by the first new ruling elite as the 'end' of the process, in which for a while there was an almost total change in the top political elite. It is true that this power transition led to significant changes; but it was not an absolute turning point in systemic change, since continuity prevailed in many other ways. This could be seen mainly in its institutional and cultural – although not in personal –

dimensions. First, the previous state socialist elites have not lost their power and influence completely, even in the ECE countries, for only the old party elite has been excluded from power and the other, governmental and economic management elites have partly survived. Paradoxically, not only the survivors of the old elite but first of all the newly elected politicians, represented in the early 1990s the strongest continuity in mentality and patterns of behaviour, preserving the model of state socialism. Such continuity is much stronger, however, for party elites and leading politicians in the Balkans and in the Western republics of the former Soviet Union than in the ECE region. Second, the elite change was neither completely new nor sudden, since the competitive fight for power between the various counter-elites, at least in Poland and Hungary, dates back to the period of pre-transition crisis. Third, political transformation itself cannot be reduced to a change in the elite holding power. Systemic change has also economic and social dimensions, each with their own elite continuities and discontinuities, overlapping at least partly with the political elite.

The transitional political elite has some obvious common features – its sudden rise to power and its lack of professionalism. This is true for the entire political elite and not just for its dominant part, that is, not only for the ruling or governing elite. Taken together, these political elites appear before society as one elite. For the non-elite there is only *one* actor, monopolizing politics and exercising control over all of social life. It is only within this monopolized sphere of politics that elite fragmentation and internal rivalry become manifest. This exclusive political elite is composed of four characteristic 'transitional' types of politicians and a fifth group which has become 'permanent'.

The first are **politicians of morals** – that group of politicians which played a role in the opposition and was seriously at variance with the previous regime. Thus, they gained moral legitimation in the democratic transition process as public figures. As liberal-democrats, they tended to be the most important actors in the very first period of power transition. Their special style of moralizing politics, however, turned from an asset to a liability, since it meant the preservation of a closed, secretive and improvised political style dating from their earlier oppositional activities. The claim to be a 'revolutionary aristocracy' (a term coined by the Czechs), destined for political leadership 'by birth', was weakened by their inability to transform themselves into professional politicians. This is because their moral background and principles had not conditioned them for rational compromises in politics. These non-compromising personalities, who had a direct link to their 'heroic' past, were marginalized in all ECE and Balkan states step by step in political life, including within their own parties.

The second type are the **politicians of historical vision**. These are the politicians who arrived on the political scene just before the power transition, without real oppositional legitimacy but with a determined historical vision of restoring the historical continuity of the nation and recreating the past in the coming future (like József Antall, the late prime minister of Hungary and so many other politicians of the region). They represent, in turn, an indirect continuity, that is, a continuity with the 'pre-communist' past, because they historicize politics and politicize history. They compromised with the previous regime, so they could not present themselves as politicians of morals (although they claimed this title, but without too much credibility). As advocates of paternalistic elitism, they were not able and ready to compromise with other elite groups.

The politicians of morals maintained the previous political approach, even unwillingly, through their black-and-white, polarizing and moralizing political style, by deep-freezing the old political divides. A direct political continuity was reproduced also by the politicians of historical vision in a completely different way, namely, by preserving the ideological manner and political style of the state socialist regime. Although they challenged the ideas and values of the previous regime – turning them from 'communism' into 'nationalism' – they also reinforced its continuity. This is because they claimed a monopolistic representation of general interests on behalf of the nation, in contrast to the so-called particularistic and short-term interests of civil society. The situation was the same in both cases with their arrogant and uncompromising elitist political style. Both types of politicians were, of course, negative products of the previous regime; they opposed it but at the same time they continued it. The differences, however, between the two groups involved here were very important.

The politicians of historical vision were also notorious in governing positions because of their non-professionalism in politics. At the same time, they disliked the 'man in the street' and tended to disregard his/her everyday problems. They concentrated on the mythical 'National History' and considered the hardships of the population as trifles and temporary discomforts that should not demand too much attention and effort. Thus, they neglected economic and social crisis management and gave preference to the restoration of the facade of nationhood (symbols, decorations etc.) and a national identity through culture, the media and social sciences. They hovered above social reality and felt deeply offended if the suffering population did not appreciate their historical vision and their efforts to return to the 'History That Never Was'. They feel bitter even now after having fallen out of power, but expect that their roles will be properly treated in the school history books of the future.

Thirdly, are the **politicians by chance** – that group of politicians (the largest in number) who came to power only because of the chaotic circumstances of the transition. There was an 'overpersonalization' of political life in general, that is, political personalities mattered more because of weak institutional development, but it was demonstrated as a problem above all by the 'small men in politics'. Both the other groups mentioned above contributed to the alienation of the population from politics to a great extent; but they were still talented people of some merits. This very 'transitional' third group, however, had no special talent and as 'political clowns' they virtually pioneered this alienation process, since their striking political inability was constantly on display. It was marked by an aggressive exhibitionism and an emphasis on personal career, and these became for them the only real public issues. It is very difficult to illustrate this group by mentioning some of their representatives, because they were characteristically small people trying to catch the public eye by arranging (organizing or provoking) scandals and making absurd declarations in the spirit of social and national demagogy.

Fourthly, we must consider the **old nomenklatura**. This group has survived to some extent and in different ways in the ECE countries as well. In some countries, like Hungary and Poland, there were counter-elites, half-oppositions and reform wings within the ruling parties, although in Czechoslovakia none of them could emerge under state socialism. Still, the old nomenklatura has survived also in Czechoslovakia, more so in Slovakia (Meciar and many others) than in the Czech Republic; and there has been more reform than continuity in Hungary and Poland in the reform wings of the former ruling parties. In general, however, one has to look at the succession *process* and not for successor *parties*, because in the early 1990s the most active former party members could have been found in the new ruling conservative parties throughout the region, including the Czech and Slovak Republics, and not in the so-called successor parties. These people have often turned out to be the best-known extremists within the newly emerging right-wing parties, carrying on the behaviour and political culture of the former authoritarian regimes. Presumably the biggest change in the old nomenklatura happened to the Polish elite in the first period of transition, since there was a counter-elite to take over the elite's roles, but the new Solidarity elite also soon lost its popularity. Thus, the least compromised and youngest members of the former reformist elite could arrange a come-back in September 1993 in Poland with a good chance of developing into a professional elite; and the case was even more so in Hungary, as the May 1994 election indicated.

Finally, **the new professional political elite** in East Central Europe, and partly in the Balkans, appears as a fifth group. This group is a mixture of new and old, with experts and professionals from the previous regime and new politicians mainly from the younger generation. The latter are on the way to becoming the real professionals in politics. This fifth group has become the trendsetter in politics in the ECE region, dominating political life in the second half of the 1990s. As the existence of democrats is not essentially the precondition but the result of democratic transition, professional politicians, too, do not appear in the first period of transition in large numbers; their mass emergence is primarily connected with the consolidation period.

Elite–mass linkages

The ECE transitions began earlier than those in the Balkans, and the (counter-)elite–mass linkages had many more precedents. The democratic political culture also had more traditions and institutions upon which to build. The populations were more mobilized and therefore the counter-elites were more motivated and influenced by the populations. However, the Balkan transformations were started only by the snowball effect of the ECE 1989 revolutions. They were violent, ranging from civil war to regular street riots and mass demonstrations, and were marked by elite–mass antagonism, even in the case of the 'new' oppositional elites. The political struggle in East Central Europe was articulated within an institutional framework and channelled within alternative party programmes, but in the Balkans it remained more or less on the level of inimical clashes. In the former region the elite–mass linkages led to a more or less articulated political structure with quite clear elite profiles and roles. Being 'gatekeepers', these ECE elites responded to the social demands in an 'Eastonian' way – that is, more or less according to the Western model, albeit in its initial stage. In the Balkans, the elite–mass linkages were not only inimical and antagonistic, but also disruptive or 'revolutionary'. In other words, communication between elite and mass was too often through the medium of mutual violence. Neither elite commands nor social demands were moulded into packages of alternative political programmes.

The level of articulation of the elite–mass linkage lies behind the emergence of a political elite as an organized entity against mass movements. This level differs from country to country in the Balkans, with Bulgaria for example much closer to the ECE type and with Yugoslavia as the extreme case of non-articulated politics. Political analysts have taken for granted that in the ECE countries the masses or movements did not play any important role in the pre-transition crisis, and 'pacts' have usually been treated as a usurpation of historical decisions by elites. However, the judgement above on 'pacts' reflects only the demobilization of the masses by the new elites. There was an important turning point at the time the former ruling ECE elites relinquished power, especially with respect to patterns of elite–mass linkages. Before the power transfer the masses had been mobilized and active; they had been optimistic with high expectations about political participation. Yet, soon after the takeover by the new, transitional elite they became bitter, disillusioned and pessimistic, because this transitional elite then tried to demobilize them and to remove them as influential actors in politics. In other words, all party leaderships as political sub-elites wanted to demobilize the masses in order to give themselves a free hand. At the same time, since then each sub-elite has tried to remobilize the masses against other sub-elites. The main beneficiaries from this demobilization and ensuing mass frustration have been the national-populists. Summing up the relations between elites and masses in the revolutionary transformations one can state that in ECE states the masses acted first and the elites reacted to these mass demands by arranging negotiated transitions, while in the Balkans the ruling elites acted first in order to avoid the major changes and the masses reacted angrily to these elite manoeuvres to 'steal the revolution'.

The contrasts between the smoother ECE elite–mass articulations and the sharper Balkan confrontations can be seen clearly not only in the period of pre-transition crisis but that of the democratic transition as well. In Summer 1990 the political changes in East Central Europe slowed down and it became apparent that the new power elites had neither the capability nor the capacity to cope with the economic crises confronting them. Political elites in ECE states thus began their de- and/or remobilization strategies. Nevertheless, these new elite–mass confrontations have not been similar to those parallel events in the Balkan countries, because the new mass movements and rising political mass dissatisfaction in the ECE region have so far followed the normal channels for articulated political pressure. They have not threatened to create public disorder or pursue campaigns of violence. In East Central Europe the elites of the political transition were usually *transitory* elites. There has been a permanent effort on their part to monopolize the power they recently assumed: by excluding the possibility of a wider political elite; by refusing to form partnerships with other elites; and by denying the need for any type of social pact or social dialogue. This caused a 'premature senility' or lack of development in the young democracies as well as an early ossification of their political systems. The new ECE democracies were born as elite democracies and turned to partyist democracies because of the construction of a new democratic order and its institutions which began from above in the political macro-sphere. After the power transfer between the old and new elites following the first free, so called 'founding' elections, the new political elite tried, once again, to 'deep-freeze' inter-elite relations and elite–mass linkages. It is clear, however, that it is only the permanent process of an elite incorporation, as the extension of a multiparty system into a 'multi-actor' system, that can produce a successful democratic transition.

Continuity and change

There has been a contrast between cultural continuity and organizational discontinuity in the democratization process and this distinction can be very helpful in the analysis of this early and relative degeneration of transitory elites. After 1989 the biggest surprise for everybody was the extent to which the former political sub-cultures, that is, value and belief systems, the patterns of behaviour and the outdated, anachronistic ideas, had survived. They had persisted even through the very long period of state socialism under authoritarian conditions. The persistent survival of these old values has been even more intensive among the intellectuals who have come to power, that is, among those of the new political elite. This feature has been much less in evidence among the administrative and technocratic elites and the population in general. The first political elites of the new democracies were trapped, or taken hostage, by the past. The new rulers arrived with ideas that are too old and/or too abstract. Their 'deep-frozen' values of the past embody a traditional conservatism made up of dogmatic-moralistic ideas posing as a neophyte liberalism. The contrast between the continuity of sub-cultures and the discontinuity of their original institutions has been marked. Not so much have the old institutions been revived, but rather these surviving sub-cultures have created new institutions for themselves. This model, with the survival of political sub-cultures in the authoritarian period to create new institutions for themselves in the new democratic period, is crucial in understanding the party formation process – first of all the failure of 'historical' parties in the ECE and Balkan states.[3]

The confrontation of outdated values and new realities has been clear from the beginning of the power transfer. It provoked a very painful political learning process right from the early 1990s for the political elite – a sobering process that warned many either to give up or fundamentally change ideas. On the other hand, for some governing circles and 'conservative' party elites it produced a voluntaristic and over-historical attitude of despising the facts or the present reality. This syndrome of provoking reality with wishful thinking was general in the ECE countries and caused a confrontation with the interests of all social strata. On behalf of History, this conservative attitude led to a 'societal war'. Certainly, the traditional conservatives in the ruling elites had no understanding at all of the European reality of the late twentieth century. After the power transfer there was a need to change political identities and personalities in order to bring about a permanent adaptation to the new democratic system. However, most members of the emerging political elites failed even in the first phase of adaptation. Opposition intellectuals were required to redefine their political identities completely, for example trade union leaders had to become ministers of privatization, etc. This was not just because of their own changing roles and duties, but also because of the transformation of the whole system within which they were to play their new roles. The new politicians were required to place themselves unambiguously within the structure of the democratic polity instead of preserving the old identities and patterns of behaviour. Yet in the event most of the transitional elite were unable to do so consciously – neither individually, nor collectively as a 'self-definition of elite identities'.

Beyond the problem of the first adaptation there was the problem of adapting to democratic life from clandestine politics, with its rather different requirements and skills. The ultimate problem for the political elites was the need to adapt permanently to the changing circumstances and to maintain openness for 'transactions' and compromises. In the first political elite, skills for both permanent adaptation and compromise-making were missing. They thought they were entitled to deal with political matters because of their moral legitimation or historical mission. Therefore, in most cases elites were simply not ready to adapt or to change. It is realized now that a democratic transition is a kind of 'permanent revolution' which needs a second opening or, at least, a series of 'transitions in transition'. Therefore, elites had to face a cruel natural selection process while performing the gigantic tasks of systemic change. This was indeed a transitional elite which 'withered away', as was the case in Southern Europe where the overwhelming majority of new politicians disappeared after eight years, that is, after the third free elections. This historical case reinforces the need for elite change and the necessity for the emergence of a new generation of political elites – the professional politicians with proper skills and a European commitment.

There are two extremes to be avoided when describing the ECE and Balkan political elites: the over-rationalization of elite behaviour on one side, and its primitivization on the other. The first argument is more frequent in the former region, the other in the latter. It would be completely misleading to describe ECE political elites as rational actors who negotiated consciously with regard to 'opening' and power sharing, nor did they have an adequate idea about their own interests, opportunities, bargaining power and room for manoeuvre. They made big efforts to act rationally, but to a great extent they were captured by the 'false consciousness' mentioned above and limited by their inexperience and lack of information. It is due to such factors that the new elites were confined to 'short-termism'. In other words, they had to react suddenly to accelerating domestic events and to overwhelming changes in the international system. Yet, at the same time elites cannot be 'primitivized', since they have also been major actors, above all in the Balkans. They have directed changes and made decisions about the fates of their populations. This leadership role has been done rather arrogantly in East Central Europe; thus, the populations have been treated simply as puppets in the historical show of recent re-democratization. As usual, ECE elites are in a comparatively in-between situation, being less conscious and articulated than their South European (particularly Spanish) counterparts, but more developed than their Balkan counterparts which have only had very sophisticated Byzantine manoeuvres to manipulate masses.

The pre-transition crisis was very different in the ECE countries, but the above-mentioned problems and the emergence and formation of new, transitional political elites are very similar. Using Huntington's terms, we have seen, for example, some kind of a *transplacement* in Poland where democratization resulted largely from joint action by government and opposition groups. In Hungary there has been a *transformation*, where the elites in power initiated democratization. In Czecho-Slovakia, in my view, there has been a *replacement*, where opposition groups took the lead in bringing about democracy. Similarly, in Bulgaria there was a transformation, but in the other Balkan countries much more elite continuity prevailed (see Huntington, 1991: 113–14). These terms express to some extent the divergencies in elite actions in the pre-transition crisis and at the time of the power transfer. Nevertheless, they do not explain the present similarities and dissimilarities. For the recent problems, the distinction between a disunified elite and a consensually unified elite is very useful. The former indicates the previous situation, in which structural integration and value consensus are minimal; the latter is the emerging stage of elite formation in which elites are relatively inclusive, and there is a positive-sum game instead of the former negative-sum game. This new professional elite develops an articulated relationship with organized interests and civil society at large. It is certain that the invention of democratic tradition, like the democratic transition and consolidation as a whole, is and will be much easier for the masses than for the elites.

Democracy and nation-building

After the 1989 revolutions it immediately became quite clear that the democratic transitions cannot be reduced even to the three simultaneous processes of the triple transition – namely, political, economic and social. A fourth process of nation-building has been equally important for all countries of East Central Europe and the Balkans, not only as a 'negative' task to restore national sovereignty after decades of having been part of the Soviet external empire, but also positively in terms of the creation of a modern civic nation with a rule of law. In some cases it means establishing the new national state itself with its internationally recognized borders, but in all cases it means overcoming the consequences of unfinished, inorganic national developments and creating belatedly modern national states of a West European type.

The task of nation-building presupposes four processes:

1 Organizing a democratic polity and a social market economy with its institutions, since the democratic polity needs a national frame with its socio-economic organizations as well as an efficient democratic state within clearly defined and internationally recognized borders.

2 Establishing a citizenry with political and human rights and with democratic traditions and political culture in civil society. The states concerned have to decide finally who are their citizens and what kinds of basic human rights they are entitled to, and what is to be their treatment of 'outsiders', such as migrants or economic refugees.

3 Shaping a healthy national identity without xenophobia and national hatred. The national consciousness of these countries has still been

'erratic', that is, burdened with the two extremes of both national superiority and inferiority complexes towards their neighbours and to the West European states, respectively.

4 Forming good neighbourhood policies and relations with the countries in the region. What these countries need first is a 'historical reconciliation' instead of the mutual accusations for the black pages of the common history. Only a historical compromise can be the solid and sober base for the elaboration of mutually advantageous, pragmatic relationships in trade, transport and environment protection etc. that the neighbouring countries are 'doomed' to have in common.

It is true, as Dimitrije Djordjevic notices, that 'It is always easier to be an emotional nationalist than a rational democrat' (Djordjevic, 1992: 341). But the democratic polity is about the rationalization of conflicts and their solutions. It can be done to a great extent in one country separately, but the real solution can be only regional. National-ethnic minorities, as a rule, are related to other countries; therefore, all political processes take place in a 'triangular configuration'. There is a dynamic interplay between the ethnically heterogeneous 'nationalizing state' – whose ruling elite tries to promote the language, the culture, the demographic position, the economic well-being and political hegemony of the nominal state-bearing nation – and the politically more or less alienated national minorities, but the external national homelands of those minorities also enter the game as the third actor. Actually, we can expect a positive-sum game only if all three actors use a democratic strategy and are ready to compromise. Since the same national minorities appear in some other countries and vice versa with large overlaps, internal democratization and regional cooperation are inseparable to a great extent, making the whole problem more difficult.

Roger Brubaker points out that a national minority itself is a political situation and not simply a question of different ethnicity:

> A national minority is not something that is given by the facts of ethnic demography. It is a *dynamic political stance*, or more precisely, a family of related yet mutually competing stances, not a *static ethnodemographic condition*. Three elements are characteristic of this political stance, or family of stances: 1. the public claim to membership of an ethnocultural nation different from the numerically or politically dominant ethnocultural nation; 2. demand for state recognition of this distinct ethnocultural nationality; and 3. the assertion on the basis of this ethnocultural nationality, of certain collective cultural and/or political rights. (Brubaker, 1995: 112)

The most important question is why and under what conditions the ethnic groups mobilize themselves as national minorities. In previous centuries, right until the end of the Second World War, the answer was simple: it was because of the great power interventions or their national homelands. The present activization of 'nationalism' after 'communism' is, however, a much more complicated issue. Beyond the deep-freezer effect described earlier, there have been some other, similar theories to explain the phenomenon that dozens of national minorities have entered the scene as conscious and active political actors in Central Europe and the Balkans. Some argue with a vacuum hypothesis, according to which nationalism replaced communism as a collective identity filling the political vacuum; some others refer to the credibility gap between the new elites and their populations, bridged by nationalist slogans on the part of new elites; there are also arguments that some large national-ethnic groups – Slovaks, Croatians etc. – felt that this was the 'final' opportunity for them to become an independent nation in the historical process of nation-building in Central Europe and the Balkans.

All these theories discover some real determining factors, but, in my view, they miss the point. Beyond the collapse of communism and the external Soviet empire, *democratization* has to be 'blamed' for the activation of national minorities in Central Europe and the Balkans. In fact, these are but the two, negative and positive, sides of the same coin. The collapse of the Soviet empire has resulted in the third wave of democratization, meaning not only the failure of the classical 'imperial solution' of oppressing and silencing all minorities, but also that of the more 'modern' solution of the nationalizing and centralizing states oppressing particular national minorities in an effort to create the homogeneous national state. There is a danger, not from minorities fighting for their legitimate rights but from the rampant nationalisms of aggressive 'majoritarian' states, that the problems of ethno-national identity will overwhelm weak democratic institutions unless their aggression is curbed by international efforts.

Some states still try the 'nationalizing' and centralizing solution in various ways, but their ethnic minority groups have realized that the international drive for democratization has changed the situation in their favour beyond recognition. The silent groups have become activated in the strong belief that international circumstances will give them enough support domestically, and that the new governments seeking an international democratic legitimacy cannot prevent them from presenting their claim for political participation and legal recognition. Thus, the activation of national minorities has become a genuine part of the general democratization process after a long period of fear and oppression. It also fits well within the Western tendency of 'new politics', which emphasizes local community and postmaterialist values *vis-à-vis* the formalistic macro-political dimensions of democracy. Consequently, the problem is not in the activation of minorities but in the missing legal-political devices of consensus democracy (see later conclusions in Chapter 8).

This legitimate tendency for democratization as proper interest representation and political participation of all kinds of minorities should not be confused in Central Europe and the Balkans with the militant nationalisms of the aggressive nationalizing states. *In the Age of Democracy there can be no return to the situation of 'silent' and passive ethnic minorities.* This Western nostalgia is absurd and unjustified: these minorities will not be silent in order simply not to hurt the comfort feeling of Westerners. The ethnic minorities have not been silent and passive in the West either. Quite the contrary, these actors in the 'East' have been encouraged by the Western practice through the actual democratization process, the promotion of democracy and democratic principles, including new community values advocated by the West. It is not a 'side effect', it is the *major* effect, because this process concerns all 'minorities' as interest groups, that is, it parallels the efforts of local communities for self-government versus the 'state' administration, and those of the business people to form their chambers and interest associations etc. Thus, the international community has to face the dual task, to condemn and contain aggressive 'majoritarian' nationalisms on one side and to support, or at least tolerate, minority claims for legitimate, non-extreme interest representation on the other, as one of the major preconditions for the general democratization in Central Europe and the Balkans.

There has been a new European public order emerging from consensus democracy and the protection of minorities. The All-European organizations, such as the Council of Europe, the Organization of Security and Cooperation in Europe (OSCE), the European Court of Justice and the European Union, have issued a series of decisions and declarations protecting minority rights in Europe, in the spirit of the Declaration on the Rights of Persons Belonging to National or Ethnic, Religious, and Linguistic Minorities (adopted by the UN in December 1992), like the European Convention on Human Rights and Fundamental Freedoms, the European Charter on Self-Government, the European Charter on Regional and Minority Languages and Recommendation 1201 of the Parliamentary Assembly of the Council of Europe. Both the nationalizing states and their national minorities have to accept these international regulations and act accordingly, since this 'European' road leads to consensus democracy and a rational conflict resolution of national-ethnic minorities.

Consequently, the new meaning of democracy, with its values focusing on the direct communities and the internationalization of democractic standards as the greatest achievements of the late twentieth century, is inseparable from the activation of all kinds of minorities, including ethnic-national minorities. This has increased the conflict potential in both the Central European and the Balkan regions. Still, democratization is the basic and dominating process in East Central Europe, and to a lesser extent, in the Balkans as well. The solution to ethnic conflicts cannot be a return to authoritarian rule, that time of nationalizing states instead of the repressive former empires which would 'solve' the problem by silencing all minorities. The final conclusion is, indeed, that against all excesses by agressive majorities in Eastern Europe, 'we should not forget the positive side of this situation.... The rediscovery of paths towards autonomy which would show regard for the wishes of the greatest number of people could quite rightly be considered very encouraging. After all, our era is also "the age of rights" and among fundamental rights, it now seems legitimate to include the recognition of diversity which safeguards the identity of each individual as well as the existence of various "collective identities"' (Giordan, 1994: 1).[4]

Despite all the problems and setbacks, nation-building is a positive and progressive process in East Central Europe and in the Balkans. It has, however, two paradoxes characteristic of this situation of systemic change. The first paradox is that the claim for regaining national sovereignty after decades of being imprisoned in the Soviet external empire, collides and conflicts with the claim of the neighbouring states and unleashes for some time a negative-sum game, even in the ECE countries, which turns painfully slowly in the mid-1990s to a positive-sum game of regional cooperation. The other paradox is that this newly regained national sovereignty has to be given up immediately, although partially but voluntarily, through the Europeanization process. European integration presupposes the dominance of supranational organizations, which has to be accepted by the new entrants as well. It is necessary and positive, but the first steps are more difficult for those countries that have just become liberated from the prison of unwanted, large-scale international integration.

Notes and further reading

1 The economic transition has a broad literature and would need a separate analysis. The social transition has been much less analysed in a coherent and comparative way, therefore I deal with it at some length, but I have to refer first of all to the book edited by Pestoff (1995). I mention for illustration that, for instance, in Hungary before 1989 only 10 per cent of the population lived below the poverty line; in early 1992 this figure was already 25 per cent. Most notably, more than one million retired people fell under the poverty line in the space of two or three years. A small proportion, 10–15 per cent, of citizens suddenly became rich – in both income and wealth – in these years. The distance between the poorest and richest decile was 1 to 4.9 in the 1980s, and 1 to 6 in early 1992 (it was much higher because of tax evasion). The other pole with the worst conditions may be represented by Serbia, Albania or Macedonia.

2 The national idiosyncrasies in nationalism and ruling classes have been analysed by many authors in the historical literature, recently and from a primarily political angle by George Schöpflin (1993).

3 I have described this asymmetrical continuity in my papers on the party formation process in detail (see, e.g., Ágh, 1994b). Here I summarize it only briefly and
   return to its implications when discussing the emergence of the parties.
4 The minority issues will be discussed in detail in the concluding chapter. For a
   comparative summary of the ethnic issues in East Central Europe and the
   Balkans, see, e.g., Bugajski, 1995a, 1995b.

Appendix: The economic situation in 1996 in East Central Europe and the Balkans

East Central Europe

Czech Republic:	Nominal GDP $51 billion; GDP per capita $4,904; GDP growth 4.2 per cent; inflation 9 per cent.
Hungary:	Nominal GDP $44 million; GDP per capita $4,272; GDP growth 1.0 per cent; inflation 18 per cent.
Poland:	Nominal GDP $129 billion; GDP per capita $3,351; GDP growth 6 per cent; inflation 18 per cent.
Slovakia:	Nominal GDP $17 billion; GDP per capita $3,148; GDP growth 6.7 per cent; inflation 5 per cent.
Slovenia:	Nominal GDP $17.5 billion; GDP per capita $8,750; GDP growth 3 per cent; inflation 9 per cent.
Croatia:	Nominal GDP $15 billion; GDP per capita $3,191; GDP growth 7.0 per cent; inflation 4 per cent.

The Balkans

Albania:	Nominal GDP $2.3 billion; GDP per capita $697; GDP growth 5.5 per cent; inflation 19 per cent.
Bosnia–Hercegovina:	Nominal GDP $2.7 billion; GDP per capita $587; GDP growth 30 per cent; inflation n.a.
Bulgaria:	Nominal GDP $10 billion; GDP per capita $1,136; GDP growth −10 per cent; inflation 311 per cent.
Macedonia:	Nominal GDP $4.2 billion; GDP per capita $1,556; GDP growth 1.6 per cent; inflation 4 per cent.
Romania:	Nominal GDP $34 billion; GDP per capita $1,466; GDP growth 4.6 per cent; inflation 57 per cent.
Yugoslavia:	Nominal GDP $15.3 billion; GDP per capita $1,430; GDP growth 4.0 per cent; inflation 59 per cent.

Altogether the six ECE states have 71.3 million inhabitants and nominal GDP $273.5 billion and the six Balkan states have 53.3 million inhabitants and nominal GDP $68.5 billion.

Source: *Central European Economic Review*, May 1997

4

Building Institutional Democracy:
Parliamentary and Presidential Systems

Democratic institution-building in general and the establishment of parliamentary institutions in particular is the main task of a democratic transition. Its blueprint has been formulated by the new democratic constitutions. East Central Europe is, by and large, a zone of parliamentary democracies, although some countries show, transitorily, some semi-presidential features. In the Balkan countries (except for Bulgaria) the presidential systems dominate with a personal rule, but parliaments even there play a significant role. For both regions our point of departure is the statement made in the previous chapter that *parliaments are the central sites and parties the major actors of democratic transition.* Therefore, in the presentation of the democratic institution-building in the ECE and the Balkan countries the parliamentary system is to be discussed first, in its constitutional arrangements and actual workings as connected with the role of the central government and the state president.

Institutions in transition

Democratic transition produced initially a series of institutions that were specially designed for that process, or even for the pre-transition; other fundamental institutions, in turn, had only some transitory features, such as the parliaments and the governments. The lifespan of these transitory institutions varies from a very short period to many years. The first is the case with the political institutions proper, the second is more character-istic of the socio-economic institutions. The central transitory political institution is the national roundtable; in the socio-economic field this is the central agency for privatization and marketization. The political tran-sition with all of its problems can proceed more quickly, the socio-econ-omic one much slower; therefore the latter has kept its institutions for a much longer time.[1]

The **national roundtable** is a particular ECE institution, although some elite negotiations have occurred in all new democracies. The national roundtable as an institution, as a device for negotiations in its role of 'constituent assembly', came to the ECE countries from Spain, but it gained a greater significance in the Eastern forum, where it also worked as a legitimation device, since there was a large legitimacy vacuum; the ruling parties of the former system were not legitimate for the popu-lations any longer, but the new opposition forces as yet did not have their own democratic legitimacy before the election. To cut this Gordian knot, these chief actors accepted each other as legitimate partners with whom to talk. By starting national roundtable negotiations 'everything' was already decided, namely that there would be no revolution but peaceful and evolutive change; that this change would have a lawful, constitutional character, through step by step transformations always making decisions within the existing legal order, but moving ahead with this legal order progressively and gradually towards democratization; and that there would be no retrospective legislation or punishment, that is, the partners accepted each other as legitimate forces, and therefore, after the transfer of power in this negotiated way, nobody could be pun-ished or hanged for former political roles, except for public crime. It is true that these results of the negotiated transition were questioned in all countries concerned in the ensuing wave of 'decommunization', but they have by and large been kept against the new right-wing extremism. There were, in fact, real negotiations only in Poland, Hungary and Slovenia, the Czechoslovak case involved some sort of capitulation of the former elite. In the Balkans we have seen a lot of the intermediary type solutions; Bulgaria for example is close to the ECE type of negotiations and in Serbia there have been no talks between the new–old government and the opposition at all.

The partners at the national roundtable negotiated about the basic con-stitutional arrangements and the electoral law, and set a date for the first democratic elections – called **founding elections** because they led to the foundation of the new democratic system. Most of the ECE and Balkans countries have opted for some kind of a proportional electoral system, based on party lists, in order to promote representativeness of the new parliaments. Only Hungary has introduced from the very beginning a mixed (proportional and majoritarian) system with a preference to governmental stability. The particulars of election regulations have been often-changing in Croatia, with its very complex electoral system. In Poland there have also been some important changes for each election, but smaller amendments from election to election have been made in most countries. The electoral law has played a significant role in shaping the party systems, although the fragmentation of parties has stemmed from many other, more basic, reasons than the proportional electoral systems. Finally, free and fair elections have everywhere been the minimal requirements for democracy, which are not sufficient for full democratization but have served as its base, and even this minimal democracy has been violated in a series of Balkan countries like Albania, Serbia and Romania.

A democratic transition, in fact, consists of many shorter or longer transitions. The most visible part of this 'transition of transitions' is the start, duration and end of negotiations, usually finished by signing a pact, followed by a short period between the pact and the first free elections. These short transition periods of negotiations and electoral campaigns, however, were packed into a longer period of **transitory parliaments**, still before the first free elections, but already after these pacts. Actually, these transitory parliaments, which were no longer 'rubber stamps', appeared in Poland and Hungary before the negotiations, and some erosion of the former power structure became more or less manifest everywhere, with the 'reformers' or 'openers' (*aperturistas* in Spain and Latin America) turning against the 'conservatives' or 'hardliners'. In Hungary and Poland we can even talk about the 'transitory governments' before the national roundtable talks, making steps for marketization and liberalization, and these transitory governments appeared in all ECE and Balkan countries before the first free elections.

Constitutional change

The first acts of the young democracies involved constitutional changes establishing the new rules of the game for the democratic polity. Constitutional changes quickly transformed macro-politics with its major institutions, but it took more time to transform the whole polity with its minor institutions in meso- and micro-politics; and it was even more difficult to change the political culture and behaviour which enables these institutions to work properly. Following the collapse of state socialism, there has been a general drive for democratization. Its concrete itinerary, however, has been determined by the internal nature of institutionalization going necessarily from the transformation of macro-politics through meso-politics to that of micro-politics. This itinerary has been identical in broad outline, but has been different in form and speed, in the various

ECE and Balkan countries. Democratic institutionalization has had three major stages. The first concerned the parliamentary and constitutional changes; the second involved change in the central government, state administration and 'functional governments', that is, nation-wide interest organizations; and the third changed the self-governing civil society institutions, primarily, local and regional self-governments. In the first stage the focus is on the constitutional arrangement of the major power sub-centres through the constitution-making process of the *parliament, president and government*, and on the regulation of the parliament itself as the mother and model institution of the 'parliamentary' democracy.[2]

In the second stage, the transformation of *government*, its reorganization and the modernization of the central government machinery with state administration and its connections with the functional or 'private' governments of the major interest organizations, becomes the most important activity in democratic institution-building. In the third stage, however, the so far relatively neglected or just abstractly regulated civil society associations come to the fore, as the democratic institutionalization of micro-politics with their specific and detailed regulations for various *associations* and *self-governments*. These stages, of course, can be separated only analytically. In the real world they run parallel and/or overlap to a great extent, but the focus of the institutionalization has been clearly changing between them, which delineates the itinerary of democratization unambiguously. The internal logic of the democratic institutionalization suggests that the macro-political institutions can and have to be shaped first, before those in the meso- and micro-political spheres, since the latter can only be articulated in a political space more or less already arranged by the macro-political institutions as parliament, president and government.

The constitution-making process provides a polity based on the rule of law and the stability of democratic arrangements based on the separation of powers. In newly democratizing countries, usually, we distinguish *macro-choices* between democracy and authoritarianism, *meso-choices* between parliamentary and presidential forms of democratic power and *micro-choices* among different forms of democratic government. The macro-choices were made in favour of democracy already by the national roundtable negotiations, but the meso- and micro-choices were left for the constitution-making process in the new parliaments. In order to describe this process of meso-choice and micro-choice in a more detailed way, we have to distinguish between the *Big Power Triangle* (parliament – president of republic – government), as the classical triangle of power sub-centres in macro-politics – and the *Small Power Triangle* (central government – functional governments – local governments), as the vertical and horizontal balance of power among many political actors of meso- and micro-politics. Again, the actors of meso- and micro-politics enter the political scene somewhat later than those of macro-politics, because they can move freely and develop their self-identity only in the democratic political space provided by the macro-political actors. At the same time, these subsequent stages do not come fully to an end before a new one begins. Constitutions, for instance, are made to a great extent in a rare historical moment of consent, but these constitutions usually are not comprehensive and coherent enough. They contain some contradictions and legal gaps, that is, they are not yet completely finished. Still, with these basically democratic, although to some extent 'imperfect', constitutions the first stage can be closed and the focus shifted to the next challenge.

The sequencing of the institution-building, from macro- to meso- and micro-politics is the general rule of democratic institution-building, with the task mostly, but not fully completed in each stage, and some parallel developments can also be observed from the very beginning at different levels of institutionalization. In the first stage of democratic institutional-ization the problem of the parliamentary versus presidential systems had to be decided. In the ECE countries parliamentary systems came into being in the early 1990s, except for the war-ravaged Croatia. In the Balkan countries presidential systems have been formed, except for Bul-garia, and for this region we can say, that *the more presidential the form, the less democratic the system*, since in these countries the necessary checks and balances do not exist at all. Therefore, the early democratic institutional-ization was a process of parliamentarization, as a dominant process in East Central Europe and a more secondary one in the Balkans. The organ-ization of a new democratic parliament has not only been the major task of the early democratization, it has also determined and articulated all the other ongoing functions of institutionalization. Parliaments were the mother and model institutions for the entire democratization process, which led to a particular dominance of parliaments ('over-parliamentar-ization') in the first phase of democratic transition. This was accompanied by a similar process of particular dominance of the parties as major actors ('over-particization'). It means that, for some years, the parliaments as central sites of democratization were almost the only sites and parties as major actors of democratization were almost the only ones. This is a typical contradiction of early democratization and institution-building, which comes from the necessity of beginning the democratization process 'from above', that is, in macro-politics, and from the ensuing uneven development, since the new institutions and actors dominate until others emerge.

Parliaments are central sites and parties are major actors of democratic transition – this is the major principle which connects East Central Europe with Southern Europe, where this principle was first formulated (see Liebert and Cotta, 1990). This principle at the same time separates East Central Europe from Latin America on one side and Eastern Europe proper on the other, where parliaments and parties are weak and have not played a decisive role in democratization, with the Balkans situated between East Central and Eastern Europe. In contrast to Western Europe where parliaments are in decline, in the new ECE democracies they are certainly on the rise because of their decisive role in democratization. This role may decline after democratic consolidation, that is, in mature democracies in a Western way, but it will certainly be maintained while democratization is going on.

Consequently, parliamentarization has a special meaning in new democracies. It is a special and decisive aspect of democratization, namely both democratic institution-building and the acquiring of democratic political culture have come into being in and through the parliaments. The moulding and modelling of other institutions and all the patterns of political behaviour has also taken place according to the parliamentary rules and designs. Parliaments have been so far the meeting place, the forum and battlefield for parties, and for all political forces and tendencies. They have also been, to a great extent, 'governing parliaments', that is, even the governments have acted in and through the parliaments, since they have had limited time and energy for the tremendous tasks of transformation. The preparation of bills, for instance, has been rather insufficient everywhere, in such a way that parliaments have not only 'passed', but also prepared and processed the bills. Parliamentarization, therefore, has an almost 'technical' meaning as well, as procedure of political processes to be learned by all actors in order to be able to act in and influence the other actors through the parliament. Parliaments in the ECE, and to some extent the Balkan, countries have enjoyed high visibility and exposure, since they have been the venue and forum of all political struggles. This high visibility brings about some negative consequences as well. The populations of these countries have closely followed the parliamentary debates, most of which have been broadcast live by TV in all countries, and because of the high visibility of parliaments, people have connected all the weaknesses and contradictions of democratic transition with the parliaments. Hence, despite their very positive and innovative role in democratization, the parliaments are very unpopular, perhaps more than the parties, just as they were in the Southern European countries during their democratic transition. Paradoxically, the parliaments have been the most important and the least popular institutions of the young ECE democracies.[3]

Parliamentarization

Parliaments have been the most important institutions of the democratization process in the ECE and Balkan countries (see Olson and Norton, 1996). Yet, parliaments are less popular than governments, since they represent all the vices and mistakes of the new regimes in the public eye, and they embrace and put on display all the political actors and processes. They concentrate in themselves the accumulated *institutional* as well as *cultural* deficits of the region in general and the historical heritage of the former authoritarian regime in particular. Still, compared to the 'decline' of Western parliaments, in East Central Europe and in some Balkan countries we have certainly been witnesses to the 'rise' of parliaments, that is, there has been an extraordinarily high importance placed on parliaments, although in a transitory and contradictory way. However, the institutional and cultural deficit is a missing capacity in and for democratization. It appears in the forms of missing institutions and missing cultural patterns, to a greater extent in the Balkan countries and to a lesser extent in the ECE countries. As David Olson notes,

> The new parliaments lack an experienced membership. They lack a structure of parties and committees, and they also lack the support facilities of space, equipment, and staff. Most importantly, the newly democratized parliaments established procedures for both raising and resolving policy disagreements. New members in new parliaments are not well-equipped to face their tasks.... Communist legislatures typically had a skeletal staff who themselves had little experience in providing support to an argumentative and busy parliament. (Olson, 1994: 37)[4]

The institutional deficit can be easily formulated into two aspects: the presence of immature parties and missing or half-made internal parliamentary institutions (structures and procedures). The cultural deficit, in turn, is bigger and it is more difficult to identify. However, it irritates the public more than the institutional deficit, since it appears to be an arrogant form of behaviour on the part of the new parliamentary party elite. Parliamentary elites have provided a much less democratic pattern of behaviour than the masses. The arrogant behaviour of the new, transitory elites has led to a great extent to the delegitimation and unpopularity of the new democratic parliaments. This has been apparent in direct anti-parliamentary feelings, movements and slogans; these have shown the limitations of this narrow 'parliamentary', that is, a transitorily 'over-parliamentarized' democracy. The democratic deficit in these 'parliamentary' democracies as a gap between elites and masses, leaders and followers, has at least three causes.

1 The elite–mass linkages changed dramatically after the first democratic elections, since the new elites wanted to demobilize the masses and transform movement parties to well-institutionalized ones; therefore, they used all means available to remove the masses from politics. The ways and means of direct democracy as plebiscites were pushed back and people had no real chance to have their voices heard. The politics, once again, became a remote realm for most of the ordinary people and this alien politics was represented for them by the parliament and the parliamentary elite.

2 Cultural struggle (*Kulturkampf*) and ideological confrontation began in the new elite immediately after the power transfer, following the inter-war intellectual traditions. The elites, fragmented in such a way into many overcompetitive sub-elites, turned away in parliamentary discussions and in their typical parliamentary discourse from the most pressing issues of socio-economic crisis management – which was, in turn, extremely important for the population – and engaged in obscure ideological fights.

3 Unlike the Western elites, socialized for tolerance and compromise-seeking behaviour, the new ECE political elites have been thinking in terms of 'final victory' and have tried to push out their competitors from politics as 'enemies'. The masses, however, would have preferred gradual and peaceful changes, and consensus-oriented behaviour to the doctrinaire radicalism of the transitory elites, and they expected model behaviour of tolerance and politeness from the parliamentary delegates throughout the entire democratization process. Therefore, they turned against the new politicians appearing with a 'moral vision' or 'historical mission' in the parliaments and they supported the incoming new pragmatic professional politicians learning the rules of efficient decision-making.[5]

Thus, the negotiated transition came to an end abruptly after the so-called founding elections, as the first free elections, and the establishment of the first democratic parliaments and governments, that is, with the transfer of power between the old and new elites. This elite transfer did not produce a 'negotiated' democracy between the new governments and new oppositions, nor between the new elites and mobilized populations. Politics has been 'running amok' in this early 'post' period. These features, which dominated in the first half of the 1990s, have become weak-ened by the later years of the decade, as the first transitory elites have gradually changed to more professional and pragmatic elites; and yet, the new gap between politics and the ordinary people has remained to a great extent. In the early 1990s the parliaments became symbols of this isolated, self-centred politics, which was far from the common people and from the everyday problems and interests of the populations concerned. This politics was primarily and typically made by self-styled and awkward parties that acted with low efficiency in the parliaments. The most characteristic case of these ill-famed ECE parliaments, as symbols of 'politics running amok', was the Polish Sejm between 1991 and 1993, which had an overfragmented party structure and many co-alition failures. The situation has now significantly improved but, to a lesser extent, these negative features have remained for longer with other new parliaments and their elites.

Discussing the paradoxes of parliamentarization as the first period of democratic institution-building, we have to put it into the broader framework of the entire systemic change. The first stage of systemic change starts with the initial or pre-transition crisis, in which the politico-cultural side plays an important role and the masses are very active. In the second stage (democratic transition), however, institutionalization, above all in the form of parliamentarization, comes to the fore and the masses are abruptly demobilized. Democratic consolidation, which embodies the third stage, can only be reached with the re-mobilization of masses for the creation of their own organized interests and civil society organizations. This common institutionalization and 'culturalization' process would be capable of leading these countries beyond the narrow confines of 'just' parliamentary democracy, by enabling them to overcome both over-parliamentarization and over-particization through the consolidation of genuine parliamentary democracy.

Thus, the parliamentarization process represents a special phase and form of democratization in East Central Europe and, in some ways, also in the Balkan countries. It shows that there are many difficulties in institutionalization and even more in 'culturalization', that is, in elite recruitment and socialization. Therefore, the transitory parliamentary elite has changed very quickly, as also happened to the South European parliamentary elites during their democratic transition. At every election about 70 per cent of delegates 'fall out' of the ECE parliaments and newcomers step in. As a result of this very low incumbent retention rate, after three elections about 5–10 per cent of the parliamentary elite remains in many of these countries. A new professional political elite has gradually emerged in the parliaments, that is to say, even in the 'natural selection' of elites, the parliamentarization process is the most important dimension of democratic transition. The latter is a chaotic whirling of the old and new, and as a creative chaos, it 'tames' political actors in and around the parliament. At the same time, it is only through this process of parliamentarization that the parliament itself can accomplish its own internal systemic change.

Separation of powers

The Big Power Triangle (of parliament, president and government) varies in its particular shape from country to country, and so do the national parliaments within this triangle. In Poland, for example, the president had the right to appoint three important ministers (home affairs, foreign affairs and defence), which limited markedly the powers of parliament and government. The parliaments vary not only in strength but also in their internal structure. In Poland, the Czech Republic, Slovenia, Croatia, Romania and Yugoslavia the parliaments are bicameral. Hungary, Slovakia, Bulgaria and Macedonia have unicameral legislations. In the Balkan states the governments are constitutionally weaker, while in Hungary – with its prime ministerial system – government is stronger than in the other ECE countries. Compared to the actual political strength

of the central governments, however, all ECE parliaments can be classified as 'subordinate' legislatures, because they are made up by party
factions with rather strict party discipline and, therefore, the governing
parties control parliaments to a great extent. In the Balkans parliaments
are even weaker compared to the power of the presidents and these
governments, therefore, can be classified as 'submissive' types. Initially,
parliaments may also be of 'coordinate' or 'intermediate' type as far as
their relationship with the executive power is concerned, but later on this
relationship stabilizes into the subordinate or submissive types. At the
same time, the parties are rather weak sociologically, that is, as social
organizations, but they are very strong as (the only) political organizations. Thus, parties exist mostly as parliamentary parties, in and through
the parliament. Their leadership has actually been merged with the
parliamentary faction. They spend most of their active time in the parliaments and have most of their infrastructure and expert staff there. They
communicate with the public, including their own membership, mostly
from the parliament. There is no doubt that the 'partyness' of parliaments
is high, but the 'parliament-embeddedness' of parties is high, too.

Whereas the Western parliaments have a clear functional division of
labour with the other political institutions and relatively narrowly
defined tasks, in the ECE and Balkan countries the parliaments have, as
an 'infantile disease', a much more extended role, since they replace other
institutions. In my understanding, the parliaments of young democracies
have five major functions, and most are directly connected with the
formation of the new democratic system. All five have been very important for this 'genesis', though their actual importance varies from stage to
stage in democratization. The major functions are the following.

1 The *legislative function*, which has taken place in East Central Europe
   above all in the constitution-making process, that is, the establishment
   of the basic rules of the political game for the whole transition and for
   the consolidation of democracy. The production of laws for the new
   social and political order has also been a very important task and the
   parliaments have produced a great number of laws and amendments
   every year. I have identified this function of parliaments as a 'legislative
   factory'.
2 The *controlling function*, in which the parliament has played the role of a
   distributor of powers, and has balanced the executive in order to prevent
   the rise of a new power monopoly. So far this role has been only partly
   and inefficiently fulfilled by the new legislatures, whereas the Constitutional Courts have performed a more important role in this respect.
   The legitimate role of the opposition, in general and in the control of
   parliament in particular, has been acknowledged and institutionalized
   in most ECE countries, but this has still been the major bottleneck in the
   democratic workings of most of the Balkan parliaments.
3 The *conflict management function*, which has been particularly important

in the period of deep socio-economic crisis associated with democratic transition. The transition has been accompanied by acute conflicts, and these have arisen in a cumulative way. Therefore, in this period the parliaments have had to be the major means of conflict resolution. It is also unavoidable that the parliaments have been the central targets of all mass protests and demonstrations.

4 The *socialization function*, involving the schooling of the new elite after its recruitment process by providing an 'arena' for its 'natural selection' and establishing the rules of 'parliamentarized' elite behaviour. The culturalizational–educational process of parliamentarization has been as important as the institutionalization process, and it deserves special attention and analysis.[6]

5 The *legitimation function* can be regarded as the most essential one in the first period of the democratic transition, since the young democracies have emerged from a legitimacy gap or vacuum and badly need a strong legitimation device. Parliament as a central site provides a forum for the major political actors and they mutually legitimize themselves and the new democratic order. The creation of a parliamentary framework for democracy should facilitate at the same time the building of a bridge between the parties and ordinary citizens in the form of a social and political dialogue, in and through the parliament.

Parliaments as central sites of democratic transition are still unfinished or half-made institutions and they work with a rather low efficiency. They have been 'legislative factories', producing a great number of Acts every year, but this extensive overproduction has not been accompanied by intensive internal workings. There has been a tradition of parliamentary procedures, and yet still the new Standing Orders have emerged after great delay and with many contradictions concerning the legitimate role of the opposition in the young democracies. Because of poor preparation of draft Bills and hastily passed Acts, a significant proportion of Acts have had to be amended or proved to be unfit for implementation. The new parliaments, however, have learned very quickly; for instance, they have already an extended system of parliamentary committees, paralleling the structure of governmental departments. Political and policy dimensions of parliamentary work meet in these parliamentary committees and they symbolize the efforts of the new legislatives in developing towards efficient and genuine parliamentary democracies.[7]

Democratic governance

After parliamentarization, the second stage of democratic institutionalization comprises the organization of the new democratic (central) governments and/or governance. This process happened first and foremost in the parliament, where the new parties learned the new and changing roles of governing and opposition parties. As we know, the new parliaments have been to some extent 'governing parliaments', since the governments have been absorbed by the many tasks of the parliamentary decision-making process. This has significantly changed, and yet some major executive decisions are still made in and through the parliament, including preparation and completion of Bills etc. The parliamentary factions of the governing parties have almost merged with the government, since to the small top leadership these everyday tasks overlap to a great extent. Yet, the distance between the legislative and executive powers has become ever wider, and the governments have focused more and more on their own internal institutionalization and democratization. They have also turned from ideologically oriented 'systemic' issues to more pragmatic, policy oriented ones; hence the switch from democratization to political modernization has been manifest in the workings of central governments as well.

The new democratic governance was organized first in the central government, then throughout the entire state administration, which itself has been constitutionally separated from the public administration managed by local self-governments. Public administration has become a separate branch of power and, therefore, the first local government elections had a special political significance in changing local elites. Public sector reform and the efficiency of the new democratic polity came to the forefront. With administrative modernization, the separation of politics and administration ('elected and selected') became the basic rule, from ministries to local communities. Politicians appeared as figures democratically controlled by elections, administrators as career civil servants with clear professional criteria. The modernization of the central government machinery led to the establishment of specific organs of government dealing with the administrative modernization – as committees for public administration reforms, organized in Hungary, Poland and the Czech Republic in 1992.[8]

The third stage of democratic institutionalization was initiated and prepared for by these public sectors reforms. There is a clear dividing line between the stages, however, in that the first two stages were much more politically oriented and directly connected with systemic change and general democratization. The third stage, however, is much more policy-centred and pragmatically oriented. It has focused on the specific process of democratization and on the efficiency of the entire polity. The new democratic constitutions, evidently, already contained provisions on self-governing functional and local units, but these provisions initially were of an abstract/general nature and the detailed, specific regulations as 'fine-tuning' were missing. They were formulated in the early 1990s as very minor issues, far from the real battlefields of the political parties. Local government regulations, of course, were passed and elections held in 1990–1 in order to change and/or legitimize the local elites, but local power and its regulation gained significance only later. As parties became organized nation-wide, or after the first elections, they immediately realized the salience of these local political issues. The nation-wide party organizations with their general electoral bases have had to face the resistance of local powers, as opposing or supporting the central power, and have therefore tried to penetrate local and regional self-governments. Thus, the second local government elections were much more politicized and particized than the first in the ECE and Balkan regions. Two contradictory tendencies appeared at the same time: the increasing legal autonomy of local self-governments with a higher level of organization and professionalization on one side, and the increasing effort of political parties to make local self-governments subservient to their political lines and to turn them into agents for the parties in national politics on the other. The states in both the ECE and the Balkan regions have latterly also made some efforts towards recentralization, usually under the banner of economic crisis management, arguing for more efficiency in the case of a bigger institutional centralization. These recentralization efforts have clashed with the autonomy of resurgent civil society in general and that of the local self-governments in particular, which indicates that the national system of public administration has been the least developed part of the democratic institutionalization process.

Yet, democratic institutionalization had reached a turning point in East Central Europe by the mid-1990s, and more and more political modernization has come to the fore. In the Balkans this process has been lagging behind and is still unfinished, since it has been a process of *re-democratization* in East Central Europe and the beginnings of *democratization* in the Balkans. The emergence of the Constitutional Courts has been one of the new decisive elements in both regions, strengthening democratic institution-building and providing a control function over both executive and legislative powers. These courts have represented a rule of law and have played a vital role in the 'checks and balances' mechanisms of the young democracies, often confronting the overwhelming presidential rule in the Balkans, in Serbia and Albania for example. The 'perils of presidentialism' have been the biggest danger in the Balkans, which could lead to a new reverse wave, and therefore the checks and balances mechanisms have to be strengthened against these perils as far as possible. As a bottom line, however, democratic institution-building has been going on in most of the countries at an incredible speed.[9]

Notes and further reading

1 These transitory institutions have been carefully studied in Poland and Hungary, together with the newly emerging parliamentary and party systems, see Ágh, 1994a; Ágh and Kurtán, 1995; and Ágh and Ilonszki, 1996.

2 The constitutional developments in East Central Europe and the Balkans have been discussed in the book edited by Howard (1993) and by the periodical *East European Constitutional Review*.

3 Concerning the South European developments, see first the various works edited by Pridham listed in the Bibliography and also Bonime-Blanc, 1987, and Wiarda, 1989.

4 The most recent assessment of parliamentary developments in the ECE and Balkan regions is the book edited by Olson and Norton (1996).

5 The unpopularity of the South European parliaments has been documented by the contributions in the volume edited by Liebert and Cotta (1990) and by Bonime-Blanc (1987). The Hungarian Centre for Democracy Studies has edited, in Hungarian, every year since 1988, *The Political Yearbook of Hungary*, a thick volume with analyses, documentation and public opinion surveys. Wyman et al. (1995) give a comparative overview of the popularity of parliaments (p. 540), which shows that it is somewhat above the parties (22–29 per cent versus 11–24 per cent) and below all the other organizations (president, government and mass media).

6 The role of parliamentary delegates and their socialization process have been analysed in the studies of W. Patzelt, G. Ilonszki and others in volumes edited by Ágh (1994a) and Ágh and Ilonszki (1996).

7 It is not by chance that the Legislative Research Committee organized an international conference about the role of parliamentary committees in June 1996 in Budapest, since the committees have been the scenes of some of the most important moments of the recent political modernization of parliaments, especially in the young democracies. For the conference papers see Longley and Ágh, 1997.

8 I was a participant in the project on the public sector reforms in East Central Europe led by J.J. Hesse, and I benefited greatly from this project in writing this chapter. Concerning the problems of the ECE public administrations, see Hesse, 1993.

9 In a well-known paper (1990, in Linz and Valenzuela, 1994) Juan Linz has discussed the 'perils of presidentialism' for young democracies and I share his worries, since the developments in Croatia, Serbia and Albania have very much illustrated his arguments.

Appendix: Constitutional order and electoral systems

Albania	Unicameral parliament (140 seats), presidential system with direct, popular election of president, mixed electoral system with individual single member constituencies and party lists with 4 per cent threshold (no final constitution).

Bulgaria

Unicameral parliament (240 seats), parliamentary system with direct, popular election of president, proportional electoral system with party lists and 4 per cent threshold.

Croatia

Bicameral parliament (138 and 68 seats), presidential system with the direct, popular election of president, mixed (both majoritarian and proportional) electoral system with 5 per cent threshold.

Czech Republic

Bicameral parliament (200 and 81 seats), parliamentary system with indirect election of president, proportional electoral system with party lists and 5 per cent threshold.

Hungary

Unicameral parliament (386 seats), parliamentary system with indirect election of president, mixed (both single member individual districts and party lists) electoral system with 5 per cent threshold.

Macedonia

Unicameral parliament (120 seats), parliamentary system with direct, popular election of president, proportional electoral system with party lists and no threshold.

Poland

Bicameral parliament (460 and 100 seats), parliamentary system with direct, popular election of president, proportional electoral system for the Sejm with 5 per cent threshold, majoritarian electoral system for the Senate.

Romania

Bicameral parliament (341 and 143 seats), presidential system with direct, popular election of president, proportional electoral system with 3 per cent threshold.

Slovakia

Unicameral electoral system (150 seats), parliamentary system with indirect election of president, proportional electoral system with 5 per cent threshold.

Slovenia

Bicameral parliament (90 and 40 seats), parliamentary system with direct, popular election of president, proportional electoral system with 3.4 per cent threshold.

Yugoslavia

Bicameral parliament (138 and 40 seats), presidential system with direct, popular election of president, proportional electoral system with 5 per cent threshold. (Note: this is the federal regulation, the Serbian parliament is different.)

Chronologies

Negotiating mechanisms

February–April 1989	National roundtable in Poland
June–September 1989	National roundtable in Hungary
November 1989	National roundtable in Czechoslovakia
January 1990	'Soft' National roundtable in Bulgaria
January 1990	Some fake negotiations in Romania
February 1990	Negotiations in Slovenia
January 1991	Talks between government and opposition in Albania

First free and/or multi-party elections

June 1989	First (semi)democratic elections and parliament in Poland
March 1990	First democratic elections in Hungary
April 1990	First democratic elections in Slovenia
April 1990	First multi-party elections in Croatia
May 1990	First multi-party elections in Romania
June 1990	First democratic elections in Czecho-Slovakia
June 1990	First multi-party elections in Bulgaria
November 1990	First multi-party elections in Bosnia and Macedonia
December 1990	First multi-party elections in Serbia and Montenegro
March 1991	First multi-party elections in Albania
May 1990	First democratic local elections in Poland
September 1990	First democratic local elections in Hungary
November 1990	First democratic local elections in Czecho-Slovakia
February 1992	First local elections in Romania

Constitution-making

23 October 1989	The new constitution of Hungary
July–August 1990	Amendment of the new constitution in Hungary
21 December 1990	The new constitution of Croatia
25 June 1991	The new constitution of Slovenia
23 December 1992	Amendment of Slovenian constitution
12 July 1991	The new constitution of Bulgaria
19 November 1991	The first constitution of Macedonia
8 December 1991	The new constitution of Romania

27 April 1992	The constitution of (small) Yugoslavia
1 September 1992	The first constitution of independent Slovakia
17 October 1992	The 'Small Constitution' of Poland
16 December 1992	The first constitution of the Czech Republic
6 November 1994	A referendum disapproves the draft constitution in Albania
25 May 1997	A referendum approves the new constitution in Poland

5

The Role of Political Parties: Political Culture and Electoral Behaviour

CONTENTS

Parties and party systems in democratic transition

Parties have been the chief actors of systemic change in its first two periods: in the pre-transition crisis and democratic transition. By now they have achieved a partial consolidation in East Central Europe and some stabilization in the Balkans. A more detailed analysis of the ECE parties gives us a point of departure for the description of the Balkan parties which have shown more 'infantile disorder' than those in the ECE region. The new democratic systems have been formed as multi-party systems. They have already made great strides from *polarized pluralism* to *moderate pluralism* and from *movement parties* to *cartel parties* in developments in East Central Europe and in the emergence of most relevant parties in the Balkans (see the list of all important parties in the ECE countries and the Balkans in the Appendix to this chapter).

There have been some very characteristic tendencies of political and electoral behaviour in the ECE states and, to some extent, in the Balkan countries (most markedly in Bulgaria), which may be summarized in the following:

1 Electoral and party fragmentation (Table 5.1).
2 High electoral volatility and protest voting.

TABLE 5.1   *Electoral and party fragmentation*

Poland	1989 6+0	1991 29+0	1993 6+9	1997 5+7
Hungary	1990 6+5	1994 6+4		
Czech Republic	1990 4+4	1992 8+1	1996 6+10	
Slovakia	1990 7+2	1992 5+4	1994 7+10	
Slovenia	1990 9+2	1992 8+2	1996 7+3	
Croatia	1990 4+12	1992 7+10	1995 10+18	
Serbia	1990 14+0	1992 9+0	1993 7+0	
Macedonia	1990 10+0	1994 7+2		
Bulgaria	1990 6+0	1991 7+0	1994 5+0	1997 5+0
Romania	1990 18+0	1992 7+4	1996 6+3	
Albania	1990 4+0	1992 5+0	1996 5+0	1997 3+3

The first figure given is the number of parliamentary parties and the second the number of relevant non-parliamentary parties.

3 The return of the 'post-communist' vote and parties (Table 5.2).
4 Growing abstentionism at elections (Table 5.3).
5 Declining confidence in parliaments and parties.[1]

These five tendencies are, however, the normal features of the party formation process leading to the emergence of a multi-party system. The first two tendencies indicate merely the temporary 'high temperature' of the political body in the first years of democratic transition. In the initial stage of democratic transition a 'hundred-party system' came into being which was reduced by the two or three consecutive free elections. The electoral and party fragmentation is, in fact, not that high; it has been sharply decreasing in the parliaments, and the largest two or three parties control the overwhelming majority of popular votes and parliamentary seats. The surprisingly strong wave of traditionalist conservatism and nationalism was also defeated in East Central Europe: these are

TABLE 5.2   *Return of the 'post-communist' vote (per cent)*

Poland	1991 11.99;	1993 20.41	1997 27.1	
Hungary	1990 10.89	1994 32.99		
Czech Republic	1990 13.24	1992 14.05	1996 10.33	
Slovakia	1990 13.34	1992 14.70	1994 10.41	
Slovenia	1990 17.30	1992 13.58	1996 9.03	
Croatia	1990 33.8	1992 5.4	1995 8.93	
Serbia	1990 46.1	1992 28.8	1993 36.7	
Macedonia	1990 25.8	1994 48.3		
Bulgaria	1990 47.15	1991 34.36	1994 43.5	1997 22.2
Romania	1990 66.31	1992 27.71	1996 22.2	
Albania	1991 56.17	1992 25.73	1996 20.37	1997 53.4

TABLE 5.3   *Growing abstentionism (per cent)*

Poland	1989 37.68	1991 56.80	1993 47.94	1997 52.1
Hungary	1990 36.9	1994 31.1		
Czech Republic	1990 3.21	1992 14.9	1996 23.5	
Slovakia	1990 3.21	1992 15.8	1994 24.8	
Slovenia	1990 16.49	1992 14.16	1996 26.8	
Croatia	1990 15.53	1992 34.39	1993 36.24	1995 31.21
Serbia	1990 28.5	1992 30.3	1993 38.4	
Macedonia	1990 15.2	1994 22.7		
Bulgaria	1990 9.2	1991 15.9	1994 24.8	1997 41.9
Romania	1990 13.8	1992 23.7	1996 23.8	
Albania	1991 1.1	1992 9.7	1996 11.0	1997 35

great achievements in a few years. The traditional conservatism was the major cause for the high electoral volatility in the early 1990s, since when it has significantly diminished. The third tendency proves that the first period is already more or less over, that is, we are at the end of the beginning in the transition process. The return of a post-communist vote arises from very different causes in East Central Europe and in the Balkans. In the ECE countries these parties have gone through a fundamental reform and in the Balkans they have simply kept power, in most cases turning to national-communism. The reasons for the fourth and fifth tendency are much deeper, since they are connected with the drastic social transformation, as a cumulative effect of all economic, social and political transformation or that of the high social price paid by the population for the political collapse and the following transformation. These tendencies will hold on until economic consolidation is reached, the first signs of which can be seen in most of the ECE countries. This leads us to the hypothesis about the *'early freezing'* of the ECE parties (and to some extent the Bulgarian party system) as a partial consolidation of a partial system. The nationalist-populist based party systems have also consolidated, to some extent, in the Balkans, with their 'charismatic' leaders.

From movement parties to cartel parties: party organization

1   The particular type of political organization which emerged in East Central Europe is the so-called *movement party*, and competition among the movement parties created the first multi-party systems (see Batt, 1991: 55-6). They represented to a degree the 'original' and 'ideal' unity of society and party, even though they were fragile and transitory political phenomena, not yet suitable for the roles of political parties in a competitive multi-party system. They had no stable and definite memberships, just participants in their actions. The cult of spontaneity was characteristic of them, since they tried to overcome the division between everyday life

TABLE 5.4   *Umbrella organizations and movement parties*

Poland	Solidarity
Hungary	Hungarian Democratic Forum
Czech Republic	Civic Forum
Slovakia	PAV – Movement for Democratic Slovakia
Slovenia	Demos (seven-party coalition)
Croatia	Croatian Democratic Community
Serbia	Serbian Renewal Movement – Depos, Together
Macedonia	Alliance for Macedonia (three parties)
Bulgaria	Union of Democratic Forces, Alliance of Democratic Forces
Romania	Democratic Convention of Romania
Albania	Albanian Democratic Party

and politics, which brought also a domination of horizontal ties over vertical ones. Leadership roles were based on personal authority and not on the elected posts of the party hierarchy. The programmes were vague, emotionally supported and directly connected with such actions as mass demonstrations. These movement parties and their social movements played a big role in East Central Europe immediately before and after the collapse of the former system, but they had to transform themselves step by step into real parties. This turning point came in Hungary in late 1989, in Poland and Czecho-Slovakia in 1990. It has not yet been fully achieved in Slovakia, where the Movement for Democratic Slovakia, as the biggest party, has tried to preserve the national-emotional features in order to maintain itself as a large populist movement (see Szomolányi and Meseznikov, 1995: 99), close to the style of the Balkan parties (see Table 5.4).

2   In the early 1990s, however, the ECE parties collected some stable memberships, initially as networks and/or movement parties, and through this they took the first steps to becoming national organizations with party programmes. Prior to the first, founding elections the early political organizations were under pressure to decide whether they would or could become real parties instead of the previous '*travestita*' or embryonic proto-parties. This was the honeymoon period for newly emerging parties, since the new legal regulations favoured parties over meso-political organizations, for example over organized interests and civil society associations. Therefore, many interest organizations opted for a party existence in order to be able to exert pressure upon politics; since then the border line between macro- and meso-systems, parties and organized interests, has remained blurred. Actually, all bigger 'baby' parties had already won some power, or at least political influence, through negotiating mechanisms between the government and the opposition. Their specific political strength, however, was still unclear before the elections. In the Balkans the former ruling parties have remained mass parties with membership continuity and many parties have become mass parties as movement parties.

The *overparticization* process was already under way in this early period. Parties became the major actors of political transformation, and during their formation process they used and abused all their available resources. This is why virtually all socio-political forces sought to be organized as parties, otherwise they would have been left out of politics. Parties were, however, more successful outside than inside; that is, they succeeded in pushing out other actors from politics, but they were not very successful in organizing themselves. This organizational deficit was clear even in this dynamic period. The ECE societies were activated and overpoliticized, but the parties' social ties remained minimal, since people did not join parties in great numbers and the national organizations remained weak. Therefore, the biggest difficulty for the parties in the early institutionalization process was to transform themselves from movement parties with loose organization and spontaneous action (which had the broad but diffuse support of the population), to organized parties with disciplined memberships, regular and formalized meetings, and extended party bureaucracy and professional leaderships. Even the most successful baby parties were only elite parties led by a small group of intellectuals, with a minimal and rather inactive membership. Actually, in the early 1990s the cultural or tribal wars led to the emergence of the first 'real', that is organized, parties but they emphasized first of all their ideological character. Therefore, the first ECE party systems can be characterized in Sartori's term as ideologically based *polarized pluralism* (Sartori, 1976/1990: 328). The most characteristic features of this period are the reform and transformation of the post-communist parties in East Central Europe and their conservation in the Balkans. Obviously, the partyist ECE regimes are much more democratic than the facade democracies or elitist democracies in the Balkans.

3   The crucial turning point for the parties came after the first elections through power transfer and the start of the *parliamentarization* process. In this period the overparticization was reinforced by the winners, the parliamentary parties, which acted aggressively to exclude both all the other socio-political actors and the non-parliamentary parties from politics. Their justification was based upon the particularistic nature of other organizations compared to parties, which represent more general, if not national, interests. The exclusion was also seen as protecting parliamentary democracy from the 'corporative' pressure of organized interests which were, supposedly, in most cases delegitimized by their participation in the former political system. At the same time, parliamentary parties concentrated all resources in political and public life on themselves, raising the 'entrance fee' into politics too high for the other parties. There was one historical occasion following the first elections when parties received big office buildings as their headquarters, along with many other privileges. The democratic institutionalization of macropolitics – parties, parliament and government – had to take place quickly, and its actors asserted their rights emphatically and aggressively.

The biggest challenge for the parties' organizational structure was certainly their participation in power with all its consequences. The parties were, even before the elections, organized from above by small groups of intellectual elites taking the initiative. After the elections this top-down organizational character became absolutely and shockingly quickly predominant. *Overparticization* and *overparliamentarization* reinforced each other, and politics once again became a remote realm for people, but this time on a multi-party base. The size of party memberships first quickly increased in the parliamentarization phase, reaching a peak in 1991–2, and then began to decline slowly. Parliamentary parties re-mained relatively small – except for some post-communist parties with membership continuity – but still have monopolized the public scene by securing privileged access to the media for themselves. This cruel selection process among parties by the first elections was necessary and unavoidable, and it has mostly been successful. But the selfishness of the 'successful' parliamentary parties and their eagerness to become the only actors of the political game backfired and isolated the parliamentary parties even more from society. The parliamentarization of parties has played a positive role even in the presidential systems, where the parliaments have been weak and subdued.[2]

The political parties had to turn inside in order to organize themselves under the new, powerful pressure of parliamentarization. This occurred in two ways: in the parliament as party factions with their leaderships and expert teams; and within the party as a relationship between the newly 'parliamentarized' leadership and the whole membership. For some time, the parties had very few leading personalities and an even smaller group of experts. The leaderships of party and parliamentary factions merged very closely; therefore, the gap suddenly increased between the narrow party elite and rank-and-file members. In the early 1990s a special 'congressing' way of working among the ECE parties began. Since then they have very often convened party congresses or national meetings to mobilize the membership and to give the activists a chance to participate and control the leadership. This 'congressing' has obviously been a substitute for everyday party life, missing so far because of the low density of party membership and low intensity of usual party activities.

The relative social vacuum in and around the new ECE parties was reinforced by the overparticization in the parliamentarization stage in the early 1990s. It weakened their 'conversion' function, that is, they were not able fully to articulate and aggregate social demands into programme packages as political alternatives at the national level. The more effort they made to achieve an independent political profile of their own, the more similar they looked. They were indistinguishable regarding basic issues of social and economic policy. The genetic defect of the ECE party systems was that most parties claimed to represent the whole nation directly and without distinction or special preference for the particular interests of some social strata or classes. It should be noted, however, that there is a second group of parties which are still '*travestita* interest organizations', and they represent the highly particularistic interests of some social strata directly and rigidly. But these organized interests, in the form of parties, have been the exceptions, and 'national' parties have dominated on the political scene. Earlier these 'national' parties were exclusivist and overcompetitive, but as premature or pseudo catch-all parties they were yet faceless to the general population. They lacked a solid party *identity* of their own; consequently, their party *identification* was also very weak among their voters. Since they were so weak in the social wilderness, the parties relied more on their privileged political power existence, which created, by means of this vicious circle, more and more social alienation from politics.

There are three major tendencies which have undermined the organizational strength of the ECE parties:

1 The *'senilization'* of party memberships, that is, the growing age of the members with all of its consequences, since it is mainly the senior citizens or the elderly who have time and energy for political activities. The young and middle generations are too busy trying to earn a modest income in the circumstances of the economic crisis and, in general, the most active and talented people tend to avoid political careers. After a peak period the younger people usually left the parties, so that local party meetings, if any, resemble senior citizens' clubs, where those present put forward their individual frustrations and outdated ideas.

2 The *'law of small numbers'*, meaning that even within the small memberships those with extremist and radical views tend to stay inside the parties and to dominate the party's grassroots activities. This leads to the 'fundamentalization' or radicalization of party memberships. Thus, a small number of true believers try to determine the party profiles from below. The radicalism of true believers usually creates a credibility gap between the party membership and its constituency, that is, between the 'inner' and 'outer' party. The small radical core in this way alienates the voters concerned and tries to take the party leadership hostage, making party democracy more dangerous, if there is any wish at all on the part of the party elites to move in this direction.

3 The *top-down construction and truncated pyramid* are characteristic of the ECE parties, in contrast to the interrelationships of different levels of party existence and to the normal organizational pyramid of Western parties. First, in my view, parties exist in forms or levels of social existence (membership party and organization party) and political existence (programme party and power party). The political existence of the ECE parties is much stronger than their social existence, and within the political existence the power party is the dominant form. Therefore, the parties have been built from the top down; that is, from the power party down to the membership party. Second, concerning the internal organization of parties, among its five layers – top leaders,

middle-level leaders, activists, members and supporters or voters – the first three are relatively large, but strangely enough almost equal in size. The membership layer, in turn, is very small compared to others, and even more so in comparison with the fifth layer, which is relatively too broad. This structure is similar to a truncated pyramid, but stands on 'moving sands', because the party identification of voters has been largely uncertain. Even with increasing party consolidation, the party support of about half the citizens has still been very volatile.

New organizational pressure appeared in the relationships of (a) the party elite and the basic party organizations, (b) the party and its original social movement, and (c) the party elite and the media. In these premature 'media democracies' the relationship to the media turned out to be vital for these new parliamentary parties in at least three respects.

1 The new party leaders were intellectuals and they had an extreme sensitivity and vanity concerning the press, the opinions of their former colleagues and those of their own former socio-cultural milieu.
2 The new parties were engaged in a cultural war among themselves because of their vague and over-ideologized programmes and 'tribal', sub-cultural political profiles. In this cultural war the media was crucially important for them.
3 Intensive media contacts compensated the party leaders for the organizational deficit and for the weakness of the national organization with its missing communication channels within the party. In fact, the media messages (or 'congressing') were substitutes for regular party meetings.

As this analysis shows, in the first half of the 1990s the ECE parties were not yet real, fully developed parties, since they were either above this level claiming to be the only 'national' party (state–party complex) or below this level being the barely concealed representatives of specific organized interests (interest organization complex). With all these setbacks, parties developed significantly in the parliamentarization stage, first of all in an organizational–institutionalizational aspect. There was a large structural differentiation inside the parliamentary parties among various party institutions, in the forms of special departments in the party headquarters, and in roles along the lines of the Weberian division of labour between political leaders, party administrators and special expert teams. Parties were the major actors also in the parliamentarization process but they were, at the same time, the most important products of this process, although still unfinished products with both institutional and cultural deficits. They developed, however, in this period toward a limited or *moderate pluralism*, in Sartori's terms, through the political learning process in the first coalition governments. The ECE parties reduced their internal heterogeneity ('many parties in one') to a great extent and created clearer party profiles (although not yet unambiguous in many respects), while the Balkan parties have been kept, at most, in the early parliamentarization stage.[3]

4   By the later years of the 1990s, however, the ECE parties and party systems entered a new – the fourth – stage of their emergence. The widening of politics has now become a vital necessity for the parties, although they have given up the monopoly of their political roles only with some hesitation. Yet, the opening up of the national political scene has begun, step by step, to include organized interests, local–regional self-governments and civil society associations, in terms of both an institutionalization of the pre-parliamentary stage in the decision-making process and as a manifest or covert political pressure on macro-politics. The low organizational level of the political meso-systems (the missing middle) and its fragility has always been the weakest point of the ECE political systems and it has been the missing link between parties and the population. There has been a lack of functional democracy which could provide the interest articulation and aggregation for the macro-politics, and this negative historical heritage has now to be overcome.

In the present period the ECE parties have turned into cartel parties under the external pressure of other actors and because of their own social weakness. They rely almost completely on the state for their resources, and share these resources exclusively among themselves (on cartel parties, see Katz and Mair, 1995). Similar moves can be noticed in all ECE countries where parties have common economic interests, drawing about 90 per cent of their incomes from state support. Consequently, the major contradiction in the ECE party formation process is that *the newly emerging parties, with many difficulties, switched very quickly, in a matter of years, from loose movement parties, representing some kind of spontaneous unity of parties and society, to rigidly organized cartels as power parties, expressing a new separation of parties and society – these being close to the traditional type of Central European hegemonic parties.* This analysis suggests that instead of the former hegemonistic or state party, a hegemonistic party system as a cartel of parties or a 'partyist' democracy may emerge in the ECE countries.[4]

Towards a relative consolidation

The South European and then ECE developments have proved that strongly organized parties opt for strong parliamentary governments, while weakly organized parties in Latin America and the Balkans encourage presidential systems and personal leadership. This approach can explain the contrast between the Latin American and South European developments, but our concern here is only to show the relative closeness between ECE developments and the South European democratizations. The 'strong parties and strong parliamentarism' connection has increasingly characterized four countries in East Central Europe. The tyrannical majority has taken a presidential form only in Croatia, but in Slovakia it has had a purely parliamentary form. Democratic consolidation as the next step in the institutionalization process has to be prepared and accomplished by the consolidation of the party systems through a *'ruptura'* with traditionalism–provincialism and by promotion of Europeanization. In the case of individual party development, Europeanization means new types of linkage between parties and society, and a social dialogue, institutionalized also by the solid contacts between political parties and interest organizations. Thus, political party consolidation has at least two aspects. The first is the above-mentioned 'external' consolidation, that is, through social contacts and establishing firm relationships between macro- and meso-politics, parties and organized interests. The second aspect is, so to speak, internal, through a further and 'final' institutionalization process of parties in terms of a smooth and efficient working relationship between the major decision-making bodies, or, in general, between leadership and membership. The maturation of these two processes can pose arguments to the hypothesis of the *early freezing* of parties in East Central Europe.[5]

This first stage of maturation may be considered as only the partial consolidation of a partial system, but it is an important and necessary precondition of the final democratic consolidation of the entire polity. It means that the specific political profile of the individual parties and the whole structure of party systems have become almost completed and quasi consolidated. It has a long way to go to reach West European stability, and even after travelling some way, the ECE party systems will keep their regional particularities, as the South European party systems have kept theirs after their first phase of Europeanization. Therefore, we suggest a formulation of the early freezing hypothesis through Olson's statement, based on the findings of ECE analysts:

> Parties now developing in Central Europe may very well evolve their own distinctive traits, not closely resembling those currently known in western democracies. The range of possible structure and behavior is much wider in the new democracies simply because they are starting anew.... We are perhaps witnessing the 'freezing moment' of the new party systems of post-communist countries. (Olson, 1993: 620)

This hypothesis, seemingly, contradicts the mainstream argument regarding the relative social vacuum in and around these 'half-created' parties and party systems, but in fact it does not. There has been a rapid advancement of the ECE party systems in the past years. If we take all the international and domestic factors into account, we can see why this early freezing has occurred to the ECE party systems. The first determining factor is rather obvious: the ECE parties can survive internationally and domestically only if they fit into the West European party systems, into the party Internationals. These Internationals have given a mandatory framework for cooperation to all major types of ECE parties as their respective partners. They are ready to support and protect them, but only by forcing them through a political learning process. This is a multi-faceted process, in which the Euro-connection of parties, including both the demonstration effects of, and the organizational constraints from, Western parties have to be considered as milder or tougher forms of this forced cooperation. The Western parties provide informal channels for the practical operation of their ECE partners and make official declarations to protect their counterparts, also giving them moral and financial support in electoral campaigns. The snowball effect has been in force in this respect as well, inasmuch as these 'import' models have to be increasingly applied by the ECE parties as they compete vigorously with each other.

All in all, the EU expects ECE parties to meet the European model of individual parties and structure of party systems in order to be accepted as partners. There is therefore not much chance for latecomers, not having West European 'parents', or for the 'non-standard parties' as the Slovak political scientists call these 'outsiders' (see Meseznikov, 1995: 106–8). But there is a strong chance of a further selection, fusion or disappearance of parties belonging to the same family of parties. The inner party structures may be fragile, and therefore some smaller parties can still emerge and/or disappear, but the major actors are already on the political scene and the future structural transformations in the ECE party systems (except for Slovakia and Croatia) will be only marginal. The 'election filter' has worked efficiently by eliminating the 'hundred-party system'; many smaller parties have already been removed from political life and/or been reduced to a mere formal existence. The ECE party systems are getting closer and closer to the balanced European model of a centre–left versus centre–right based multi-party system.

The second conditioning factor operates domestically and is much less obvious than the international one but still operates intensively. The existing bigger parties have already embraced the major political alternatives and occupied their political space; therefore, there is no longer any chance for a new party to gain a large constituency. Furthermore, currently, in the present stage of the party formation process not only are the parties looking for a solid social base but also the newly emerging social strata are seeking political representation by reconquering the parties and making them more and more suitable to represent their views. Thus, after the 'culturalization' phase the parties have entered now the 'socialization' phase, that of socio-economic constraints and pressures which create closer commitments between some parties and their respective social bases. Both the individual parties and the party structures have become more and more arranged according to the cleavages of the Lipset–Rokkan model. After at least two general elections the parties have developed more capacity for social dialogue and particular preferences for the specific demands of social strata. There is still a long way to go to the well-established 'Rokkanian' parties and party systems, but it is mostly the same parties and the same party systems that have to go through the further maturation process.[6]

The final – and also very important – conditioning factor in this historical development from movement parties to cartel parties has been the creation of a *political class*. It has been one of the major functions in the party formation process. This political class has already emerged and become more or less consolidated. The parties have been the chief actors in democratic transition and they have played an almost monopolistic role in the creation of the new political elite, and beyond it, of the new political class. The *political elite* embraces only the top and middle ranking party leaders, so it is an eminently party and government elite (about 10,000 people in the ECE countries). But the political class includes all those elected in (national and local) politics and those employed in public administration who are 'state-dependent' and live from politics and for politics (altogether around 100,000 persons, including the political elite in the average small countries, more in Poland and less in Slovakia, Croatia or Slovenia). There has been a lot of debate on elite change, succession or continuity in East Central Europe. Cultural and social capital has undoubtedly played the dominant role in the emergence of the new professional elites, including the new political class, the formation of which is a very important factor in the stabilization of politics and the consolidation of party systems.[7]

The competitive party system has already produced this new political class in the ECE countries, with an increasing professionalization, but so far with a fusion of the economic and political spheres until the privatization process ends. This has been a very positive development on one side, with the creation of an active and relatively well educated political class, but a very negative one with regard to the merger of politics and economics on the other. The next few years will decide whether the ECE countries after the privatization period, which has made the clear separation of political and economic interests impossible, will take the 'Italian Road' as partyist democracies with the clientura system of structural connections between politics and business, or turn towards the 'Austrian Road', as some kind of neo-corporatist democracy, with more or less regulated relationships and articulated separation of these two worlds. The latter is more likely, since the tripartite institutions are already relatively well developed in all ECE countries. They have not worked properly so far because of the domination of privatization eagerness in politics, penetrating the entire political class (see Ágh and Ilonszki, 1996). Further consolidation of the ECE party systems can be expected at the end of the 1990s when privatization ends and laws on conflict of interest can be brought into play to achieve separation of the worlds of politics and business.

Party types: the party formation process

In the conventional literature on the ECE and Balkan parties the problems of party *systems* and *individual* parties have usually been treated without a careful distinction, creating many confusions. After having analysed party systems through four periods of development from movements to cartel parties, we deal here with the specific party formation process concerning only the main individual party types and their internal maturation processes.

There are several ways of characterizing the ECE and Balkan parties by using typologies. The following analysis outlines the most common typologies, adding my own functional and genetic approaches as well. This analysis of the development of the individual parties and their types will, hopefully, provide further arguments for the hypothesis of 'early freezing' in East Central Europe.

Descriptive–quantitative typology   Parties may be characterized according to their size as far as membership or parliamentary seats are concerned. It is easy to conclude that the 'hundred-party system' still exists in the ECE and Balkan countries, since formally/legally there are more than one hundred parties everywhere, but actually the zones of the large, medium-sized and small parties have been differentiated sharply. The *small* parties still exist in great numbers, but they are completely marginalized politically and do not play any significant public/political role. Yet, we should not forget about them, because some are very aggressive small groupings on the extreme right and as 'happening' or 'performance' parties they sometimes produce a great deal of noise and public scandals. Most of the *medium-sized* parties have their own social, political and/or ethnic base by now, therefore their number in a country (usually below ten, close to five) and public/political role have already been consolidated. There are only two to four *bigger* parties in ECE countries, usually arranged around the centre–left and centre–right axis, which play the decisive role in public/political life, with 80–90 per cent of all members of parliament (Table 5.5).

Functional typology   The party formation process in East Central Europe has produced typical functions for parties, among which two party types have proved to be predominant. The first and most characteristic party type of the emergence process, the *movement party* as an *umbrella organization*, has already been described. 'Popular fronts', so to speak, came back in the late 1980s in the ECE countries as movement-oriented parties, which at the same time were representative of the general interests of the whole nation, since they were above parties as 'fora' instead of following 'narrow' party interests. These umbrella organizations have disintegrated in the ECE and Balkan regions, but their successor parties inherited the

TABLE 5.5   *Party concentration: the three biggest parties*

Poland	Social Democracy of the Republic of Poland; Polish Peasant Party; Union of Freedom 1991: 32.98 – 170 (36.8); 1993: 46.40 – 377 (81.7); 1997 48.2 – 251 (54.4)
Hungary	Hungarian Socialist Party; Alliance of Free Democrats; Hungarian Democratic Forum 1990: 55.01 – 292 (75.5); 1994: 64.47 – 318 (81.86)
Czech Republic	Civic Democratic Party; Left Bloc; Czech Social Democratic Party 1990: 66.85 – 143 (71.5); 1992: 50.31 –1 27 (65.5); 1996: 66.39 – 151 (75.5)
Slovakia	Movement for Democratic Slovakia; Common Choice; Hungarian Coalition 1992: 59.38 – 117 (77.9); 1994: 55.55 – 96 (64.4)
Slovenia	Liberal Democratic Party; United List of Social Democrats; Slovenian Christian Democrats 1990: 44.8 – 37 (46.2); 1992: 51.55 – 51 (56.65); 1996: 45.6 – 44 (48.8)
Croatia	Croatian Democratic Community; Croation Social Liberal Party; Social Democratic Party of Croatia 1990: 88.89 – 78 (97.4); 1992: 66.4 – 101 (84.1); 1995: 65.71 – 95 (74.79)
Serbia	Serbian Socialist Party; Serbian Renewal Movement; Serbian Radical Party 1990: 61.9 – 213 (85.2); 1992: 68.3 – 224 (89.8); 1993: 67.1 – 207 (82.8)
Macedonia	Social Democratic Union of Macedonia; Alliance of Reform Forces of Macedonia; Party for Democratic Prosperity in Macedonia 1990: ?– 71 (59.0); 1994: ?– 97 (80.7)
Bulgaria	Bulgarian Socialist Party; Union of Democratic Forces; Movement of Rights and Freedoms 1990: 89.38 – 378 (84.4); 1991: 75.05 – 240 (100.0); 1994: 73.1 – 209 (86.9); 1997: 81.9 – 214 (89.8)
Romania	Party of Social Democracy; Democratic Party of Romania (SDU); Christian Democratic National Peasant Party 1990: 68.87 – 275 (71.0); 1992: 57.90 – 242 (74.1); 1996: 66.1 – 266 (77.5)
Albania	Albanian Socialist Party; Albanian Democratic Party; Omonia 1991: 95.61 – 239 (99.6); 1992: 90.72 – 132 (94.2); 1996: 79.9 – 135 (96.3); 1997: 82.7 – 145 (93.6)

First figure gives the percentage of the vote, the second the number of seats and the figure in brackets the percentage of seats in the national parliament concerned. Further details can be found in the Appendix.

idea of representing the whole nation directly as 'the party above parties'. Actually, all bigger parties more or less followed the pattern of the defunct umbrella organizations and determined their party profiles as national parties, that is, parties serving and concerting the interests of all important social strata. *These national parties, with their claim to represent 'national interest' directly, were in fact close to the type of state parties of the authoritarian periods, and this turn took place very quickly in the early 1990s from loose, action-oriented movement parties to rigidly organized quasi state parties.*

This ECE 'definition' of parties above the 'normal' party level was accompanied by the other extreme, by the stubborn existence of some medium-sized parties below the party level, that is, too close to organized interests. (The ethnic parties are also typical middle-sized parties, but we discuss them later.) This *narrow interest party* is also an 'archaic' type from the party formation process, since in the early stages some interest organizations (for example, the peasant parties and the parties of entrepreneurs etc.) became parties in order to exert political pressure. There is still a grey zone between parties and interest organizations in which, to various degrees, the organizations appear legally as parties yet act politically as organized interests. This duality of national parties and interest parties, as two main functional types, is still – although decreasingly – an 'infantile' feature of ECE party systems, a point of departure for the parties' further development. There is a tendency nowadays for national parties to be socially more selective, so that they can anchor themselves more in particular social strata and also for interest parties to open up beyond their direct constituencies. The early freezing process of parties is definitely going on, yet this duality is going to stay with us as a long-term functional feature: the bigger parties are usually national parties or premature catch-all parties competing for the votes of all strata, and the medium-sized parties as interest parties still rely more on the 'automatic' votes of their direct constituencies (Table 5.6).

Genetic typology   Parties may be differentiated by the roles and places they had in the party formation process. In this respect, we can describe three major cleavages which originally arranged the types of the newly emerging parties with their twins or 'anti-parties'. We have in this way six major types of parties, as discussed below.

The **first** cleavage line is between the former ruling, now *reformed post-communist*, parties and the *new opposition* parties. This confrontation through negotiations led to the formation of multi-party systems, and – with mutual deep transformations on both sides – these 'first generation parties' of both types are still the major players. They have mobilized the most talented people as well as the other resources, and have organized the most important parties along ideological lines most successfully. The former ruling parties disintegrated, but from among them successor parties have gone through a modernization process and in East Central Europe we now see everywhere new socialist/social democratic parties with a consolidated social and political background. The old opposition parties meanwhile have developed into the new leading parties in many cases, being the trendsetters of political development in the first years of democratization. Some of these have become parliamentary parties, eliminating or marginalizing the others from the parliamentary/political scene by politically and electorally outcompeting them. What looked like an 'original organizational chaos' in the late 1980s and early 1990s, was in fact a quick and cruel natural selection process on a 'first come, first

TABLE 5.6   *Functional typology: 'national' and 'interest' parties*

National parties

Poland	Social Democracy of the Republic of Poland; Union of Freedom
Hungary	Hungarian Socialist Party; Alliance of Free Democrats; Fidesz–Hungarian Civic Party
Czech Republic	Civic Democratic Party; Czech Social Democratic Party; Left Bloc
Slovakia	Movement for Democratic Slovakia; Christian Democratic Movement
Slovenia	Liberal Democratic Party; United List of Social Democrats
Croatia	Croatian Democratic Community; Croatian Social Liberal Party; Social Democratic Party of Croatia
Serbia	Serbian Socialist Party; Serbian Renewal Movement
Macedonia	Social Democratic Union of Macedonia; Alliance of Reform Forces in Macedonia
Bulgaria	Bulgarian Socialist Party; Union of Democratic Forces
Romania	Party of Social Democracy; Democratic Party of Romania
Albania	Albanian Democratic Party; Albanian Socialist Party

Interest parties

Poland	Polish Peasant Party; Solidarity Trade Union
Hungary	Independent Smallholders Party; Christian Democratic Peoples Party
Czech Republic	Society for Moravia and Silesia; Agrarian Party
Slovakia	Workers Association of Slovakia; Agricultural Movement
Slovenia	Slovenia Peoples Party; Socialist Alliance of Slovenia
Croatia	Croatian Peasant Party; regionalist parties (IDS, DA, RDS)
Serbia	(Democratic Community of Hungarians in Vojvodina; Albanian Democratic Party)
Macedonia	Socialist Party of Macedonia
Bulgaria	Bulgarian Agrarian National Union; Bulgarian Business Bloc
Romania	Christian Democratic National Peasant Party
Albania	(Omonia)

For details of parties, see Appendix.

served' basis. As we realize now, the most important parties established a place for themselves at a very early stage of the transition process. In the later stage, they have only further transformed internally, but there have been no newcomers among the bigger parties since the beginning. The first cleavage line determined the broad landscape of the party system, on both sides, although immediately after the collapse of the former system it seemed as if the ruling parties or their successors might be completely eliminated. Just the contrary has happened to the reformed leftist parties. With a relatively quick social democratization – the degree of which varies tremendously from country to country – the reformed post-communist parties in the ECE countries have been able to survive any delegitimizing efforts of their competitors and to articulate the demands of the larger society for a renewed leftist perspective.

At the same time, in the first period the original opposition parties had the legitimacy of fighting against the one-party system. They also benefited from the early mobilization of the masses, and attracted the most talented leaders and activists as well. Although the transitional political elites are already gone to a great extent in all ECE countries, these 'priority birth rights' remain valid. The reformed leftist parties and the most important former opposition parties have captured both the largest memberships and the most skilled professional politicians, remaining the leading parties since the beginning. These two types of parties have been connected, as twins, by the same formation process described above. Both types are successor parties in some ways, since most of the former party members joined the newly emerging opposition parties in this succession process. Therefore, not only the formal/legal continuity matters in the reformed post-communist parties but also the continuity of mentality, membership and organizational principles between the old ruling parties and the newly emerging opposition parties. These two types of parties have converged in their major features, becoming national parties or early, premature catch-all parties. When the early movement parties left the stage, not only the 'legal', post-communist successor parties, but also the new parties inherited the model of the quasi state parties to a great extent.[8]

The former big opposition parties, seizing power after the first free elections in East Central Europe, became the new ruling parties and showed sometimes more resemblances in this period to the features of the former ruling parties than did their legal post-communist successors, since the latter were forced into opposition. Political life became over-ideologized, above all because these new parties emphasized first of all their ideological confrontations against the former political system with a loud anti-communist rhetoric, but also because the new leading parties built up clientelistic organizations rather similar to the old state parties. Thus, for various reasons, this original *dominating* cleavage between the reformed versions of the previous ruling parties and the newly emerging parties mostly lost its force and validity in East Central Europe as the 1990s wore on, although some new larger parties still try to keep and reinforce it for electoral and political advantages, as a delegitimizing device against the reformed leftist parties; and it is still the dominant cleavage in the Balkans (Table 5.7).

The **second** major cleavage between the ECE party types has been the confrontation between the *old* and *new* parties. The old, 'pre-communist' parties usually reactivated themselves only after the first new parties

TABLE 5.7   *The early rivalry: post-communist and post-opposition parties*

Poland	Social Democracy of the Republic of Poland *vs* UF, LU and Fatherland etc.
Hungary	Hungarian Socialist Party *vs* Hungarian Democratic Forum (and Alliance of Free Democrats)
Czech Republic	Left Bloc *vs* Civic Democratic Party
Slovakia	Common Choice *vs* Movement for Democratic Slovakia
Slovenia	United List of Social Democrats *vs* Christian Democrats and Liberals
Croatia	Social Democratic Party of Croatia *vs* Croation Democratic Community
Serbia	Serbian Socialist Party *vs* Serbian Renewal Movement (Depos)
Macedonia	Social Democratic Union of Macedonia *vs* Alliance of Reform Forces
Bulgaria	Bulgarian Socialist Party *vs* Union of Democratic Forces
Romania	Party of Social Democracy *vs* Christian Democratic National Peasant Party (Democratic Convention)
Albania	Albanian Socialist Party *vs* Albanian Democratic Party

In Hungary and Slovenia there have already been governing coalitions across this divide (Hungary: HSP–AFD; Slovenia: LDP, ULSD, SCD, SDPS)

For details of parties, see Appendix.

had emerged and were formed as 'second generation' parties; the small 'third generation' parties woke up even later. In that situation a strange contradiction came to the surface of political life, namely, soon after their emergence the new parties received both subjective and objective resources and tried to monopolize them. The belatedly arrived 'historical' parties, however, protested against that and wanted to get back their former party fortunes. They hoped to play a dominant role in political life as in good old times, that is in the 'pre-communist' period. This belated attempt at political takeover by the historical parties failed in all ECE and Balkan countries. The historical parties as second generation parties have usually been relegated to the lower positions of party politics (the Czech Social Democratic Party can be considered the only exception). They have been dwarfed, or at least significantly reduced in size, in both their social and political forms of existence and most of them have survived only as medium-sized interest parties of secondary importance. Originally these historical parties were connected to particular social strata, and to their values and interests as social democratic, Christian democratic or peasant parties which led to their 'automatic' revival in some cases, but only in a reduced form. In addition, because of their archaic style and outdated programmes, and primarily of their old and senilized leaderships, they have sometimes not even been competitive enough as interest parties. Hence, some new interest parties have been

TABLE 5.8   *Party generations: historical and new*

Important historical parties	
Poland	Polish Peasant Party; Democratic Party
Hungary	Independent Smallholders Party; Christian Democratic Peoples Party
Czech Republic	Czech (oslovak) Social Democratic Party; Czechoslovak Peoples Party
Slovakia	Democratic Party (62 per cent of votes in the 1946 Slovak election)
Slovenia	Slovenian Christian Democrats
Croatia	Croatian Party of Rights; Croatian Peasant Party
Serbia	Serbian Radical Party (chetniks)
Macedonia	Internal Macedonian Revolutionary Organization
Bulgaria	Bulgarian Agrarian National Union
Romania	Christian Democratic National Peasant Party; National Liberal Party
Albania	None
Dominant new parties	
Poland	Union of Freedom; Social Democracy of Republic Poland; Labour Union
Hungary	Alliance of Free Democrats; Hungarian Socialist Party
Czech Republic	Civic Democratic Party
Slovakia	Movement for Democratic Slovakia; Common Choice
Slovenia	Liberal Democracy of Slovenia; United List of Social Democrats
Croatia	Croatian Democratic Community; Social Democratic Party of Croatia
Serbia	Serbian Socialist Party
Macedonia	Social Democratic Union of Macedonia; Alliance of Reform Forces in Macedonia
Bulgaria	Bulgarian Socialist Party; Union of Democratic Forces
Romania	Party of Social Democracy
Albania	Albanian Democratic Party

For details of parties, see Appendix.

formed, or otherwise some trade unions or business interest associations have functioned as new interest parties. In such a way, the contradiction between the old and new types of parties has been reproduced at the level of interest parties, although not among the national parties. Altogether, the (non-communist) historical parties have some continuity and relevance in East Central Europe, but much less in the Balkans (Table 5.8).

The **third** cleavage is between ethnically and or locally/regionally based parties on one side and nationalist parties on the other. The ECE and Balkan countries are multi-ethnic societies where ethnic rights and interests have been traditionally oppressed and their organizations banned or paralysed. These interests have come back with a vengeance in the democratization process through the formation of ethnic or regional parties trying to represent these national minorities at the highest level, that is, at macro-political level. At the same time, there has been the phenomenon of rising nationalism even in those ECE and Balkan countries that have not produced any significant extreme right-wing, nationalist–populist, 'single issue' parties like in Hungary or Albania. The only political issue for them is the representation of the interests of 'true' Polishness or Slovakness etc., against the international and/or domestic 'conspiracy' of other ethnicities, that is, their own national minorities and/or the Jews (see Bugajski, 1995a; Hockenos, 1993).

There is no doubt that the ethnically based parties sometimes overdo their legitimate cases because they are single issue parties, formulating almost exclusively ethnic or regional demands without a differentiated ideological and political stance. But to a great extent they have been forced to do so, because it is about the general understanding of democracy as a confrontation between its 'majoritarian' and 'consociational' varieties. The new ECE democracies are not yet ready to protect vital minority rights by incorporating the ethnic-regional interests in some ways into the national policy-making process. The ethnically based parties are also medium-sized parties, like some interest parties, receiving electoral support almost 'automatically'. Opposing them, there is at least one small or medium-sized extreme nationalist party in each ECE country. These extreme nationalist single-issue parties, however, have a very limited electoral support, and their political strength varies greatly from country to country. The nationalist–populist parties in East Central Europe may also be considered phenomena of the political transition, expressing the frustration and disappointment of some groups in the population, and as a reaction to Europeanization and modernization. They emphasize only the nation as a symbolic pre-modern community, the promotion of which will definitely solve all the other social and political problems. It has been much worse in the Balkans where nationalism has become the major organizing principle for almost all parties and the national–populist parties of different kinds have been dominant. In most cases the new ruling parties are ultra-nationalistic and the ethnic parties are defensive (Table 5.9).

The party systems of the ECE and Balkan countries consist of these six major types of parties, as three couples or pairs of twins. The predominance of the first cleavage line characterized the early stage of the party formation process but from the very beginning it has also shown a rather quick maturation process. Therefore, by now this early feature has mostly been abandoned, although the parties still bear the signs of their particular emergence from different party 'families'. Yet, nowadays the first two cleavage lines already play a less and less decisive

TABLE 5.9   *The deepest divide: (ultra-)nationalist and ethnic-regionalist parties*

Poland	Confederation for Independent Poland and Fatherland vs German minorities, represented in parliament (no ethnic party)
Hungary	Independent Smallholders Party vs National Roundtable of Minorities (no ethnic party)
Czech Republic	Republican Party vs Society for Moravia and Silesia (no ethnic party)
Slovakia	Slovak National Party and Movement for Democratic Slovakia vs Hungarian Coalition (three parties)
Slovenia	Slovenian National Party vs minority representation in parliament (small ethnic organizations)
Croatia	Croatian Democratic Community and Croatian Party of Rights vs Serbian Democratic Party and regionalist parties (minority representation in parliament)
Serbia	Serbian Socialist Party, Serbian Radical Party and Serbian Renewal Movement vs the Albanian parties and Democratic Community of Hungarians in Vojvodina
Macedonia	IMRO-DPMNU vs Party for Democratic Prosperity in Macedonia
Bulgaria	Union of Democratic Forces vs Movement for Rights and Freedoms
Romania	Party of Social Democracy, Party of Romanian National Unity and Greater Romania Party vs Democratic Alliance of Hungarians in Romania
Albania	Albanian Democratic Party vs Omonia

For details of parties, see Appendix.

role, and the parties have been arranged more or less according to the Europeanization–traditionalism and left–right axes. The significance of the third cleavage has not yet been diminished; its two party types will stay with us for longer because, first, the issues of minority rights and representation even in the ECE countries are still unresolved, and secondly, the socio-economic crisis and difficulties of the European integration have produced new tensions facilitating the survival of the nationalist–populist parties, and even giving them a new push in their extravagant activities.

At the same time, this genetic party typology also shows the huge difference between the ECE and Balkan parties. First, there is a genuine, although unfinished, social democratization process of ECE leftist parties, but the successors to the former ruling parties in the Balkan countries have simply changed the facade by renaming themselves 'socialist' parties, when in fact they are mostly 'national–socialist' parties. Secondly, the historical parties have revived as significant parties in the Balkans to a lesser degree than in East Central Europe, but the former communist parties, as special 'historical' parties of the Balkan region, still dominate in their slightly changed forms against the newly organized parties.

Thirdly, both the nationalist and ethnic parties are much stronger in the Balkans than in East Central Europe. The national and ethnic issues clash in the Balkans in a violent way, producing hidden or open civil wars, while these clashes are rather minimal and peacefully controlled in the ECE countries.

Ideological typology   The conventional Western typology describes the party families first of all as liberal, conservative or Christian democratic and socialist or social democratic etc. This approach has been most frequently applied from the very beginning to the ECE parties as well, and the ECE parties have been categorized according to those headings available in West European countries. This typology is evident and almost unavoidable but it was misleading because of two manifest limitations. First, ideological labels such as liberal, conservative etc. could not be directly transferred from the West to the ECE region, and much less to the Balkans. These terms are rather blurred even in the West and their local meanings are absolutely idiosyncratic. Secondly, the basic information from the countries concerned was not easily available and the profiles of the ECE parties were not clearly demarcated. Nevertheless, in the ECE countries these broad party families may be observed, and the parties are moving closer to the West European types.

There are, however, also some further complications, given the fact that the information on parties has been contaminated with the ideological prejudices of either the local survey teams or those of Western analysts – in most cases both. This approach is still fruitful and necessary, however, and there have also been some very instructive studies which have identified 10 types of parties (communist, socialist, ecologist, liberal, religious, conservative, farmer, nationalist, ethnic and other) and this typology has offered deep insights into the party dynamics of both East Central and East European countries. The typology of ideological families was originally very arbitrary and misleading, but nowadays it is increasingly correct and meaningful, not only because the theoretical and empirical analysis of the ECE parties has developed a lot, but primarily because these parties themselves have developed and changed a great deal. Therefore, after many mergers and splits and internal transformations, they are closer now to the Western types. It is one of the most characteristic signs of the early freezing and maturation process that the major ECE parties by now have acquired rather clear political profiles and they can be more or less unambiguously identified along these ideological lines and labelled as member parties of the European party Internationals. They are not completely along the lines of the parties of Western Europe, and they still have a long way to go to become really Christian democratic, social democratic or liberal parties. The Balkan parties have kept their idiosyncrasies, and no significant similarity can be observed between them and the Western parties.[9]

Summing up the different typologies, we can conclude that, first, the genetic approach – combined with the functional one – gives us the most correct description of party types, since it appears the selection of major parties was decided very early in the party formation process. Later on, after this first turning point or rather solid point of departure, the ECE parties have come closer and closer to the West European party types, and now they can be seen more or less as proper members of the ideological party families. They have become mostly 'standard' parties, as Slovak political scientists term them, because in Slovakia they still have some bigger 'non-stardard' parties, that is, those without Western parallels or counterparts, such as the Democratic Movement for Slovakia, and in this spirit the whole Balkan region can be considered as 'non-standard'. The second turning point came in the mid-1990s, by which time the first crisis of the ECE parties along the lines of Europeanization versus provincialism, modernization versus traditionalism had been solved to some extent. The parties with a clear engagement for modernization cum Europeanization gained the upper hand at least in Hungary, the Czech lands, Poland and Slovenia.

Secondly, after having overcome the crisis of the nationalist-traditionalist deviation, the West European roles of centre–right and centre–left parties (or party alliances) have manifestly emerged and have stabilized among the ECE parties. Thus, the early freezing means that the ECE parties have been significantly Westernized from outside, but still much less so from inside. The parties' places and roles, as institutional frameworks, are already defined in the ECE countries, but the parties as both social networks and political organizations are still underdeveloped and immature. Yet, some ECE parties have progressed also in this field, and their success in the internal transformation, through a snowball effect, will force other parties to speed up their internal changes as well, in order to remain competitive with the most successful ones. In the Balkan region the parties have been less developed and important in the presidential systems, and yet still have played a central role in the lopsided development, that is, in both the paralysis and progress of democratization. The former ruling parties have usually kept their places in the Balkans and there has been an acute contradiction between the 'tyrannical' nationalist parties and the defensive ethnic parties.[10]

Notes and further reading

1 The Appendix illustrates the high volatility in the first period. In the Appendix, as throughout the following chapters, the full names of the parties are given in their English version and generally I use their English abbreviation

(e.g. Hungarian Democratic Forum, HFD); but when I refer to a party for the first time, I also give the abbreviation in the original (e.g. *MDF* – Magyar Demokrata Fórum), these being italicized for clarity in the Appendix.

There are no comparative figures about the declining confidence in parties and parliaments, just in selected countries; two cases are given below:

I (see Wyman et al., 1995: 540) – Czech Republic: 24–29%; Hungary: 11–22%; Slovakia: 16–21%; (Russia: 6–12%).

II (see Plasser and Ulram, 1996: 16) – Czech Republic: 24–32%; Hungary: 11–23%; Poland: 8–24%; Slovakia: 16–22%; (Russia: 14–12%).

2 Wyman et al. (1995) present very rich data about parties and party behaviour in some ECE countries (Czech Republic, Slovakia and Hungary) compared to the countries of Eastern Europe proper (Russia and Ukraine), although in attempting to give a common picture about 'post-communist Europe', they make sweeping overgeneralizations, which reflect usually the EE situation. Yet, the data describe fairly well the party formation process concerning the ECE countries: (1) the party membership in these three countries is around 2 per cent of population (trade union membership is 20–39 per cent); and (2) trust in the parties (11–24 per cent) has been the lowest among all social and political organizations (22–29 per cent for the parliaments and 32–45 per cent for the media). These data suggest that the overwhelming majority of the ECE populations accept the multi-party system. It is striking, however, that supporters of the governing parties are much more willing to ban opposition parties than vice versa. The depth of party identification, of course, remains weaker than in Western Europe: still 82–89 per cent of the ECE populations favour at least one party, which is the beginning of the consolidation of individual party identifications.

3 The Civic Democratic Party was considered to be one of the stablest parties in the Czech Republic, yet there was a Czech saying that the CDP was a conservative party with social democratic politics and with a Bolshevik leadership style on the part of Vaclár Klaus; or it was a 'liberal party of Leninist type'.

4 In 1996 the Hungarian parties negotiated about giving property 'forever' to all parliamentary parties and to the bigger non-parliamentary parties and sociopolitical organizations. The parties have to publish their budget every year in the *Official Gazette*; based on those documents, we can show their dependence on the state budget, which is between 85 and 95 per cent. The tendency is clear – state support has continuously grown and the membership fees have usually declined, in some cases drastically, so that Hungarian parties have relied more and more on state support in their activities.

5 In this respect, Pridham emphasizes: 'Consolidation through parties is characterized, above all, by the organization and expansion of the party structures and the party system as a whole, which is then able to control and, if needs be, moderate and integrate all forms of participation.... Clear, long term alignments between parties and social groups are established. Identities and rules of internal competition among the party elites are formed' (Pridham, 1990: 37). Parties consolidate themselves 'incrementally through piecemeal changes', as Haggard and Kaufman suggest: 'Party-system consolidation can be encouraged through a number of different institutional reforms ... Party systems, of course, often reflect social and cultural cleavages that will persist even after the implementation of changes in electoral rules. Even so, such changes can make

a considerable difference in reducing party-system instability' (Haggard and Kaufman, 1994: 15).

6 There have been some regular sociological surveys in Hungary on the stabiliz-ation of relationships between the political parties and their respective social bases, see Ferenc Gazsó and István Stumpf, 'Pártbázisok és választói magatar-tástípusok' (Party support and types of voters' behaviour)', in Sándor Kurtán et al., *Political Yearbook of Hungary 1995*, Budapest: Hungarian Centre for Democracy Studies, 1995. These data, by the way, show much less volatility among Hungarian voters than the data in Wyman et al. (see note 1). The only larger change between the 1990 and 1994 election results is between that of the HSP and HDF (which is an eminent case of high volatility or a 'substantial pendulum swing' for some analysts, see Wyman et al., 1995: 537, 546). Other-wise, the other four parties had almost the same results twice. But even this change between the HSP and HDF proves that electoral behaviour is stable and consistent, as the HDF presented itself to a great extent as a leftist move-ment party in 1989–90 and only later became a centre–right party instead of a large umbrella organization. Thus, leftist voters cast their vote in 1990 mostly for the HDF and in 1994 for the HSP. This is the only 'change', which shows, in fact, a remarkable consistency of rational voting behaviour.

7 First, although the transition from 'cultural' politics, based on subcultures and values, to 'political' politics, based on social strata and their interests, has been very positive, cultural and social capital even now still plays a great role, much more than 'physical' or economic capital. Second, Iván Szelényi argues in his latest writings and interviews (see for example, Szelényi, 1995) that a mana-gerial capitalism has emerged in East Central Europe, at least in Hungary, in which cultural and social (network) capital is the most important vehicle to get coopted.

8 As to the membership continuity of all parties, Wyman et al. write that, 'Just who were the party members? ... One of the most striking features of our survey is that in each of our countries they are also overwhelmingly former members of the communist party. In other words, it is largely the same people active in politics now as were active in the communist period' (Wyman et al., 1995: 538–9).

9 There have been several classifications of party families, e.g. Michael Smart has identified eleven 'party streams': communist, independent socialist, social democratic, liberal radical, liberal conservative, centre–Christian democratic, conservative, nationalist, extreme right, ethnic, regional, and ecologist (see Smith, 1983: 329–31).

10 The key issue is, indeed, the emergence of balanced centre–left and centre–right parties which has taken place in most ECE countries, but the degree and character of which varies from country to country. In Hungary and Poland the centre–left is well organized, but the rightist parties are fragmented and un-consolidated to a great extent; in the Czech Republic and Slovenia the centre–right is well organized and the leftist parties are fragmented to some extent; in Slovakia and Croatia both sides are still weak and fragmented.

Appendix: The most important political parties of East Central Europe and the Balkans

---

The first figure given indicates the percentage share of the vote, the second the number of seats and the third (in brackets) the percentage of seats in the national parliament concerned. 'Lost vote' is the vote cast for parties not gaining parliamentary representation. Note 1 above gives details of the system of abbreviations.

East Central Europe

Poland

In the 1989 semi-free election 65 per cent of seats were reserved for the **Polish United Workers Party** (PUWP; *PZPR*) and its allies (**United Peasant Party, Democratic Party** and three small Catholic satellite organizations). Among the Catholic organizations, **Pax** had 10 seats in the contractual parliament and was organized later as **Christian Democracy**, but after 1991 these three organizations had no parliamentary representation. On 28 January 1990 the PUWP was dissolved and the **Social Democracy of the Republic Poland** (SDRP; *SdRP*) was organized, creating an electoral coalition with the Confederation of Polish Trade Unions (*OPZZ*) and smaller leftist groups, called **Democratic Left Alliance** (DLA; *SLD*); membership 60,000.

   1991: 11.99 – 60 (13.0); 1993: 20.41 – 171 (37.1); 1997: 27.1 – 164 (35.6).

Polish Peasant Party (PPP; *PSL*), organized on 5 May 1990 from the United Peasant Party (*ZSL*) and from other peasant organizations; membership 250,000.

   1991: 8.67 – 48 (10.4); 1993: 15.40 – 132 (28.6); 1997: 7.3 – 27 (5.8).

In the 1989 election **Solidarity** gained 35 per cent of seats (161), all of those contested; it organized the Civic Parliamentary Club which disintegrated in parliament into smaller groups. The biggest ones were as follows. In May 1990 the Centre Alliance (*PC*) – or **Citizens Centre Alliance** (*POC*) – emerged to support Walesa and in July 1990 the **Citizens Movement for Democratic Action** (*ROAD*) emerged as the liberal wing, which was organized in December 1990 into the **Democratic Union** (DU; *UD*) and the **Christian–National Union** (CNU; *ZChN*) (first organized in October 1989 inside Solidarity). Between 1990 and 1993 a dozen post-Solidarity parties emerged which split and rejoined each other, more or less following a left–right, conservative–liberal, nationalist–European and religious–secular orientation (see the major ones below).

Freedom Union (*UW*), formerly the Democratic Union (DU; *UD*), organized on 2 December 1990, joined by the Liberal Democratic Congress, merging in 1994 to UW; membership 15,000.

   1991: 12.32 – 62 (13.4); 1993: 10.59 – 74 (16.0); 1997: 13.8 – 60 (13.0).

Labour Union (LU; *UP*) from June 1992, formerly Solidarity of Labour (*SP*), which was organized on 4 August 1990; membership 8,000.

1991: 2.06 – 4 (0.8); 1993: 7.28 – 41 (8.9); 1997: 4.9 – 0.

Fatherland (*Ojczyzna*), its predecessor in the 1991 election was the Catholic Electoral Action (CEA; *WAK*); it emerged as an electoral coalition in 1993, the main force behind it being the Christian-National Union, formed from Solidarity in 1990.

1991: 8.74 – 49 (10.6); 1993: 6.37 – 00 (one seat in the Senate); 1997: 5.6 – 6 (13).

Liberal Democratic Congress (*KLD*), organized on 15 February 1990; after the 1991 elections it was represented in the Sejm by the **Polish Economic Programme** (*PPG*) and **Polish Liberal Programme** (*PPL*) as parliamentary factions, but it failed to get into the parliament in 1993. After this failure the Liberal Democratic Congress joined the Democratic Union and they formed the Freedom Union together (see above).

1991: 7.49 – 37 (8.2); 1993: 3.99 – 00 (0).

(Citizens) Centre Alliance (CCA; *PC–POC*) organized behind Walesa but turned against him. Almost defunct in 1992, since two groups left: the right wing formed the Movement for Republic (*RDR*), while the liberal wing joined the Polish Liberal Programme.

1991: 8.71 – 44 (9.7); 1993: 4.42 – 00 (0).

Non-Party Bloc for the Support of Reform (NBSR; *BBWR*), organized by Walesa before the 1993 election.

1993: 5.41 – 16 (3.4).

Solidarity Trade Union (*NSZZ*), the trade union wing of Solidarity Organized by Marian Krzaklewski, the leader of Solidarity after Walesa. It is a trade union party, that is, its organization has been based on the trade union network in working places, its membership is about 1.8 million. In 1996 it established the **Electoral Action of Solidarity** (*AWS*) for the centre–right parties.

1991: 5.05 – 27 (6.0); 1993: 4.90 – 0 (0); 1997: 33.8 – 201 (43.7).

Peasant Accord (*PL*), the peasant wing of Solidarity.

1991: 5.47 – 28 (6.2); 1993: 2.37 – 00 (0).

Confederation for Independent Poland (*KPN*), a third party family, neither post-communist, nor post-Solidarity, organized in September 1979; membership 25,000.

1991: 7.50 – 46 (10.2); 1993: 5.77 – 22 (4.7); 1997: 0.

Electoral threshold: in 1993, 5 per cent for parties, 8 per cent for coalitions; the 5 per cent threshold to get seats from the national list (69 seats) was raised to 7 per cent from 4 per cent in 1992.

Participation: 1989: 62.32; 1991: 43.20; 1993: 52.06; 1997: 47.93 per cent.

Lost vote: 1989: 0; 1991: 0; 1993: 35.14; 1997: 11.8 per cent.

Hungary

The former ruling party, the **Hungarian Socialist Workers Party** (HSWP; *MSZMP*) was dissolved in October 1989 and the **Hungarian Socialist Party** (HSP; *MSZP*) emerged, with no membership continuity between HSWP and HSP; membership 37,000 (2,500 basic organizations and about 300 party employees).

1990: 10.89 – 33 (8.5); 1994: 32.99 – 209 (54.1).

Hungarian Democratic Forum (HDF; *MDF*), membership 25,000 (587 basic organizations and 136 party employees).

1990: 24.73 – 165 (42.7); 1994: 11.74 – 38 (9.8).

Alliance of Free Democrats (AFD; *SZDSZ*), membership 32,000 (740 basic organizations and 102 party employees).

1990: 21.39 – 94 (24.3); 1994: 19.74 – 71 (18.5).

Independent Smallholders Party (ISP: *FKGP*), membership 60,000 (1,700 basic organizations and 76 party employees).

1990: 11.73 – 44 (11.4); 1994: 8.82 – 26 (6.7).

Alliance of Young Democrats (**Fidesz**), in 1995 added the name of **Hungarian Civic Party** (*MPP*); membership 15,000 (300 basic organizations and 45 party employees).

1990: 8.95 – 22 (5.7); 1994: 7.02 – 20 (5.2).

Christian Democratic Peoples Party (CDPP; *KDNP*), membership 27,000 (750 basic organizations and 24 party employees).

1990: 6.46 – 21 (5.4); 1994: 7.03 – 22 (5.7).

Electoral threshold: 4 per cent in 1990, 5 per cent in 1994.

The biggest non-parliamentary party is the **Hungarian Socialist Workers Party** (now **Workers Party**, WP; *MP*), vote 1990: 3.68; 1994: 3.19 per cent.

Participation: 1990: 63.1; 1994: 68.9 per cent.

Lost vote: 1990: 10.99; 1994; 9.97 per cent.

Czech Republic

Czechoslovak Communist Party (CCP; *KSC*) or later **Communist Party of Bohemia and Moravia** (CPBM; *KSCM*) (organized on 31 March 1990), after the first elections turned into **Left Bloc**, but separated from it for the 1996 elections; membership 200,000.

   1990: 13.24 – 16 (8.0); 1992: 14.05 – 35 (17.5); 1996: 10.33 – 22 (11).

Civic Forum (CF; *OF*), organized on 19 November 1989 and split in 1991 into **Civic Democratic Party** (CDP; *ODS*), organized on 20 April 1990, membership 22,000, and **Civic Movement** (CM; *OH*), organized on 27 April 1990; membership 30,000 – but this latter party has lost its membership and significance. In the 1992 elections the Civic Democratic Party was in electoral alliance with the **Christian Democratic Party** (ChDP; *KDS*); it was organized already in 1989, but this small religious party could survive only in alliance with the CDP and in 1996 the two parties merged.

   Civic Forum: 1990: 49.50 – 127 (63.5).

   CDP–ChDP: 1992: 29.73 – 76 (38.0) of which CDP: 66 (33.0), ChDP: 10 (5.0); 1996: 29.62 – 68 (34.0).

   Civic Movement: 1992: 4.49 – 00 (0).

Civic Democratic Alliance (CDA; *ODA*), was organized as a small rightist group before the November events, became a party in December 1989, and later joined Civic Forum in a 1990 election alliance. With the disintegration of CF it became an independent party again. It tries to be the competitor of the CDP from the right; membership 2,500.

   1992: 5.93 – 14 (7.0); 1996: 6.36 – 13 (6.5).

Society for Moravia and Silesia (*HSD–SMS*), left the Civic Forum as a regionalist party in January 1990.

   1990: 10.3 – 22 (11.0); 1992: 5.87 – 14 (7.0); 1996: 0.42 + 0.27 – 00 (0).

Christian Democratic Union (CDU; *KDU*), membership 80,000; organized on 3 December 1989 with Christian Democratic Party (*KDS*) in an effort to form a federal party with the Slovak counterpart; in 1992 and 1996 in electoral alliance with **Czechoslovak People's Party** (*CSL*), the latter was founded in October 1918, and survived during the state socialist period as a member of the National Front. It combines a rural orientation with the Christian Socialist traditions.

   1990: 8.42 – 19 (9.5); 1992: 6.28 – 15 (7.5); 1996: 8.08 – 22 (11.0).

Czech(oslovak) Social Democratic Party (CSDP; *CSSD*), founded in 1878, re-organized in December 1989, a historical party as the leading force of the Europeanizer left; membership 13,000.

   1990: 4.11 – 00 (0); 1992: 6.53 – 16 (8.0); 1996: 26.44 – 61 (30.5).

Liberal Democratic Party (*LDS*), organized in November 1898 from the Czecho-slovak Democratic Initiative (1987) and ran in the 1990 election with the Civic Forum; the **Liberal Social Union** (*LSU*) was organized after the 1990 election as a coalition of the **Czech(oslovak) Socialist Party** (*CSS*), the **Agrarian Party** (*CSSZ*) and the **Green Party** (*SZ*); membership 11,000.

1990 (separately): 10.89 – 00 (0); (together) 1992: 6.52 – 16 (8.0); 1996: 0 (party disbanded).

Republican Party–Alliance for Republic (RP; *SPR-RSC*), formed in December 1989, in the 1990 election ran with the Civic Forum, then separated as an extreme right, nationalistic party; membership 55,000.

1990: 0000–00 (0); 1992: 5.98 – 14 (7.0); 1996: 8.01 – 18 (9.0).

The parliamentary data refer to the Czech National Council.

Electoral threshold: 5 per cent for parties; in 1992 7 per cent for coalitions of two parties, 9 per cent for three parties.

Participation: 1990: 96.8; 1992: 85.1; 1996: 75.7 per cent.

Lost vote: 1990: 18.11; 1992: 19.11; 1996: 11.15 per cent.

Slovakia

Communist Party of Slovakia (CPS; *KSS*), renamed on 20 October 1990 as the **Party of the Democratic Left** (PDL; *SDL*) and decided on a re-registration of members in January 1991; it organized an electoral coalition called **Common Choice** (*SV*) for the 1994 election, joined by the Green Party, the Social Democratic Party of Slovakia and the Agricultural Movement; opposed by the Workers Alliance of Slovakia, representing the close CPS tradition; membership 48,000.

1990: 13.13 – 22 (14.6); 1992: 14.70 – 29 (19.3); 1994: 10.41 – 18 (12.0).

Public Against Violence (PAV; *VPN*), emerged on 20 November 1989 as an umbrella organization, it ceased to exist in the original form in March 1991 as a result of a split between the pro-federation PAV and the emerging anti-federation Movement for Democratic Slovakia .

1990: 29.34 – 48 (32.0).

Movement for Democratic Slovakia (MDS; *HZDS*), founded by Meciar on 6 March 1991 and organized as an independent party on 22 June 1991; the MDS has become the biggest Slovak party, although it has had some further splits; membership 34,000.

1992: 37.26 – 74 (49.3); 1994: 34.96 – 61 (40.6).

Civic Democratic Union (CDU; *ODU*): the remaining PAV members formed another party (PAV–Civic Movement, then CDU); it could not survive but it is one of the precursors of the Democratic Union of Slovakia.

1992: 4.03 – 0 (00).

Democratic Union of Slovakia (DUS; *DUS*), emerged from the split in the MDS, joined also by the residual CDU; membership 2,000.

1994: 8.57 – 15 (10.0).

Christian Democratic Movement (CDM; *KDH*), founded in December 1989; the ultra-nationalistic elements were pushed out in March 1992. Solid conservative party; membership 27,000.

1990: 19.20 – 31 (20.6); 1992: 8.88 – 18 (12.0); 1994: 10.08 – 17 (11.3).

Hungarian Coalition (HC; *MK*), composed of the **Coexistence** (*Együttélés*, organized in February 1990), **Hungarian Christian Democratic Movement** (*MKDM*, organized in March 1990) and **Hungarian Civic Party** (*MPP*, organized in January 1992); membership 36,000.

1990: 8.66 – 14 (9.3); 1992: 7.42 – 14 (9.3); 1994: 10.18 – 17 (12.0).

Slovak National Party (SNP; *SNS*), organized in February 1990; membership 7,000.

1990: 13.94 – 22 (14.6); 1992: 7.93 – 15 (10.0); 1994: 5.40 – 9 (6.0).

Democratic Party (DP; *DS*), founded in 1944 as the Party of Slovak Renewal (gained 62 per cent in the 1946 Slovak election and was liquidated in 1947–48); reorganized in December 1989 as DP, formed an alliance in 1992 with the **Civic Democratic Party** (*ODS*), which is a small Slovak party and has no connection with the big Czech party under the same name.

1990: 4.39 – 7 (4.6); 1992: 3.31 – 00 (0); 1994: 3.42 – 00 (0).

Green Party (*SZ*), in 1994 electoral coalition with the Common Choice.

1990: 3.48 – 6 (4.0).

Workers Association of Slovakia (WAS; *ZRS*), emerged before the 1994 election as a split-off party from the Party of the Democratic Left; membership 20,000.

1994: 7.34 – 13 (8.6).

The parliamentary data from 1990 and 1992 also refer to the Slovak National Council.

Electoral threshold: 3 per cent in 1990; 5 per cent for one party, 7 per cent for two-three party coalitions and 10 per cent for more than three parties in 1992 and 8 per cent for two parties in 1994.

Participation: 1990: 96.8; 1992: 84.2; 1994: 75.2 per cent.

Lost votes: 1990: 7.65; 1992: 23.81; 1994: 13.06 per cent.

Slovenia

The **League of Slovenian Communists** (LSC; *ZKS*), renamed on 7 February 1990 as the **Party of Democratic Renewal** (PDR; *SDP*) and organized as a coalition for the 1992 election as the **United List of Social Democrats** (ULSD; *ZLSD*) jointly with the Workers Party, Social Democratic Union and Democratic Party of Pensioners (*DSP*).

1990: 17.3 – 14 (17.5); 1992: 13.58 – 14 (15.55); 1996: 9.03 – 9 (10.0).

Demos (Democratic Opposition of Slovenia), seven-party coalition organized for the 1990 election, disintegrated in late 1991 (SCD, SDPS, GS, SDA, SFP – see below; Democratic Party of Pensioners and Party of Craftsmen).

1990: 54.4 – 47 (58.7).

Liberal Democratic Party (LDP; *LDS*), organized on 10 November 1990; on 12 March 1994 organized a bigger liberal party coalition as **Liberal Democracy of Slovenia** (*LDS*), joined by the Democratic Party and the Greens.

1990: 14.5 – 12 (15.0); 1992: 23.46 – 22 (24.44); 1996: 27.01 – 25 (27.7).

Slovenian Christian Democrats (SCD; *SKD*), historical party, reoganized on 10 March 1989.

1990: 13.0 – 11 (13.7); 1992: 14.51 – 15 (16.66); 1996: 9.62 – 10 (11.1).

Slovenian Farmers Party (SFP; *SPL*) – later **Slovenian Peoples Party** (SPP; *SLS*), organized on 12 May 1988.

1990: 12.6 – 11 (13.7); 1992: 8.69 – 10 (11.11); 1996: 19.38 – 19 (21.1).

Slovenian Democratic Alliance (SDA; *SDS*), later **Democratic Party** (*DS*), organized on 11 January 1983; in 1994 joined the LDP but ran again independently in the 1996 elections.

1990: 9.5 – 8 (10.0); 1992: 5.01 – 6 (6.66); 1996: 2.68 – 0.

Greens of Slovenia (GS; *ZS*), organized on 11 June 1989; in 1994 joined the LDP, but ran again independently in the 1996 elections.

1990: 8.8 – 8 (10.0); 1992: 3.70 – 5 (5.55); 1996: 1.76 – 00 (0).

Social Democratic Party of Slovenia (SDPS; *SDSS*), reorganized on 16 February 1989 and became a rather right-wing party.

1990: 7.4 – 6 (7.5); 1992: 3.34 – 4 (4.44); 1996: 16.13 – 16 (17.7).

Socialist Party of Slovenia (*SSS*), organized on 9 June 1990.

1990: 5.4 – 5 (5.75); 1992: 2.8 – 00 (0).

Slovenian National Party (*SNS*), organized on 17 March 1991 from a faction of SFP as an ultra-nationalistic party.

   1992: 10.02 – 12 (13.33); 1996: 3.22 – 4 (4.4).

The parliamentary data in 1990 refer to the socio-political chamber which was the main chamber of the three former chambers (it had 80 seats) and has become the parliament (with 90 seats). Sixteen parties participated in the 1990 election and 9 became parliamentary parties, 26 and 8 in 1992, 20 and 7 in 1996 respectively.

   Electoral threshold: 2.5 per cent in 1990; 3.4 per cent (3 seats) in 1992.

   Participation: 1990: 83.51; 1992: 85.84; 1996: 73.2 per cent.

   Lost vote: 1990: 8.0; 1992: 17.69; 1996: 11.29 per cent.

Croatia

The **Croatian League of Communists** (CLC; *SKH*) became the **Social Democratic Party of Croatia** (SDPC; *SPDH*). In 1990 the **Socialist Party of Croatia** (*SSH*) had both common candidates with SDPC and separate ones (here counted together). The SDPC in 1992 received also three Serbian seats (not counted here).

   1990: 34.97 – 20 (25.00); 1992: 5.40 – 3 (2.50); 1995: 8.93 – 9 (7.08).

Croatian Democratic Community (CDC; *HDZ*) as an umbrella organization was formed on 17 June 1989; it split in 1993 and the **Croatian Independent Democrats** (*HND*) left, but gained only one seat in 1995.

   1990: 41.93 – 55 (68.75); 1992: 43.72 – 85 (70.84); 1995: 45.23 – 75 (59.05).

For the 1990 election a four-party coalition was formed under the name of **Coalition of People's Agreement** (*KNS*), but one member of the coalition, the Croatian Democratic Party (*HDS*), also ran separately and had one seat (here counted together and these figures are repeated below at CSLP).

   1990: 15.34 – 3 (3.75).

Serbian Democratic Party (*SDS*), organized on 17 February 1990 as an ethnic party and later pushed into the background during the war; the **Serbian National Party** (*SNS*) was organized as a party loyal to the Croatian government but not representative. In 1992 the three seats it received as an ethnic party were given to SDPC. In 1995 the Serbian minority received three seats.

   1990: 1.62 – 1 (1.25); 1992: 1.06 – 00 (0); 1995: (–) 3 (2.36).

Croatian Social Liberal Party (CSLP; *HSLS*), organized on 20 May 1989; a member of the four-party coalition in 1990 (see above).

   1990: 15.34 – 3 (3.75); 1992: 17.33 – 13 (10.84); 1995: 11.55 – 11 (8.66).

Croatian Party of Rights (CPR; *HSP*), historical party from 1861, reorganized on 25 February 1990, ultra-nationalistic.

1990: –; 1992: 6.91 – 5 (4.17); 1995: 5.01 – 4 (3.14).

Peoples Party of Croatia (PPC; *HNS*) organized on 31 January 1991. In 1995 joined an electoral alliance with the Croatian Peasant Party and regionalist parties.

1990: –; 1992: 6.55 – 4 (3.34); 1995: {18.26 – 21 (16.53)}.

Croatian Peasant Party (CPP; *HSS*), founded in 1904, reorganized on 20 November 1989; in 1995 joined electoral alliance with the PPC and regionalist parties.

1990: –; 1992: 4.16 – 3 (2.50); 1995: {18.26 – 21 (16.53)}.

Coalition of Regionalist Parties, the Istrian Democratic Assembly (*IDS*, Pula: February 1990), the Dalmatian Action (*DA*, Split: December 1990) and Democratic Alliance of Rijeka (*RDS*, in early 1990). In 1995 joined an electoral alliance with two other parties (PPC, CPP).

1990: –; 1992: 3.11 – 6 (5.00); 1995: {18.26 – 21 (16.53)}.

Electoral regulations: very complicated and arbitrarily changed several times by the CDC tyrannical majority. For 1990 only 80 seats of the socio-political chamber which has become the parliament are counted; in 1992 only 120 seats, because 18 other seats (for minorities) were distributed by the Constitutional Court. In 1995 there were 127 seats (108 elected in Croatia – both on party lists and in single member individual districts – 12 in diaspora and 7 given to minorities). In 1995 28 parties ran for the election and 12 parties gained seats in the parliament (five of them only with one seat). In some ways all opposition parties formed electoral coalitions against the CDC, both on party lists and in the single member individual districts.

The Coalition of People's Agreement was organized in 1990 by the Croatian Social Liberal Party, Croatian Christian Democratic Party, Croatian Democratic Party and Social Democratic Party; in the 1992 election several party coalitions were formed; in 1995 all opposition parties organized resistance against CDC in some ways, but the CPP, the PPC and the regionalist parties formed a direct electoral coalition.

Participation: 1990: 84.47; 1992: 75.61; 1995: 68.79 per cent.

Lost vote: 1990: 3.1; 1992: 11.8; 1995: 0 per cent.

Balkan parties

Serbia

Serbian Socialist Party (SSP; *SPS*), formerly **League of Serbian Communists** (LSC; *SKS*), reorganized on 16 July 1990 with full organization and membership continuity.

   1990: 46.1 – 194 (77.6); 1992: 28.8 – 101 (40.4); 1993: 36.7 – 123 (49.2).

Serbian Renewal Movement (SRM; *SPO*), began during 1989 as **Serbian National Renewal** (*SNO*); organized in January 1990 and turned by the charismatic writer and orator Vuk Draskovic to SRM as a party in August 1990. It follows the line of ultra-nationalism for Greater Serbia but formed an alliance of Depos (Democratic Opposition of Serbia) against Milosevic in May 1992 with the Democratic Party of Serbia (DOS; *DSS*), the Serbian Liberal Party (SLP; *SLS*), the New Democracy – Movement for Serbia (ND–MS; *ND-PS*) and the Peasant Party (PP); the 1992 and 1993 figures indicate the results of the Depos bloc.

   1990: 15.8 – 19 (7.6); 1992: 16.9 – 50 (20.2); 1993: 16.6 – 45 (18.0).

Serbian Radical Party (SRP; *SRS*) began from the SNO–SPO line but Vojislav Seselj founded a new ultra-nationalist party in January 1990. As a follower of cetnik tradition it has been the most militant nationalist party, sponsored and bolstered by the Milosevic regime as a shield for its own nationalist policies, but it turned later against Milosevic.

   1990: –; 1992: 22.6 – 73 (29.2); 1993: 13.8 – 39 (15.6).

Democratic Party (*DS*), founded on 3 February 1990, middle-sized Europeanizer rightist party.

   1990: 7.4 – 7 (2.8); 1992: 4.2 – 6 (2.4); 1993: 11.6 – 29 (11.6).

Democratic Party of Serbia (DOS; *DSS*) – small, pro-monarchist party; in May 1992 left the Democratic Party and joined Depos for the 1992 elections.

   1990: –; {1992: 16.9 – 50 (20.0)}; 1993: 5.1 – 7 (2.8).

Democratic Community of Hungarians in Vojvodina (*VMDK–DZVM*), Hungarian ethnic party organized on 31 March 1990, later splitting on the question of autonomy and the more conciliatory **Organization of Hungarians in Vojvodina** (*VMSZ*) was created.

   1990: 2.6 – 8 (3.2); 1992: 3.0 – 9 (3.6); 1993; 2.6 – 5 (2.0).

Albanian Democratic Party, a small pro-Serbian party in Kosovo; ran only in the 1993 elections.

   1993: 0.7 – 2 (0.8).

Participation: 1990: 71.5; 1992: 69.7; 1993: 61.6 per cent.

Lost vote: 1990: 10.8; 1992: 14.0; 1993: 13.9 per cent.

Macedonia

Social Democratic Union of Macedonia (SDUM; *SDSM*), renamed in 1991), formerly **League of Macedonian Communists** (LMC; *SKM*) (founded in 1943) and later **Party of Democratic Transformation** (PDP; *PDT*) (organized in 1989), led by Kiro Gligorov; for the 1994 elections an electoral coalition, Alliance for Macedonia, was established.

1990: – 31 (25.8); 1994: – 58 (48.3).

Internal Macedonian Revolutionary Organization (IMRO; *VMRO*), organized originally in 1894 as a pro-Bulgarian movement to attach Macedonia to Bulgaria. Reorganized on 17 June 1990 in Macedonia as a populist-nationalist party, adding the party name **Democratic Party for Macedonian National Unity** (DPMNU; *DPMNE*). Very militantly nationalistic and anti-Albanian, yet still split in January 1991 when an even more pro-Bulgarian and anti-Muslim group left (*IMRO–DP*). In the spirit of Macedonia only for (*pravoslav*) Macedonians, the IMRO has opposed the consolidation of the present Macedonian state.

1990: – 38 (31.6); 1994: did not run.

Alliance of Reform Forces of Macedonia (*SRSM*), emerged during the first multi-party elections, later on adding the name of **Liberal Party** (LP; *LS*) as well; urban based liberal party.

1990: – 17 (14.1); 1994: – 29 (24.1).

Socialist Party of Macedonia (SPM; *SPM*), grew out from **Socialist Alliance** (*SS*), founded on 28 September 1990; advocates socialist and ecological values.

1990: – 5 (4.1); 1994: – 7 (5.8).

Party for Democratic Prosperity in Macedonia (PDP; *PDP*), ethnic Albanian party, organized in April 1990, at the first multi-party elections in electoral coalition with the other Albanian party, the **National Democratic Party** (NDP; *PDP*, organized in early 1990), adopting more radical positions.

1990: – 23 (19.1); 1994: – 10 (8.3).

Participation: 1990: 84.8; 1994: 77.3 per cent.

Lost vote: none (majoritarian system, single member districts with two rounds).

Bulgaria

Bulgarian Socialist Party (BSP; *BSP*), the **Bulgarian Communist Party** (BCP; *BKP*, founded in 1891), changed its name to BSP in April 1990, with full institutional and membership continuity. In the 1997 election ran as **Democratic Left** (DL; *DL*).

  1990: 47.15 – 211 (52.7); 1991: 33.14 – 106 (44.2); 1994: 43.5 – 125 (52.0); 1997: 22.2 – 57 (21.6).

Union of Democratic Forces (UDF; *SDS*), organized from 16 political groups by Zheliu Zhelev on 23 November 1989 as a member organization including BANU (see below). It has become a national-conservative party; the liberal democrats left, organizing the UDF-Centre and the UDF-Liberals for the 1991 elections. In the 1997 election ran as **Alliance of Democratic Forces** (ADF; *ODS*) with BANU–NP (see below).

  1990: 36.20 – 144 (36.0); 1991: 34.36 – 110 (45.8); 1994: 24.2 – 69 (28.7); 1997: 52.2 – 137 (55.7).

Bulgarian Agrarian National Union (BANU; *BZNS*) – the great historical party, organized in 1900. It split in late 1989, with the more radical wing separating and taking the name of the post-war leader Nikola Petkov (BANU–NP). This wing separated again in 1994, when one group joined BSP (the Stamboliyski wing), and the other the Popular Union (see below).

  1990: 8.03 – 16 (4.0); 1991: 3.86 + 3.44 – 0; 1994: {6.5 – 18 (7.5)}; 1997: –.

Movement for Rights and Freedoms (MRF; *DPS*), the ethnic Turkish and/or Muslim party, founded on 4 January 1990 by Ahmed Dogan. In the 1997 election ran as Union for National Salvation (*ONS*).

  1990: 6.03 – 23 (5.7); 1991: 7.55 – 24 (10.0); 1994: 5.4 – 15 (6.2); 1997: 7.5 – 20 (12.5).

Popular Union (*NS*) emerged before the 1994 elections from the liberal wing of UDF and BANU.

  1990: –; (1991: 3.20 + 2.81 – 00 (0)); 1994: 6.5 – 18 (7.5); 1997: –.

Bulgarian Business Bloc (BBB; *BBB*), pro-Western entrepreneurial party.

  1990: –; 1991: –; 1994: 4.7 – 13 (5.4); 1997: 4.9 – 12 (5.0).

  Participation: 1990: 90.79; 1991: 84.1; 1994: 75.23; 1997: 58.1 per cent.

  Lost vote: 1990: 1.69; 1991: 34.95; 1994: 15.59; 1997: 12.3 per cent.

Romania

National Salvation Front (NSF; *FSN*), organized by Ion Iliescu and Petre Roman on 22 December 1989, based on the decomposing **Romanian Communist Party** (*PCR*). Before the 1992 elections there was a split between the traditionalist and modernizing wings, the former with Iliescu adopted the name of **Democratic National Salvation Front** (DNSF; *FSND*), later on the **Party of Social Democracy in Romania** (PSDR; *PDSR*). The modernizing wing with Roman kept the original name (NSF) and first merged with the Democratic Party and later on with the historical Romanian Social Democratic Party.

1990: 66.31 – 263 (67.9); 1992: 27.71 – 117 (35.5); 1996: 22.2 – 91 (26.5).

Democratic Party of Romania *(PDR)*, organized on 27 December 1989 as a pro-Western democratic party, merged after the 1992 elections with the NSF of Petre Roman. Before the November 1996 elections this new party merged with the small historical Romanian Social Democratic Party *(PSDR)* and Petre Roman founded the **Social Democratic Union** (SDU; *USD*) which became a member of the Socialist International at its New York conference in September 1996.

{1990: 66.31 – 263 (67.9)}; 1992: 10.18 – 43 (13.2); 1996: 13.7 – 53 (15.4).

Christian Democratic National Peasant Party (CDNPP; *PNT-cd*), one of the great historical parties, founded in 1869, refounded in 1895, banned in 1947, reorganized on 26 December 1989. Originally a peasant–populist party, although somewhat modernized recently, it has kept the inward-looking peasant orientation. It was the major force behind the **Democratic Convention of Romania** (DCR; *CDR*), the umbrella organization of the opposition in the 1992 and 1996 elections. The figures for 1992 and 1996 indicate the DCR results.

1990: 2.56 – 12 (3.1); 1992: 20.01 – 82 (25.4); 1996: 30.2 – 122 (35.5).

National Liberal Party (NLP; *PNL*), the other great historical party, originally founded in 1876, disbanded in 1948, reactivated on 30 December 1989. A more urban based, liberal oriented party, with a series of split and mergers. There have been almost a dozen successor parties with the name 'liberal'. As a junior partner, it participated in the 1992 and 1996 elections in the Democratic Convention of Romania.

1990: 6.41 – 29 (7.2); {1992: 20.01 – 82 (25.2)}; {1996: 30.2 – 122 (35.5)}.

Democratic Alliance of Hungarians in Romania (DAHR; *RMDSZ–UDMR*), the Hungarian ethnic party, organized on 21 December 1989.

1990: 7.23 – 29 (7.2); 1992: 7.45 – 27 (8.1); 1996: 5.8 – 25 (7.3).

Party of Romanian National Unity (PRNU; *PUNR*), an ultra-nationalist party, emerged before the May 1990 elections, based on the socio-cultural nationalistic organization **Romanian Cradle** (*Vatra Romaneasca*), headed by Gheorghe Funar.

1990: –; 1992: 7.71 – 30 (8.9); 1996: 3.7 – 18 (5.2).

Greater Romania Party (GRP; *PRM*), established in May 1991 by a group of journalists of the newspaper *Romania Mare* (*Greater Romania*) (created in June 1990), headed by Corneliu Vadim Tudor, as an ultra-nationalist party, it competes with the PRNU.

1990: –; 1992: 3.89 – 16 (5.1); 1996: 4.1 – 19 (5.5).

Participation: 1990: 86.2; 1992: 76.28; 1996: 76.11 per cent.

Lost vote: 1990: 0; 1992: 20.02; 1996: 20.3 per cent.

Albania

Albanian Socialist Party (ASP; *PSS*), formerly **Albanian Workers Party** (AWP; *PPS*); changed its name to ASP in June 1991.

1991: 56.17 – 169 (70.4); 1992: 25.73 – 38 (27.1); 1996: 20.37 – 10 (7.1); 1997: 53.4 – 118 (76.1).

Albanian Democratic Party (ADP; *PDS*), formed by Sali Berisha on 19 December 1990.

1991: 38.71 – 65 (27.2); 1992: 62.09 – 92 (65.7); 1996: 55.53 – 122 (87.1); 1997: 25.3 – 24 (15.4).

Unity Party of Human Rights – formerly **Omonia**, the ethnic Greek party.

1991: 0.73 – 5 (2.0); 1992: 2.90 – 2 (1.4); 1996: 4.04 – 3 (2.1): 1997: n.a.

Participation: 1991: 98.92; 1992: 90.35; 1996: 89.0; 1997: 65.2 per cent.

Lost vote: 1991: 4.11; 1992: 1.79; 1996: 0; 1997: 0 per cent.

PART THREE

THE REGIONS IN COMPARATIVE TRANSITION

6

Re-democratization in East Central Europe

The East Central European countries have had a mixed tradition, since both democratic and authoritarian features were developed in their political systems before the state socialist period. They have embarked upon democratization of their polity several times from the mid-nineteenth century on, but the unfavourable international circumstances prevented them from accomplishing this task. The latest attempt was in the early post-war period (1944–8), but the Cold War System and the attachment to the Soviet external empire stopped the democratization efforts again. Consequently, in the late 1980s a re-democratization began in the ECE countries, that is, a democratization process based on the repetition and continuation of former democratizations because they had a substantial democratic potential in both democratic institutions and culture. Obviously, the relative success of this new democratization effort was due not only to the favourable international circumstances this time, but also to the strength of the democratic traditions, which has allowed for a relatively quick and peaceful transition to democracy in East Central Europe.

The negotiated transition

The 1980s was a decade of protracted crisis within state socialism in East Central Europe, most manifestly in Poland. Poland became the trend-setter and model for changes not only during the crisis of state socialism but also afterwards, during the pre-transition crisis and breakthrough between the two systems and in the first period of democratic transition. Poland, therefore, enjoyed the advantages as well as the disadvantages of being an early-comer. Hungary had the longest and most evolutionary form of socio-economic transformation, and in the late 1980s followed very closely the Polish lead. Czechoslovakia, in turn, was a political laggard with its deeply frozen post-Stalinist structure, and it began the political transition as the latest within the region, but it enjoyed all the advantages of a late-comer in its 'Velvet Revolution', since the state socialist system collapsed in Czechoslovakia without strong resistance from the Husak leadership. Slovenia and Croatia belong to the ECE region, but we discuss them in the next chapter as post-Yugoslav states, since most of their recent political history has been connected with the disintegration of Yugoslavia.

In the ECE pre-transition crisis, the Polish Solidarity was the major force and a symbol of opposition against the state socialist system in Poland and in the entire ECE region in the 1980s. It was an umbrella organization with three different functions. Its original core was a trade union and it was organized by Lech Walesa initially, in the early 1980s, as a working-class movement. Later on, Solidarity turned into a particular kind of political party and finally became a national liberation movement. Under conditions of illegality, this huge and heterogeneous organization contained embryonically the whole multi-party system in itself, since all the forces of opposition had to unite. Therefore, during the negotiated transition, step by step, Solidarity already proved to be an obstacle to the formation of a genuine multi-party system, which emerged in Poland only much later than elsewhere in East Central Europe, through the disintegration of Solidarity (see Lewis, 1994b: 785). But in the late 1980s and at the beginning of the negotiated transition, Solidarity was still a pioneer in systemic change internationally and domestically at the national roundtable talks, and played a very active and positive role in the entire negotiated transition (see East, 1992; Mason, 1993).[1]

The negotiated transition had been a Spanish invention but it was further developed in East Central Europe. The national roundtable, as an institutionalized forum between government and opposition, became the most important institution in closing the pre-transition crisis and during the negotiated transition. In Poland, the way to national roundtable negotiations was opened by both external and internal factors. In early 1989 it became clear that, in the spirit of Gorbachev doctrine No. 1, in Poland power *monopoly* could and should be given up for a power *hegemony*. After the new waves of strikes and leadership changes in the ruling Polish United Workers Party (PUWP; PZPR),[2] negotiations began between the government and Solidarity on 6 February 1989 and, after two months of tough bargaining, finally on 5 April 1989 a pact was signed. As a first pillar of compromise, in the April Pact Solidarity was given legal status and semi-free elections were held in June. But Solidarity could compete only for 35 per cent of the seats in the Sejm (the Polish parliament). A majority of seats (65 per cent) were reserved for the PUWP and its party allies, having had parliamentary representation already in earlier decades. Still, the April Pact was a big breakthrough because it produced the first non-communist government in East Central Europe since the early post-war period. Above all, it initiated a dynamic for systemic change in Poland and for the whole Eastern part of Europe.

The national roundtable negotiations broke the political deadlock and produced two important consequences. First, the entire political transformation proceeded within a framework of constitutionality and legality. It was a 'constitutional revolution', sometimes even called a 'conservative revolution', since the negotiating partners changed the existing legal order within its own constitutional framework. The compromises at the national roundtable unleashed, however, a process of radical transformation which led to further constitutional changes through a series of new compromises. Secondly, this consensual model of peaceful revolution excluded violence as a means to achieve fundamental changes. The negotiated transition within the existing constitutionality produced a radical political transformation which, at the same time, did not allow for retrospective punishment of the political vices of former leaders because they had contributed to the peaceful transition as partners in initiating these evolutionary changes. The national roundtable and negotiated transition process, elaborated in and experimented with by Poland, provided a model for almost all ECE and Balkan countries. In point of fact, this means of solving the pre-transition crisis was elevated to the status of an obligatory route to democratic transition in East Central Europe by the demonstration effect of the successful Polish, as well as later the Hungarian, transformation. The negotiated transition heralded a new age in ECE regional developments, a deep historical rupture with the former traditions of violent political transition and social transformation. The negotiated transition operated in an opposite way in the ECE and Balkan countries. It was completely peaceful only in the former region, although this political innovation did significantly decrease the violent character of political change even in the Balkans.

In Poland, the second pillar of the April Pact was an agreement on a strong presidency to ensure a smooth transition for the ruling party. The strong presidency meant, *inter alia*, the right to appoint and control the three most important ministries (exterior, interior and defence). The ensuing dual executive power was a second genetic weakness of the Polish polity, the first being Solidarity itself as a huge and loose umbrella organization replacing the whole multi-party system. The 'moving walls' of the Polish political system, that is, a dynamism of change transcending the April Pact step by step, corrected these weaknesses. With the disintegration of Solidarity in 1990–1, a genuine multi-party system came into being and also the strong presidency eroded to a great extent up to the mid-1990s. In the 'moving walls' aspect of the institutional system after the pact signed at the national roundtable, Poland produced another general model, also valid for many ECE and Balkan countries. The 'moving walls' mean that the former opposition gains more and more strength in the real world of politics and this offsets the institutional arrangements fixed by the original pact. Each new situation generates further institutional changes through new agreements and the process is repeated again and again during the whole negotiated transition, that is, until the first free election.

The first Polish multi-party election was only semi-free. At the June 1989 election, Solidarity won all the seats in the Sejm it was allowed to compete for, that is, only 35 per cent . But in the Sejm convened in July the PUWP lost its majority through the defection of its former allies, since they wanted to ensure their political future by changing sides. In this new situation and in the spirit of moving walls, a new compromise was reached with the PUWP through a formula suggested by Adam Michnik, a leading intellectual of Solidarity: 'your president, our prime minister'. Indeed, Wojciech Jaruzelski was elected president by the new parliament in July, then Tadeusz Mazowiecki, a Catholic liberal intellectual was elected prime minister in August 1989 in the terms of the new compromise. The Mazowiecki government was the first non-communist government in Central and Eastern Europe, although originally it had some PUWP ministers, appointed by the president, but under popular pressure they soon left the government. Consequently, by the Autumn of 1989 Solidarity had seized power step by step, since the growing erosion of power of the former ruling party and the international circumstances made the completion of this power transfer mandatory.

However, the Mazowiecki government exercising full powers in Poland immediately had to face a new difficulty: it had to cope with a protracted deep economic crisis which provoked the breakdown of the state socialist regime. For radical economic crisis management, in October 1989 Leszek Balcerowicz, the finance minister, introduced *shock therapy*. Cutting state subsidies and lifting price controls 'overnight' was followed by 'a leap to a market economy'. This shock therapy came as a real shock to the population, with sky-rocketing prices, a decreasing standard of living, job insecurity and a high unemployment rate. This radical treatment of the economic crisis was necessary in Poland and after some years it proved to be successful. But in the short run the shock therapy was politically divisive and contributed much to the split in Solidarity itself, the hard core of which was a working-class movement and the Polish working class suffered the most because of this radical cure. The ensuing political shock caused widespread disillusionment and political apathy in Poland. People turned away from politics, became disappointed even in Solidarity because democracy appeared as coupled with mass poverty. Populism gained momentum and the early 1990s became a period of political uncertainty (see Tymowski, 1993: 185–8).[3]

Thus, paradoxically, Solidarity after Autumn 1989 lost and gained power at the same time. It gained power with the retreat of the PUWP and finally, with the resignation of president Jaruzelski in October 1990. Thereafter, the election of Lech Walesa as president of Poland in December 1990 completed the political takeover, the last 'wall' of former institutions was removed and Solidarity alone ruled Poland. On the other side, however, from late 1989 the disintegration process of Solidarity came increasingly to the forefront of Polish politics. The emerging post-Solidarity parties – the Democratic Union (DU; UD), the Citizens Centre Alliance (CCA; POC), the Christian–National Union (CNU; ZChN), etc., etc. – represented almost the entire political spectrum. The newly formed parties turned against each other vehemently at the first really free elections in October 1991, and well before the election they brought their bitter infighting to the centre of the election campaign. Nevertheless, despite all these transitory negative features and setbacks, the Polish developments in 1989–90 initiated a radical transformation and produced large-scale democratization, closely followed by Hungary.

After the defeat of the October 1956 Revolution in Hungary, the continued resistance against the Soviet external empire forced János Kádár, the party leader between 1956 and 1988, to produce the most liberal version of state socialism. The 1980s saw increasing socio-economic liberalization but a growing contradiction with political conservatism of the ageing leadership. This contradiction generated a political crisis in the second half of the 1980s and the pre-transition crisis had already begun in Hungary in 1987–8. In September 1987 the first opposition party, the Hungarian Democratic Forum (HDF; MDF) was organized in the spirit of Polish Solidarity but giving a model at the same time for other 'Forum' type large and loose movement parties. As a result of the deepening political crisis, at a party conference of the ruling party, the Hungarian Socialist Workers Party (HSWP; MSZMP) in May 1988, the Kádárian leadership was removed and it was followed by a 'reform communist' team. In late 1988 a party movement for reforms emerged within the ruling party, and these 'reform circles' were then organized at the national level into the Reform Alliance. The reform circles held their national conferences in May and September 1989, and they became an important social movement and political organization in Hungary. Finally, in early October 1989 at the party congress this reform faction of the HSWP succeeded in dissolving the old party and formed a new one, the Hungarian Socialist Party (HSP; MSZP), with a social democratic profile.[4]

Thus, 1989 was a crucial year for the Hungarian long pre-transition crisis. In early February 1989 the Central Committee of the HSWP voted for introduction of a multi-party system and acknowledged that the October 1956 Revolution was not a counter-revolution but a genuine national uprising. In March 1989 an Oppositional Roundtable of nine opposition groups was formed and, after having prepared a common platform, it engaged in negotiations with the ruling party in June, just some days after the Polish elections. Consequently, the Hungarian political transformation proceeded quite smoothly and proceeded from the outset on a multi-party foundation (see Swain, 1993: 66–7; Tôkés, 1996). During the Summer of 1989 the national roundtable produced an agreement on all important aspects of political transition. The agreement contained a blueprint for the further negotiated transition and democratization, and it was signed on 18 September 1989. This September Agreement not only set a date for a completely free election in Spring 1990 but also contained the basic constitutional amendments. In this spirit, a new, fully democratic constitution was passed by the Hungarian parliament in October 1989. This was still the 'transitory parliament', elected in 1985, but even at that date elections had been on the basis of mandatory multiple candidacy in each electoral district. This parliament played a major role in the pre-transition crisis and became in 1989–90 a quasi multi-party parliament through dozens of by-elections.[5]

These events show that the fight between the two wings of reform communists, that is, between the conservative power technocrats and the democratic reformers, was decided in the favour of the latter during 1989. The Miklós Németh government was very instrumental in bringing about changes. In fact, as a self-declared caretaker government, it was at the same time the last 'communist' and the first democratic government during its tenure between November 1988 and March 1990. Therefore, the Németh government is still very popular with Hungarians because of its eminent role in the negotiated transition. This government gained international fame not just through a demonstration effect in peaceful domestic transformation, but first by opening the Hungarian–Austrian borders for the citizens of the German Democratic Republic in late August and early September 1989. Through this action the Németh government significantly contributed to the fall of the Berlin Wall and by this to that of the entire GDR; and, in general, to the collapse of state socialism in Central and Eastern Europe. Hungarians acted in the terms of the Gorbachev doctrine No. 2, as if the Soviet external empire had ceased to exist in East Central Europe, albeit this was formulated only in December 1989 in Malta at the Bush–Gorbachev summit.

In Hungary no mass opposition movement existed in the 1980s comparable to Solidarity, but there was, in turn, wide mass pressure for reforms. Only a small group of democratic opposition confronted the regime manifestly from the early 1970s until the mid-1980s; they were the founding fathers of the Alliance of Free Democrats (AFD; SZDSZ). But the organized opposition gained strength increasingly in the second half of the 1980s. During the pre-transition crisis it developed two major tendencies: first, the 'national-popular' direction, emphasizing the importance of Hungarian traditions and national specificities with a need to return to them by re-establishing a genuine national continuity: secondly the urban-modernizer group, emphasizing the salience of the European model and the need for its application to Hungary. The first tendency, represented by the Hungarian Democratic Forum, in the spirit of national-conservatism, somewhat neglected mainstream European developments; and the second, represented by the Alliance of Free Democrats, in the spirit of a rather abstract liberalism, somewhat overgeneralized these common European features.

The party formation process accelerated in 1988 with some opposition parties getting legally organized after the HDF and the AFD. The AFD was initially joined by the Alliance of Young Democrats (Fidesz), which came into being as a liberal party of the young generation but later as a centre–right party it developed closer to the HDF. Two historical parties also re-emerged in 1989, the Independent Smallholders Party (ISP) and the Christian Democratic Peoples Party (CDPP), and became parliamentary parties, while others (the Hungarian Peoples Party, the Hungarian Social Democratic Party etc.) disappeared as major political forces after the first election. The ISP developed toward an extreme rightist-populist party, finding a constituency, beyond the traditionalist small peasantry, among the losers of systemic change. The CDPP remained more of a centre–right organization as a small traditionalist-religious party in the Hungarian party system, representing the conservative middle classes and the rural poor. In addition to these parties, the formation of the HSP took place also in 1989, and altogether these six became parliamentary parties, having been the earliest to appear and having organized their leadership and mobilized public support well before the others. In such a way, in Hungary not only did the multi-party system come into existence rather early, but also its six leading parties were selected out from among an emerging 'hundred-party system' at the very beginning.

With the formation of a multi-party system, and with the institutional transformations during the negotiated transition, Hungary also provided a model of peaceful democratic transformation for the rest of Central and Eastern Europe in the Autumn of 1989. The other countries followed suit, and after September 1989 the collapse of the Soviet external empire accelerated. The Berlin Wall fell on 9 November, Todor Zhivkov of Bulgaria was removed from his post on 10 November and the Christmas Revolution brought the rule of Ceausescu to an end in Romania. The 'Velvet Revolution' in Czechoslovakia on 17 November 1989 was an important part of this chain reaction, caused by the snowball effect of former transformations. The actual capitulation of the Husak regime already predicted the final demise of the external Soviet empire as a whole. Under the impact of the demonstration effect of the Polish and Hungarian negotiated transitions, the Czech population was already on high alert during September and October, and under the direct influence of the fall of the Berlin Wall, on 17 November a mass demonstration took place in the centre of Prague, in the Wenceslav Square. This peaceful demonstration won the day rather easily, since after a week or so the Husak regime gave up any resistance and began to negotiate, not seeing any chance for suppressing this mass movement by means of a new Soviet invasion in the radically changed international arena.

The ease of the 'Velvet Revolution' produced a general euphoria in Czechoslovakia. After the breakthrough at the demonstration, a new power centre arose around Vacláv Havel, an eminent playwright and leading member of the small former opposition group. The Civic Forum (CF; OF) was formed as a large umbrella organization on 19 November 1989 and its Slovak sister organization, the Public Against Violence (PAV; VPN) the following day. On 24 November the leadership of the Czechoslovak Communist Party (CCP; KSC) resigned and the new leadership resorted to negotiations. This particular national roundtable was very short-lived and conclusive, since the CCP leadership did not negotiate but capitulated, and by giving up power completely they hoped for a quiet retreat. Actually, in Czechoslovakia there had been no manifest pre-transition crisis, so no real negotiated transition took place either, because total power was given immediately to the new umbrella organizations or movement parties. The former communist deputy prime minister, Marián Calfa, was appointed prime minister of the new government on 10 December, this time as the representative of the PAV. Consequently, despite the abrupt political changes, a personal continuity prevailed everywhere in the first period because, unlike in Poland and Hungary, in Czechoslovakia the victorious opposition was small and weak and, therefore, there was no counter-elite available for a complete political takeover.[6]

Hence, we see a profound continuity in Czechoslovakia under the surface of sudden discontinuity in the Velvet Revolution, coupled with the non-democratic, elitist tradition of the Czech political culture (see Wolchik, 1992: 149–50). It was the former communist parliament that elected Havel as President and Alexander Dubcek, the hero of the Prague Spring in 1968, as Speaker of the House in the last days of 1989. Although Havel declared that, with the power transition, a system of 'civil society in power' had occurred immediately in Czechoslovakia, the reality was completely different. Despite the capitulation of the former regime, the new regime had to face many difficulties that we have also seen in Poland and Hungary. The 'revolutionary aristocracy' around Havel played the role of a transitory top elite, felt to be 'ahead of Europe' with its moral-oriented, 'postmodern' politics, and dreamt about a short and painless transition for Czechoslovakia. But this postmodern politics proved to be ineffective and the transition costs had to be paid. The CF disintegrated into a series of real parties and the generation of post-modern politicians were replaced during 1990 in the emerging multi-party system with 'organization men' in politics. The nostalgia of intellec-tuals for the loose and spontaneous movement parties, as for the direct unity of civil society and state, proved to be an infantile disease of tran-sition politics. This dream was deeper and persisted longer in Czechoslo-vakia than in Poland and Hungary, but after the first free election it gave way here also to 'ordinary' party politics (see East, 1992: 42).

First free elections and new parliamentary parties

Poland, as an early-comer, experienced its first free election later than Hungary and Czechoslovakia because of the April Pact. The first free and fair election in the ECE region was held in Hungary, in March and April 1990. Not earlier, since after the September Agreement the oppo-sition parties asked for a longer period of preparation as a prolongation of the negotiated transition, in order to organize themselves and prepare for an election campaign. Hungary during the national roundtable talks elaborated a mixed electoral system, unlike most of the ECE and Balkan countries in which some sort of a proportional electoral system was introduced. In Hungary, out of 386 seats, 176 (45 per cent) are filled from the single member individual districts and 210 seats (55 per cent) from the (regional and national) party lists. In the individual districts an absolute majority is needed in the first round, but, if this is not the case, in the second round a relative majority is enough between the two or three top candidates. This electoral regulation favours government stability over proportionality because it gives a premium to the largest party and by this it tends to create a stable government. The proportional part of the electoral system cannot compensate for the unproportional results in the individual districts, so the final result of election is also rather unpropor-tional. In addition, a threshold – 4 per cent in 1990 and 5 in 1994 – prevents party fragmentation from penetrating the parliament by denying seats to small parties.

As a result of the early emergence of a multi-party system, and owing to the electoral regulations described above, Hungary produced a relatively stable multi-party system, since the same six parties entered parliament in both free elections in 1990 and 1994. Except for the two winners, the HDF in 1990 and the HSP in 1994, the election results of the other four parties were almost the same. The distance between the smallest parliamentary party and the largest non-parliamentary party grew between 1990 and 1994, and thus the non-parliamentary parties had less and less chance of getting into parliament. Finally, the percentage of the 'lost vote', that is, the votes cast for parties not gaining parliamentary representation, was minimal in Hungary, even in 1990 (10.99 per cent) and further decreased in 1994 (9.97), both figures being very much below the regional average of 20–25 per cent. It shows that the Hungarian parliamentary party system was consolidated at an early stage and is not as fragmented as the other party systems in the ECE region. As a result, the First Parliament (1990–4) and the Second Parliament (1994–8) completed their full terms, and so did the respective governments.

In Czecho-Slovakia (as we should now term it) the first free elections took place in June 1990, in a very complicated proportional electoral system, reflecting the federal structure of the country and the growing Czech and Slovak controversy. The 300 member Federal Parliament was bicameral, so voters cast votes for both the House of the People (150 seats, 101 Czech and 49 Slovak, according to the size of populations) and for the House of Nations (150 seats equally distributed between the Czech and Slovak parts of the country). In addition, the voters elected by a third vote the Czech National Council (200 seats) or the Slovak National Council (150 seats). The endorsement of the federal government was the job of the Federal Parliament and that of the Czech or the Slovak governments was the responsibility of the Czech or Slovak National Council respectively.[7]

This system was not only complicated but produced a constitutional deadlock, with the requirement of a 'double majority' in the Federal Parliament, that is, with a need to reach a majority in both Houses, since the Slovaks could veto all legislative proposals of the Czechs and vice versa. Except for the former ruling party, the Czechoslovak Communist Party – later the Communist Party of Bohemia and Moravia (CPBM; KSCM) in the Czech lands and the Communist Party of Slovakia (CPS; KSS) in Slovakia – there were no federal parties in the first free election. Even the sister parties, for example the Christian Democrats, ran separately in the two parts of the country – Christian Democratic Union (CDU; KDU) in the Czech part and Christian Democratic Movement (CDM; KDH) in the Slovak part. The big umbrella organizations, the CF and the PAV, emerged as relative winners in both the Czech and the Slovak parts, and could form a federal government with a solid majority. The two separated party systems, however, already pre-programmed the disintegration of Czecho-Slovakia with their nationalist inertia. After the June 1990 election, both the Czech and the Slovak party systems showed only medium fragmentation – seven parties in both National Councils – with a high representation of former, non-reformed communist parties receiving more than 13 per cent of popular support in both parts of the country. The Moravian regionalist party in the Czech lands and the nationalist party in Slovakia were almost equally strong, manifesting the diverging political forces. The historical parties, represented mostly by the Christian Democrats, were stronger in the early 1990s in Slovakia than in the Czech lands.

This original party system was greatly transformed through the disintegration of both Czech and Slovak umbrella organizations as chief actors of the negotiated transition up until the first election. The disintegration had not happened before the election but occurred somewhat later, inside the first freely elected parliament. These large movement parties produced a series of smaller successor parties and by this a fragmented legislature. In February 1991 the Civic Forum split into the Civic Democratic Party (CDP; ODS) and the Civic Movement (CM; OH). The CDP, led by Vacláv Klaus, was a well-organized centre–right party *vis-à-vis* the movement oriented CM, led by Jiri Dienstbier, a close friend of Havel and supporter of Havel's ideas on postmodern politics. The CM, representing the revolutionary aristocracy, was subsequently marginalized in Czech politics. The CDP, in turn, became the largest and the most influential party in the Czech National Council by the early 1990s. Two other parties also benefited from the disintegration of the Civic Forum, the Civic Democratic Alliance (CDA; ODA) and the Czechoslovak Social Democratic Party (CSDP; CSSD), since some former members of parliament from the CF joined their factions, too. By this process, the Czech party system became rather fragmented, but only until the next election in June 1992 when voters made a new selection among them.

The disintegration process of the PAV was less dramatic in Slovakia because the party system as a whole was less affected. The major change came in March 1991 when Vladimir Meciar left the PAV with most of the members of parliament following him and founded a new party, the Movement for Democratic Slovakia (MDS; HZDS). This party, and its leader, has played a dominant role since then in Slovakian politics. The remaining members of parliament, after some temporary party transformations, finally formed the Democratic Union of Slovakia (DUS; DUS). Meciar had been the first freely elected prime minister of Slovakia after the June 1990 election, on behalf of the PAV, but by this divorce action he lost PAV's majority in the Slovak National Council and had to resign. Jan Carnogursky, the leader of the Christian Democratic Movement (CDM; KDH) formed the new government, but the June 1992 election brought Meciar back to power as prime minister.

The electoral turnout at the June 1990 election was very high in Czecho-Slovakia (96 per cent) because of the euphoria of the sudden regime change. It was much lower in Hungary in Spring 1990 (63 per cent) as a result of its slow evolutionary changes. It was even lower in Poland at the first free election in October 1991 (43 per cent) because of widespread apathy and disappointment. The Polish population at that time was already drastically shaken by the shock therapy and by the 'war at the top', that is, by the in-fighting among former Solidarity leaders. At the first free election the post-Solidarity parties also campaigned very aggressively against each other. The new electoral law, a proportional system without a threshold, used in the October 1991 election, resulted in an extreme fragmentation of the Polish party system. The largest party, Mazowiecki's Democration Union, received only 12 per cent of the popular vote and only 13 per cent of the seats. Altogether about 30 political groups were represented in the Polish Sejm, and among them 11 party groups had only one seat. It is, in fact, difficult to give a precise figure about the parties represented in the Sejm between 1991 and 1993, since these parties both formed coalitions and split all the time. So the Polish party system was fluid and volatile in the early 1990s because Solidarity as a united political organization never ran in a completely free election. The first free election came too late, at the time of a deep economic crisis when severe crisis management had already produced the full disintegration of Solidarity. As a result, the Polish party system became overfragmented with a dozen middle-sized parties in the Sejm, making coalition-forming very difficult.

A short comparison of the ECE party systems shows that Hungary created a relatively stable multi-party system at an early stage, followed by the later formation of the Czech party system and later still by the unstable Slovak one. The Polish multi-party system was formed as the last in the region. This delay was the political price paid by Poland for being the first-comer. The actual structure of the early consolidated national party systems took shape only around the mid-1990s, hence we have to analyse next the new constitutions and the activities of the new democratic governments.

Democratic constitutions and representative government

Systemic change necessitated the formulation of new democratic consti-tutions as new rules of the political game in East Central Europe. Con-stitutions provide a legal framework for basic human rights, rule of law and the market economy. Therefore, in the early 1990s all three states made great efforts for constitution-making and achieved a Western-type democratic constitutionalism. None the less, because of party compe-tition and diverging approaches to the basic constitutional issues, these new constitutions are far from displaying legal perfection and coherence. In Hungary the negotiated transition already prepared the basic consti-tutional amendments, summarized in the September Agreement, including also the democratization of local-territorial and functional-economic self-governments, that is to say, the regulation of micro- and meso-politics. The new, amended constitution was passed by the Hun-garian parliament on 18 October 1989. This legal act produced a full-bodied constitution, legally only in a form of amending the 1949 Consti-tution, although its text was almost completely re-written. On 24 August 1990 a further constitutional amendment introduced the constructive non-confidence vote or prime ministerial government according to the (West) German model. Thus, the constitution-making process in Hungary was relatively short and successful, unlike in Czecho-Slovakia where constitutional deadlock between the Czechs and Slovaks in the

Federal Parliament made possible only the elaboration of a Charter of Fundamental Rights and Freedoms, passed by the Federal Parliament on 9 January 1991. The real constitutions, therefore, were elaborated separately only during the 'Velvet Divorce', passed on 1 September 1992 in Slovakia and on 16 December 1992 in the Czech Republic. In Poland, the 1952 Constitution was amended first in April 1989 as prepared by the April Pact, then on several occasions in the early 1990s. In the fragmented Polish party system there was no chance to have a consensual constitution-making process, so finally, on 17 October 1992 the Sejm passed only a so-called Small Constitution. It was designed only for provisional regulation and, thus, it did not cover all basic constitutional issues.

The ECE constitutions stipulate that all the three – later four – countries have become parliamentary democracies, but the Polish case transitorily shows some deep contradictions in this respect. Actually, the regulation of the Big Power Triangle – the separation of powers and the relations between president, parliament and (head of) government – has proved to be a very difficult and delicate task everywhere, first of all with regard to the relationship between president and government. Similarly, the regulation of the Small Power Triangle – the separation of the independent power branches of central government, functional self-governments and local self-governments with provisions for intergovernmental relationships – has created a lot of problems. This task has been achieved only by Hungary completely; in both Poland and Czecho-Slovakia – later in the Czech Republic – the intermediary level of territorial organizations (provinces) have not yet received their final shape.

Whereas in the Czech Republic, Slovakia and Hungary rather weak presidents emerged who were elected by the national parliaments, in Poland some kind of a semi-presidential system came into existence in 1989 as a result of the April Pact. As we know, the President of Poland had the right to appoint the three key ministers – interior, exterior and defence, called in Poland Belwedere ministeries after the name of the Presidential Palace. In this way a dual executive emerged with partially overlapping rights and duties between the president and prime minister, since even the Small Constitution (1992) left many things unregulated, including the precise rules for appointing or dismissing a prime minister or the dissolution of the parliament. Lech Walesa, as the President of Poland in 1990–5, was happy to inherit the mantle tailored for General Jaruzelski in the spirit of the early transition (see East, 1992: 115). This strong presidency was originally an assurance for the PUWP, but after the period of the negotiated transition it became more and more an obstacle to further democratization. The claim for stronger presidential powers led to a fight between Walesa and the prime ministers during his term, since Walesa wanted to extend his rights to establish a full presidential system. He argued with the impotence of the 'Sejmocracy' but all the parliamentary parties resisted his efforts to control the whole of Polish political life. In this power game the Sejm refused his claim for the introduction of a presidential system several times. These efforts of Walesa to gain full power at any price contributed a great deal to his defeat in the November 1995 presidential election and to the victory of Aleksander Kwasniewski, the leader of the reformed left. The problem of the dual executive has been completely solved by the new president and by the parliament in the new constitution passed by parliament in March 1997 and confirmed by a referendum in May of that year.[8]

It is true that in the first half of the 1990s the Sejm was very fragile and vulnerable, manouvering itself very often into a legislative blind alley because of the narrow-minded party struggles. Coalition formation was also a complicated and worrisome process in Poland due to an immature and fragmented party system. After the resignation of Mazowiecki, the first non-communist prime minister who lost the presidential race against Walesa, Jan Bielecki became prime minister in January 1991. Walesa preferred Bielecki because he was not an influential politician and he came from Gdansk, the native city of Walesa. With such a relatively weak prime minister, Walesa could dominate Polish politics until the first free general election, but after the October 1991 election, the Polish parliament regained the initiative in appointing and controlling the executive. However, coalition-forming was not an easy task in this over-fragmented parliament in the period of 1991–3, with more than a dozen post-Solidarity parties. Even these post-Solidarity parties split into two major groups on the basic issue of Europeanization versus traditionalization. None had a simple majority in the Sejm; not even the five major post-Solidarity parties could have formed a stable coalition (see Jasiewicz, 1993a: 143–4). This forced them to make a compromise for a temporary coalition, first headed by the traditionalists, then by the modernizers, although both coalition formulas proved to be fragile, given their fundamental divergence concerning the basic values of Europe and the Nation.

After several weeks of negotiations, in December 1991 Jan Olszewski formed a traditionalist, right-wing coalition government from some post-Solidarity parties with the major backing of the national-conservative CNU. The Olszewski government as a minority coalition was indeed very fragile, having only 205 seats out of 460 in the Sejm and had to turn to the other post-Solidarity parties for support at every step of legislation. As a protector of the strong state idea, it was, however, very active in slowing down privatization and foreign investment. This group of arch-conservatives was preoccupied first of all with 'decommunization' as the self-declared 'first truly non-communist government since the Second World War'. The extreme nationalist and anti-market orientation, and the focus on the past grievances instead of aiming at economic crisis management, alarmed even the Europeanizer post-Solidarity parties. Widespread purges in the central government concerned not only the officials of the former regime but also those of the previous 'liberal' Solidarity governments. This hysterical anti-communist drive brought down the Olszewski government after six months and this short period put the typical infantile diseases of early transition as traditionalism and parochialism very markedly on display.

In July 1992 Hanna Suchocka from the DU formed the next post-Solidarity coalition government, which survived until May 1993. This extended coalition had a small majority – 233 seats out of 460 in the Sejm – but it was still very fragile because of its inherent political heterogeneity. The Suchocka government was supported mostly by the Europeanizer right from the post-Solidarity party family, advocating a policy of fast marketization and full democratization. But some coalition member parties were still proponents of state protectionism and supporters of the direct role of the Catholic Church in the Polish political life and legislation. Yet, this was a very successful modernizer government, albeit the compromise of modernizers and traditionalists could have only been temporary. The Suchocka government took the task of economic crisis management very seriously and prepared the conditions for the start of economic growth in 1993–4 to a great extent. The last austerity measures, however, provoked the resistance of the smallest coalition member party, the Solidarity Trade Union (STU; NSZZ), having only 5 per cent of the popular vote in the 1991 election. Although the smallest party faction in the Sejm, they still represented the workers' interest very vehemently, this time by protesting against the further decrease of standard of living in the continued crisis management. In mid-May 1993 they tabled a motion of non-confidence which defeated the Suchocka government – by just one vote. The last action of the 1991–3 parliament was to pass a new electoral law with a 5 per cent threshold to exclude the smaller parties from the Sejm. This law changed the political landscape in Poland beyond recognition at the September 1993 election, since it removed many parties, including some of those which had voted for it in May 1993.

The early consolidation of the party system and the mixed electoral system created a stable parliament and government in Hungary after the Spring 1990 election. In the ECE region only the Hungarian parliament served the four years it had been elected for and the first coalition government also completed its full term. This was a centre–right government of three parties – HDF, ISP and CDPP – with three other parties (AFD, HSP and Fidesz) in opposition. The right-wing national-conservative government, headed by József Antall, had a comfortable 60 per cent majority in the Hungarian parliament. The three-party conservative coalition kept its majority during its tenure, at least indirectly, despite the defection of the ISP from the coalition, since after a split in the ISP most parliamentary delegates (36) still supported the coalition and only eight delegates left it. This early confrontation in the Hungarian coalition government was around the restitution issue because the breakaway ISP group demanded a full reprivatization of small landed property and the Antall government resisted this challenge. In 1993 a party split occurred also in the largest coalition party, the HDF, which was the typical umbrella organization in Hungary. The break between the moderate centrist-conservatives and the radical national-populists created from the HDF a small centre–right party on one side and a series of smaller extreme rightist parties on the other, the largest among them being the Hungarian Justice and Life Party (HJLP; MIÉP). These splits did not lead to governmental instability, since the HJLP and the other breakaway groups supported the Antall government in parliament. The premature death of Antall did not shake the stability of the government and in December 1993 his deputy, Péter Boross, took over as the new prime minister. The next election took place as scheduled in May 1994 with an Antall–Boross government in office until the end of its term. Government stability was valuable even for the opposition parties and they did not try to bring the government down in the last year of its term, hoping for their electoral fortune at the next election.

The opposition, indeed, gained a landslide victory at the second free election in Hungary. This belongs to the phenomenon usually called 'the return of the post-communist vote', which began in Poland at the September 1993 election. To understand this phenomenon, we have to discuss briefly the reform process of the former ruling parties.

The successors of the former ruling parties had suffered a big defeat in the first free elections in East Central Europe and rightist governments were formed everywhere. After the electoral defeat and under the pressure of changing international and domestic conditions, the leftist parties were forced to reform themselves – as an exception, in the case of the HSP this reform took place before the collapse of the former regime – in order to be able to provide a renewed leftist alternative in a competitive multi-party system. The radical reform meant both institutional and membership discontinuity, that is, the dissolution of the former party and recruitment of a new membership for the re-established leftist party with a social democratic profile. This radical change happened only to the HSP and later on, in late January 1990, to the Social Democracy of Republic Poland (SDRP; SdRP). The Czechoslovak Communist Party was neither able nor ready for such a reform. After its separation to the CPBM and to the CPS, the Slovak party proved to be more reform-oriented. In October 1990 the Slovak Communist Party was reorganized as the Party of the Democratic Left (PDL; SDL) and in January 1991 it decided to re-register its members. Even compared to this vague discontinuity and partial reform in the Slovak Left, the CPBM has avoided any meaningful reform but has been quite successful as an unreformed conservative-communist party. Therefore, in the Czech Republic a real opportunity has been given to a historical party, the Czech Social Democratic Party, to play the role of the modern centre-left party in the Czech party system, that is, the same role which has been played in the other ECE countries by the reformed successor parties having a social democratic profile.

In the former systemic change during the period of the Cold War, the social democratic parties in East Central Europe were forced to unite with the communist parties, and were absorbed by the latter during four decades. In the present process of systemic change we can observe the opposite process. The social democratic parties have re-emerged – usually from the all-embracing ruling parties – and the (much smaller) genuine communist parties have appeared, too, for example, the Workers Party in Hungary which claims to be the real successor of the HSWP. This reform and reorganization of the left has changed the political landscape in all ECE countries concerned – Slovenia belongs to East Central Europe also in this respect – but this tendency cannot be extended to the Balkans. In the Balkan countries, as we shall see in the next chapter, so far there has been no radical reform of the ruling communist parties, just a simple change of labels from communist to socialist.[9]

The reform of the Polish left bore fruit as early as the October 1991 election, when the SDRP came in a close second with 12 per cent of the popular vote. The SDRP later formed an electoral coalition with many smaller leftist organizations in the Democratic Left Alliance (DLA; SLD), and this DLA won the September 1993 election, enjoying also the support of the Polish business community (see Zubek, 1994: 283). In 1993 the DLA received more than 20 per cent of the popular vote and 37 per cent of the seats, and the Polish Peasant Party (PPP; PSL), as the second largest party, 15 per cent of the popular vote and 28 per cent of the seats. This was a landslide victory, indeed, due also to the in-fighting in the post-Solidarity parties. But this disproportionately large victory was also because of the newly introduced 5 per cent threshold which resulted in an uneven distribution of seats, since most of the overfragmented parties of the Polish right received less than 5 per cent of the vote. The Polish left, however, has a continuity in the post-Solidarity party family as well. Among them the Labour Union (LU; UP – formerly Solidarity of Labour) also managed to get into the Sejm (7 per cent of the popular vote and 9 per cent of the seats), so in the Sejm between 1993 and 1997 the Polish right was chronically underrepresented, as was indicated by a very large (35 per cent) 'lost vote'.

This 'return of the communists', or the recovery of the reformed Polish left, caused both a sensation and a worry in the West in Autumn 1993. Both were soon dissipated by the new Polish leftist governments of this parliamentary cycle which continued privatization and marketization, as well as democratization, very actively. This change was as much a result of the defeat of the delegitimized Polish right, with its prevailing nationalist-provincialist orientation and permanent in-fighting, as the victory of the recovered left. The DLA entered a coalition agreement with the PPP and this coalition had about a two-thirds majority in the Sejm. First Waldemar Pawlak, the PPP leader, formed the DLA–PPP coalition government in October 1993. Then, in March 1995, Józef Oleksy from the DLA became prime minister, to be followed a year later by Wlodimierz Cimoszewicz from the same political party as the third prime minister of this parliamentary cycle. Overall, this was a successful coalition government, with only some in-fighting of lesser importance and with a successful political learning process. This coalition served its full term, which in itself proves the consolidation of the Polish polity, and it administered over the economic and social recovery in Poland in the mid-1990s which has shown Poland again in its trendsetter role in the ECE region.

At the May 1994 election in Hungary the party political situation was similar to that in Poland in September 1993, in that people in Hungary were tired of the national-conservative government with its orientation towards the 'glorious' past instead of a radical economic crisis management. Although the economic and social situation was better and more balanced in Hungary than in Poland in the early 1990s, the resistance was also bigger against the conservative government because of the higher expectations concerning economic growth and standard of living. Even during the 1990–4 parliamentary cycle, Hungary had a well consolidated political life, with the extreme parties marginalized. People were hurt also in Hungary by the nationally oriented traditionalist conservatism of the Antall–Boross government. In 1992–3 the HSP as an opposition party, with its modernization orientation and professional political style, became more and more popular and finally won a landslide victory like its Polish sister party. At the May 1994 election the HSP received 33 per cent of the popular vote on the party list and won most of the individual seats (149 out of 176) which was converted altogether to 54 per cent of seats. The HSP was joined by the AFD to form an oversized coalition government with a 72 per cent majority under the socialist prime minister Gyula Horn.

This socialist–liberal coalition had to introduce a small degree of shock therapy to address the economic crisis. The March 1995 crisis management package caused a political shock in Hungary, resulting in the declining popularity of both governing parties and in the increasing popularity of both the moderate and radical right, represented by Fidesz and the ISP respectively. As its high political price, however, the economic crisis management has been by and large successful: the Hungarian economy has recovered and economic growth has begun (see OMRI, 1996: 36–41). International debt has also decreased and Hungary has attracted the largest share of foreign investment in East Central Europe (16 billion US dollars up to the end of 1996). This socialist–liberal coalition government has very vigorously promoted the Euro-Atlantic integration of Hungary and it has signed bilateral treaties with its neighbours, Slovakia and Romania, to defuse tensions with them concerning Hungarian minorities, since these treaties have provided them with the hope of both collective and individual rights in their own countries. As a result of the successful crisis management, in 1997 the governing parties regained their former public support, well before the May 1998 election. With the weakening of smaller centre–right parties (HDF and CDPP), Fidesz (its new full name: Hungarian Civic Party) has become the dominant centre–right party. Thus, for the May 1998 election the Hungarian party system turned out to be bipolar, HSP and Fidesz are the dominant centres and the populist ISP and the liberal AFD play only secondary roles.[10]

The recovery of the reformed left can be noticed also in the Czech Republic, although in the first half of the 1990s this country was much more a success story for the modernizing right. It was represented by the CDP, and by its allies, the CDA and the CDU. In the independent Czech Republic after the Velvet Divorce, Klaus formed a coalition government of the moderate right. It is more accurate to say this was already the Czech government in conformity with the results of the June 1992 election, and six months later it became the government of the independent Czech Republic. Political stabilization was achieved quite easily; the first Klaus government ruled the country until the May–June 1996 election with the same coalition. Yet, the Czech party system changed a lot during those four years and the recovery of the left was felt in such a marked way that by 1996 the CSSD had become the largest competitor of the CDP.

Consequently, by the latest election the centre–right versus the centre–left party structure appeared very markedly in the Czech Republic, with the CDP winning 30 and 34 and the CSDP 27 and 31 per cent of the popular vote and parliamentary seats respectively. Klaus could form again his new government but this time only after a compromise with Milos Zeman, the CSDP leader, since he had merely 50 per cent of seats for his centre–right government and had to compensate the CSDP with parliamentary posts to get his government accepted in the Czech parliament. Still, the Czech parliamentary situation was relatively stable, although both the leftist and the rightist extremist parties had a significant presence within the Czech parliament. The CPBM received 10 per cent of the popular vote and 11 per cent of the seats; the nationalist Republican Party (RP; SPR), 8 per cent of the popular vote and 9 per cent of the seats. So these two extremist parties control 20 per cent of seats in the Czech parliament, which indicates the existence of major tensions in Czech society during the democratic transition and in the process of privatization–marketization.[11]

The ease of the Czech transition in the mid-1990s created a myth about the Czech 'wonderland', since – without the Slovak 'burden' – the Czech economy could develop very quickly and all the problems could be solved without major 'transition costs'. The Czech government, and first of all its prime minister, Vacláv Klaus, advocated this over-optimistic view and used a rhetoric of Czech exceptionalism which was accepted by most of the Western press and politicians. The illusion of the easy transition, however, broke down apparently in Spring 1997. In March 1997 an economic, then social and political, crisis began in the Czech Republic, termed euphemistically by the Czech leadership as 'velvet crisis', which came to a temporary end in July 1997. This case has shown, again, that the 'vale of tears' cannot be completely avoided, the transition costs can only be reduced, but the long-term postponement of painful restrictions produces only short-term advantages and finally proves to be more costly than tough measures – as some kind of shock therapy – taken in time. For political reasons, in order to avoid political confrontations and enjoy popularity, Klaus ignored the signs of the coming crisis and continued the 'wonderland' propaganda domestically and internationally, and this crisis, again, not so 'velvet' as propagated, may bring the end of the Klaus era and a new turning point in Czech politics.

By Spring 1997 it became clear that after the huge (about 6 billion dollar) loss in balance of trade in 1996, Czech economic growth had slowed down and, because of the lack of competitiveness the international debt was growing; it reached 20 billion dollars in 1997. The growing indebtedness was the price paid by the Czech Republic for the postponement of harsh measures. There was only a half-made privatization by vouchers, without real owners and without new resources in production. There was, however, no bankruptcy legislation and state subsidies survived which brought about low competitiveness and labour productivity but allowed for high wages and social benefits, and produced social peace and high popularity. Because of the political prestige the Czech koruna became overvalued and attracted hot money from abroad but the government was not ready to devalue it. The crisis began right here: bad news about the economic development was coupled with decreasing trust in the Czech currency.

As a reaction, on 19 April 1997 the government produced a first package for crisis management, but it was too small and proved to be ineffective. In mid-May the value of the koruna suddenly dropped by about 20 per cent and it came as a real shock for the population. The government crisis turned out to be manifest; on 21 May 1997 the coalition partners demanded the resignation of Klaus, who survived by a government reshuffle. Given the fact that the April package did not work, the economic and political crisis worsened, and on 9 June 1997 the government was forced to introduce a new package with deep cuts in social policy and salaries of public employees as well. On 10 June 1997 the Klaus government was saved on a non-confidence vote in the Czech parliament by just one vote. But the Czech miracle has dissipated and there has been a common understanding about the necessity of new elections.

This crisis had indicated that there has been no Czech exceptionalism and that transition costs have to be paid everywhere. At the same time, the Czech economy and polity have proved to be stable enough to handle the crisis without major political and social upheavals and after painful correction socio-economic and political development will continue in the Czech Republic.

The Slovak political situation, however, has always been much more controversial. The MDS as the major force in Slovak politics originally engaged in a nationalist-populist line against the traditional 'Czech centralism'. As a large umbrella organization, it still resists the simple categorization of left or right, representing 'an eclectic mix of nationalists, dissidents, and former *apparatchiks*', as a political tradition 'based on patronage, political centralization, economic *dirigisme*, and nationalism'

(Carpenter, 1997: 212). Yet, despite its leftist-populist rhetoric, this party is much more a rightist-nationalist organization than a leftist one. This party clearly shows a deviation from the general modernization-Europeanization tendency of the ECE region and it is still some kind of a heterogeneous umbrella organization. After the September 1994 election MDS was joined by the two Slovak extremist parties to form a coalition which since then has governed Slovakia. These extremist parties are the Workers Alliance of Slovakia (WAS; ZRS), the reborn Slovak Communist Party, and the Slovak National Party (SNP; SNS), the extreme rightist-nationalist party in Slovakia.

The main problem in Slovakia has always been that the traditionalist-nationalist parties have had a slight majority, broken by the temporary majority of the alliance of Europeanization and modernization oriented parties only for short periods, as the Carnogursky government in 1991 or the Moravcik government in 1994, but the Meciar government was always re-established after the next election. The Europeanizer parties so far have been weak and fragmented. Popular support for the reformed left actually declined between 1992 and 1994, from 15 to 10 per cent, since the non-reformed left came back against the PDL with the WAS, which received 7 per cent of the popular vote in 1994. The CDM usually receives 9–10 per cent of the vote, and the secular centre–right party, the more recently organized DUS, obtained only 8 per cent of the vote in 1994. The Hungarian Coalition (HC; MK) – an electoral coalition of the three Hungarian parties – received in 1992 7 and 1994 10 per cent of the popular vote. In 1994 the HC collected, in fact, all the Hungarian votes.[12]

These four parties – PDL, CDM, DUS and HC – have been unable so far to form a durable alliance of the Europeanizer parties, since they have been divided among themselves along the left–right dimension and also along ethnic cleavage lines. Therefore, Meciar has dominated the Slovak political scene, although he himself and his political attitude have been constantly criticized by Western governments and international agencies. The incumbent Meciar government, as a 'red–brown coalition' since 1994, 'has undermined the Moravcik government's democratic reforms and moved closer to outright authoritarianism' (Carpenter, 1997: 215). Thus, Slovak politics still suffers from the 'birth pangs' of a new nation, although some alternative can be provided by the new opposition forum, the 'blue coalition' formed by the CDM and the DUS, the two centre–right parties, with some smaller parties, against the MDS to stop the 'triumph of nationalist populism' in Slovakia.

Mapping common regional features

The ECE region has shown some very marked common features after the collapse of state socialism, and, in general, its regional features have further been strengthened in the second half of the 1990s. The ECE countries were, even before, strikingly different from both the Balkans and the countries of Eastern Europe proper; this distance, however, has become much larger after the systemic change. First and foremost, the ECE countries have produced so far a typical 'U' curve of recovery which contrasts with the continued economic and political crisis in the Balkans and even deeper complex crisis in the EE region.

This 'U' curve of recovery means that a drastic decline of GDP began in 1989 – with about 25 per cent of loss in GDP in the early 1990s – which came to an end in the mid-1990s such that the ECE countries have already regained the 1989 level of GDP but with a completely different – privatized and marketized – economy. The earlier decline can be described as a *vicious* circle or negative feedback between economic, social and political transformation, that is, the economic crisis caused serious social problems and both destabilized politics to a greater extent, and vice versa. The recovery, in turn, can be described as a *virtuous* circle, with its positive feedback between economic and social change and political stabilization. The worst period is certainly over in East Central Europe and the consolidation of democracy can now be reached in a matter of some few years.

In the ECE countries the political crisis has appeared in two ways. First, as the contradiction between democratic institution-building and the low performance of the new institutions, generated mainly by the insufficiencies of the new democratic political culture. Secondly, there was an authoritarian renewal in all ECE countries, with a revival of nationalist-conservative traditionalism, in the form of both moderate and radical right tendencies. It has been demonstrated how difficult it is to generate a well-working democracy, and even more a modern right as well as a modern left. But the ECE countries – except for Slovakia, which has been a controversial case – have succeeded in producing a modern democratic polity with stable democratic constitutionalism and with the provision of basic human rights. They have mostly overcome so far the infantile disease of nationalist-populist tendencies and party fragmentation.

The ECE region has produced not only a democratic macro-political system, but the democratization has penetrated the whole polity, including the meso and micro levels, unlike in the Balkan countries. It is true, however, that macro-politics has developed first and foremost in East Central Europe, sometimes even at the price of the proper autonomy of functional or territorial organization. The party systems have been more or less consolidated and the parties have joined the respective European Party Internationals. These processes of democratic transition have run parallel with those of the structural adjustment to the EU, thus, the biggest success of the ECE countries has been in the field of Euro-Atlantic integration as full NATO and EU membership gets ever closer.

The Slovak case – that is, fighting with the burden of nation-building – indicates, however, that there have also been marked national differences or idiosyncrasies in this common process. The Czech development after the Velvet Divorce proved to be the most balanced case, with the smallest socio-economic crisis followed by a relative recovery and with the slightest deformation of politics as a whole towards the extremities. In the Czech Republic the political stabilization was achieved by the modernizer right but the tough austerity measures introduced in Spring 1997 have shaken the popularity of the CDP and of Klaus himself. The modernizer left has played only a secondary role so far, but it has become the most popular political force because of the failures of the Klaus government, and in 1997 the Czech political system underwent a fundamental change. The traditionalist-provincialist forces in the Czech Republic have been rather weak, unlike in Slovakia where they have been dominating by pushing the modernizer parties – of both left and right – into an underdog position. In Poland the modernizer right (the Freedom Union; UW) has been fairly weak, and otherwise the right has been overfragmented and tended to lean towards the traditionalism-provincialism, whereas the modernizer left has managed a comeback to the centre of political life. The same has been true in the case of Hungary concerning the right, although to a much lesser extent. In Hungary the modernizer left has been very instrumental in crisis management and in promoting the socio-economic recovery, and the political stabilization has been achieved almost from the very beginning of systemic change. All in all, the three countries, Poland, the Czech Republic and Hungary, have already succeeded in creating modern polities capable of joining the democratic community of the West European countries, and Slovakia has somewhat lagged behind.

Notes and further reading

1 There is a very large literature about Poland and discussions are going on concerning all turning points which I can mention here only very briefly. I concentrate on the negotiated transition and cannot deal with the emergence of Solidarity in the 1980s in detail.

2 Throughout this chapter, the reader may find it helpful to refer to the Appendix to Chapter 5 for clarification of abbreviations.

3 It is usually taken for granted that Solidarity was ready to take power in Autumn 1989, although Zubek warns us that Solidarity had no complex socio-economic programme or a team to execute it; therefore, they hesitated to take full power. Balcerowicz, who was considered by the population a 'Bolshevik of the market', presented his shock therapy rather abruptly which came as a surprise even for most Solidarity leaders (see, for example, Kramer, 1995: 80; Zubek, 1995: 379).

4 Concerning Hungary, a large data set is available from 1988 on from *The Political Yearbook of Hungary*, edited by the Hungarian Centre for Democracy Studies. I emphasize here the special significance of the reform circles of the HSWP for the whole Hungarian negotiated transition in general and for the formation of the HSP in particular (see O'Neil, 1996).

5 There was a major conflict during the Hungarian negotiated transition concerning the first presidential election, which was intended by the September Agreement as a popular election before the general election. Therefore, the AFD and Fidesz did not formally sign the Agreement, although otherwise they did not refuse it. The AFD successfully collected signatures for a referendum and in November 1989 this referendum decided – with the smallest possible margin – in their favour. The direct presidential election was abolished and the president was elected only by the parliament after the Spring general election.

6 Linz and Stepan (1996: 316) indicate that the formally negotiated transition in Czechoslovakia was, in fact, a capitulation of the former elite. The ease of this power transition was an initial advantage which created a lot of problems later.

7 Czechoslovakia in the inter-war period was a multinational country but this problem was 'solved' after the Second World War by 'ethnic cleansing' as the Benes Decrees deprived ethnic Germans in Western Czech lands and Hungarians in Slovakia from their citizenship rights and most of them (3 million Sudenten Germans and hundreds of thousands of Hungarians) were forced to emigrate. The Czech and Slovak controversy was superimposed above this issue and both new countries inherited the controversy with their neighbours. The Czech parliament ratified a historical reconciliation document with Germany in March 1997 and Slovakia had signed a bilateral treaty with Hungary by March 1995.

8 As public surveys show, Kwasniewski in December 1995 was the candidate of the European-oriented middle strata and middle aged people; Walesa, in turn, was that of traditionalist elderly people and the rural poor. The Catholic Church supported Walesa too actively, which became counter-productive for him, since many people voted simply against the direct role of the Church in Polish politics.

9 In the extended literature about the return of the post-communist vote there are two usual overgeneralizations. The first is to put East Central Europe and the Balkans on a common denominator and give the same image to all leftist parties, and also to those in East Central Europe, based on the Balkan 'socialist' parties. Second, the common nomenklatura principle leads to the idea in all countries concerned that the post-communist parties equally monopolized privatization, although this process was very different even among ECE countries. In the Czech Republic, for example, the centre right government represents the nomenklatura in this respect and, according to Zubek (1995: 286, 289), the Freedom Union (the former Democratic Union) has also been very active in Poland.

10 The history of the Hungarian–Slovak bilateral treaty demonstrates the whole minority issue with all its problems. Although the treaty was signed by the prime ministers in March 1995, and the Hungarian parliament immediately ratified it, it took more than a year for the Slovak parliament to pass it. Meanwhile, the Slovak parliament passed some laws clearly contradicting this

bilateral treaty, for example, a language law against the public use of the Hungarian language, although in June 1995 Slovakia also signed the Framework Agreement of the Council of Europe on the protection of minorities (see Hyde-Price, 1996: 93–9; OMRI, 1995: 28–9).

11 The Senate elections in November 1996 were relatively more successful for the CDP, although since the May 1996 election the relationship has worsened with its coalition partners. The results are the following for the 81-member Senate in terms of popular vote and number of Senate seats respectively: CDP (36.47 – 32); CSDP (20.27 – 25); CPBM (14.26 – 2); CDU (9.94 – 13); CDA (8.06 – 7); with two independents.

12 About the Slovak politics and party system see Szomolányi and Meseznikov (1995), and the chapter by Darina Malová and Danica Sivaková in Ágh and Ilonszki (1996). On Meciar see Steve Kettle, 'Slovakia's one-man band', *Transition*, vol. 2, no. 17, August 1996.

Appendix: Summary of election results in East Central Europe

Poland 1991–1993

Parties	Votes (%)		No. of seats		Seats (%)	
	1991	1993	1991	1993	1991	1993
DLA (SLD)	12.0	20.4	60	171	13.0	37.1
PPP (PSL)	8.6	15.4	48	132	10.4	28.6
FU (UW)	12.3	10.6	62	74	13.2	16.0
LU (UP)	2.0	7.3	4	41	0.8	8.9
Fa (Oj)	8.7	6.4	49	0	10.6	0
CIP (KPN)	7.5	5.8	46	22	10.2	4.7
NBSR (BBWR)	8.7	5.4	44	16	9.7	3.4
STU (NSZZ)	5.0	4.9	27	0	6.0	0.0

Fa = Fatherland, i.e. Ojczyzna, its predecessor was the CEA (WAK); the NBSR is a pro-Walesa organization, its predecessor in this respect being the CCA (POC).

Parties	Votes (%)	No. of seats	Seats (%)
	1997	1997	1997
SEA (AWS)	33.8	201(51)	43.7
DLA (SLD)	27.1	164(28)	35.6
FU (UW)	13.8	60 (8)	13.0
PPP (PSL)	7.3	27 (3)	5.8
MRP(ROP)	5.6	6 (5)	1.3
GM (NN)	0.6	2 (5)	0.4
Lost votes	11.8	0	0

Turnout 47.9 per cent

Hungary

Parties	Votes (%)		No. of seats		Seats (%)	
	1990	1994	1990	1994	1990	1994
HSP (MSZP)	10.9	32.9	33	209	8.5	54.1
AFD (SZDSZ)	21.3	19.7	94	71	24.3	18.3
HDF (MDF)	24.7	11.7	165	38	42.7	9.8
ISP (FKGP)	11.7	8.8	44	26	11.3	6.7
CDPP (KDNP)	6.5	7.03	21	22	5.4	5.6
Fidesz	8.9	7.0	22	20	5.7	5.1
WP (MP)	3.7	3.2	0	0	0.0	0.0

The Czech National Council

Parties	Votes (%)		No. of seats		Seats (%)	
	1992	1996	1992	1996	1992	1996
CDP (ODS)	29.7	29.6	76	68	38.0	34.0
CSDP (CSSD)	6.5	26.4	16	61	8.0	30.5
CPBM (KSCM)	14.0	10.3	35	22	17.5	11.0
CDU (KDU)	6.3	8.1	15	18	7.5	9.0
RP (SPR)	6.0	8.0	14	18	7.0	9.0
CDA (ODA)	5.9	6.3	14	13	7.0	6.5

The Slovak National Council

Parties	Votes (%)		No. of seats		Seats (%)	
	1992	1994	1992	1994	1992	1994
MDS (HZDS)	37.2	34.9	74	61	49.3	40.7
PDL (SDL)	14.7	10.4	29	18	19.3	12.0
HC (MK)	7.4	10.1	14	17	9.3	11.3
CDM (KDH)	9.0	10.1	18	17	12.0	11.3
DUS (DUS)	0.0	8.6	0	15	0.0	10.0
WAS (ZRS)	0.0	7.3	0	13	0.0	8.7
SNP (SNS)	7.9	5.4	15	9	10.0	6.0

Chronologies

Transition in Poland

10 November 1918	Marshal Józef Pilsudski declares the independence of Poland
1 September 1939	Germany invades Poland
28 June 1945	The first post-war government
19 January 1947	Elections followed by a Communist takeover
31 August 1980	Gdansk accords are signed between the government and Solidarity
13 December 1981	Wojciech Jaruzelski declares martial law (in force until 1983)
16 August 1988	New waves of strikes begin
17 September 1988	The 'reform communist' government of Mieczyslaw Rakowski
6 February 1989	The national roundtable negotiations begin
5 April 1989	A pact is signed by the participants
4, 8 June 1989	The first (semi-)free election
4 July 1989	The 'contractual parliament' convened
19 July 1989	Jaruzelski elected president
24 August 1989	Tadeusz Mazowiecki elected prime minister
12 September 1989	The first non-communist government of Mazowiecki
21 September 1989	The Christian-National Union introduced
12 October 1989	The shock therapy of Leszek Balcerowicz
27–30 January 1990	The Polish United Workers Party dissolves itself and the Social Democracy of the Republic Poland emerges under Aleksander Kwasniewski
27 May 1990	Local government elections (turnout 42 per cent)
26 June 1990	(Citizens) Centre Alliance formed by Lech Walesa
6 July 1990	Mazowiecki replaces three communist ministers
28 July 1990	Citizens Movement for Democratic Action formed
1 October 1990	Jaruzelski resigns as president
25 November, 9 December 1990	Two rounds of presidential elections, Walesa elected
14 December 1990	Mazowiecki resigns as prime minister
12 January 1991	Jan Bielecki government
27 October 1991	The first fully free elections
23 December 1991	Jan Olszewski becomes prime minister with a right-wing coalition

10 July 1992	Hanna Suchocka broad coalition government
28 May 1993	Suchocka government voted down in the Sejm
17 October 1992	The 'Small Constitution' adopted
19 September 1993	Second free elections
26 October 1993	Waldemar Pawlak government
19 June 1994	Second local government elections
3 March 1995	József Oleksy government
5, 19 November 1995	Aleksander Kwasniewski elected president and Walesa defeated in the second round (51.72 vs 48.28 per cent)
14 March 1996	Wlodzimierz Cimoszewicz government
21 September 1997	Parliamentary elections
20 October 1997	Jerzy Buzek government (SEA and FU)

Transition in Hungary

16 November 1918	Hungary becomes independent
12 June 1948	The unification congress of the Hungarian Communist Party and the Hungarian Social Democratic Party, the emerging Party of Hungarian Workers introduces the one-party system
25 March 1985	The XIIIth Congress of HSWP, manifest political crisis
27 September 1987	Hungarian Democratic Forum formed in Lakitelek
17 March 1988	Network of Free Initiatives leading to AFD
30 March 1988	Fidesz formed as a student movement, later party
20–22 May 1988	HSWP party conference, János Kádár ousted and Károly Grósz comes in as first secretary of the HSWP
13 November 1988	Alliance of Free Democrats organized
24 November 1988	The first government of Miklós Németh
11 February 1989	The Central Committee of the HSWP allows the multi-party system
15 March 1989	Mass demonstration of the opposition
22 March 1989	The Roundtable of the Opposition formed
15–16 April 1989	The first national conference of the HSWP reform circles in Kecskemét
10 May 1989	Second Németh government
20–22 May 1989	Second national conference of the HSWP reform circles in Szeged
13 June 1989	The national roundtable between the HSWP and the Roundtable of the Opposition
16 June 1989	The reburial of Imre Nagy with a mass demonstration

1–3 September 1989	Third national conference of the HSWP reform circles in Budapest
18 September 1989	A pact is signed between the HSWP and the Roundtable of the Opposition
6–9 October 1989	HSWP dissolved; HSP foundation congress
18 October 1989	Parliament passes the new constitution
23 October 1989	The Third Hungarian Republic
26 November 1989	Referendum on the presidency
25 March, 8 April 1990	The first free elections
29 April 1990	The HDF–AFD pact
2 May 1990	The first parliament opens
23 May 1990	The government of József Antall
3 August 1990	Árpád Göncz elected president
30 September, 14 October 1990	The first local government free elections
25–28 October 1990	Taxi drivers' strike
19 June 1991	The Red Army leaves Hungary
21 December 1993	Péter Boross, minister of the interior, follows the late prime minister József Antall at the head of the national-conservative government
8–29 May 1994	Parliamentary elections
15 July 1994	The Horn government formed (HSP–AFD coalition)
11 December 1994	Local government elections
19 March 1995	Bilateral treaty with Slovakia signed
16 September 1996	Bilateral treaty with Romania signed

Transition in Czechoslovakia

28 October 1918	Czechoslovakia formed
9 May 1948	The Czechoslovak Socialist Constitution
21 August 1968	The WTO intervention in Czechoslovakia
1 January 1977	The opponents of the Husak regime publish Charter 77
17 November 1989	The collapse of state socialism following a mass demonstration
19 November 1989	Civic Forum and Public Against Violence emerge
26–30 November 1989	National roundtable talks
10 December 1989	The coalition federal government of Marián Calfa
30 December 1989	Vacláv Havel becomes interim president, Alexander Dubcek speaker of parliament
20 April 1990	Czechoslovakia changed to the Czech and Slovak Republic
8, 9 June 1990	The first free parliamentary elections
27 June 1990	Second federal government of Marián Calfa
5 July 1990	Havel elected president by the new parliament

23–25 November 1990	The first local government elections
9 January 1991	Federal Assembly passes Charter on Fundamental Rights and Freedoms
1 January 1991	Start of a 'small' shock therapy
28 January 1991	Tripartite General Agreement signed
9 April 1991	Summit meeting of Hungary, Poland and the Czech and Slovak Republic in Bratislava
20 April 1991	Civic Forum splits into Civic Democratic Party of Vacláv Klaus and Civic Movement of Jiri Dienstbier
27 April 1991	PAV splits into Civic Democratic Union–PAV and Movement for Democratic Slovakia
19 June 1991	Soviet troops leave the Czech and Slovak Republic
4 October 1991	The 'screening' (or lustration) law
17 November 1991	Campaign of Havel for extended presidential rights
31 January 1992	Constitutional Court established in Brno
5, 6 June 1992	Second free elections
3 July 1992	Ján Strasky heads the last federal government
30 September 1992	Federal Assembly passes laws on the division of the federation
1 January 1993	The 'Velvet Divorce' between Czechs and Slovaks

Czech Chronology

January 1990	Petr Pithart's interim Czech government
July 1990	Pithart government
3 July 1992	Václav Klaus government
16 December 1992	The Czech Constitution
26 January 1993	Vacláv Havel elected Czech president
17 July 1993	The Czech Constitutional Court established in Brno
8–9 November 1994	Local government elections
2 January 1996	The official application for EU membership
31 May, 1 June 1996	Parliamentary elections
4 July 1996	New Vacláv Klaus government
15–16 November 1996	Senate elections
16 April 1997	'Velvet Crisis' – economic crisis management introduced
2 January 1998	Klaus resigns, Josef Tosovsky becomes prime minister of an interim government

Slovak Chronology

14 March 1939(–1944)	Independent Slovak state under Father Tiso
January 1990	Milan Cic interim Slovak government

July 1990	Vladimir Meciar's first Slovak government
23 April 1991	Jan Carnogurski Slovak government
24 June 1992	Second Meciar government
1 September 1992	Slovak Constitution
15 February 1993	Michal Kovac elected president
16 March 1994	Jozef Moravcik government
20 September, 1 October 1994	Third parliamentary elections
12 December 1994	Third Meciar government
27 June 1995	Official application for EU membership
30 October 1996	A 'blue coalition' formed between the Christian Democratic Movement, Democratic Union of Slovakia and Democratic Party against the Movement for Democratic Slovakia

7

Democratization in the Balkans

CONTENTS

The Balkan countries had much less tradition in democratization in the late 1980s than their ECE partner states. This is mostly due to the long Ottoman rule in the Balkan region and to the late emergence of the independent Balkan nation-states. They did not have a democratization period in the early post-war, pre-Cold War era (1944–8) and had no reform cycles under state socialism either. In some ways, they began the democratization efforts seriously only after the collapse of the bipolar world order, under international pressure and through the snowball effect of the ECE states. Therefore, without proper democratic traditions, that is, without an inherited democratic culture and institutions, the process of democratization in the Balkans has been more controversial and slower, very violent in the initial stages and burdened with pre-communist and communist authoritarian traditions. After six to seven years of delay, in the late 1990s, however, the Balkan countries have begun to make a new effort for democratization, which gives a time frame for our analysis of systemic change in the region. The Yugoslav tragedy also had a great impact on Balkan developments, both positively and negatively. It had a deterrent effect in a bid to avoid similar ethnic confrontations and extreme violence, and at the same time, the war in Yugoslavia disturbed the democratization efforts in the entire Balkan region. Thus, we have to start our analysis of the democratization in the Balkans with the Yugoslav war and the post-Yugoslav developments.

The Yugoslav war and the post-Yugoslav states

Yugoslavia was formed after the First World War as a federation of South Slav nations but under Serbian dominance, which became even more marked with the introduction of the royal dictatorship in 1929. This 'first' Yugoslavia was artificially created by the French post-war arrangements which produced the most heterogeneous country of Europe with two scripts, three religions and five major languages. There were tremendous economic and cultural differences between the Western and the Eastern regions, that is, between the Central European and the Balkan parts of the country. The tension between the two regions increased much in the inter-war period, to a level that during the Second World War Serbs and Croats engaged in a civil war against each other which was not forgotten in the decades of the 'second' Yugoslavia after the war either. The post-war organization of the Socialist Federal Republic of Yugoslavia under Tito (Josip Broz), the almighty ruler, in six republics (Slovenia, Croatia, Bosnia–Hercegovina, Serbia, Montenegro and Macedonia) with two autonomous regions within Serbia (Vojvodina and Kosovo) eased inter-ethnic tensions to some extent by giving them some autonomy. This constitutional solution, however, could not solve the problems generated by extreme heterogeneity and traditional-historical animosities.

As in the other Balkan states, also in Yugoslavia there was a tradition of violent politics and ethnic cleansing which surfaced during the Second World War and the early post-war period. There was no short democratization period, since Tito's partisan army defeated also all of its internal enemies and emerged as the only political actor on the scene after the war. Socialist Yugoslavia was a very centralized state, in fact a 'Serbian empire', with almost all economic, political and military powers concentrated in Belgrade, in the hands of the Serbian bureaucracy and the Serbian top officers of the Federal Army. This created a huge resentment in the Western republics of Slovenia and Croatia, which suffered not only from the command economy in general, but also from the transfer of their economic resources from the West to the East, for investments in the less developed republics and for the costs of the huge Serbian army and bureaucracy.

Politically, Yugoslavia was ruled by the League of Yugoslav Communist (LYC; SKJ), under Serbian chief party bureaucrats but with a republican branch of party organization in each republic. There was a huge overrepresentation of Serbs in the leadership, since there were ten times more Serbs than Croats among senior civil servants, chief officers and party leaders. Tiny Montenegro alone with its Serbian population had an equal number among these elites as the Croats had altogether. In addition, a much larger 'political population' of Serbs was spread across the whole country and the 'economic population' of Serbs followed everywhere grandious industrial investment projects, with new living quarters built for them, as for example, in the new industrial zone around the Bosnian capital, Sarajevo.[1]

At the same time, Socialist Yugoslavia differed from the other state socialist countries in many ways. First, it was independent from the Soviet Union and played a great role in world politics as a chief representative of the non-aligned movement. Secondly, it introduced some elements of a market economy, and third, it experimented with some sociopolitical decentralization in the form of 'workers' self-management' (see Goati, 1995: 16). Despite these features, socio-economic and political tension was growing in the 1980s and an economic disintegration began, above all as a 'commercial war' with mutual boycotts between Slovenia and Serbia. The collapse of the state socialist world system and, particularly, its pre-transition crisis in the neighbouring states in 1989, gave a final blow to the unity of Yugoslavia. During the crucial year of 1990 no new compromise was reached between the Western republics and Serbia and in 1991 the second Yugoslavia disintegrated.[2]

The political disintegration of Yugoslavia did not produce a 'velvet divorce', but led to a terrible civil war because the Serbs were not ready to accept the desire of other nations to become independent and used the Federal Army under their command brutally to keep the 'Serbian empire' together (see Seroka, 1993: 105). Although this powerful army dominated in the ensuing civil war, the Serbs soon realized that they could not maintain the second Yugoslavia as a whole and from 1991 onward they concentrated increasingly on creating a Greater Serbia at the expense of Croatia and Bosnia–Hercegovina by uniting all Serbian populated territories in one state. This meant not only a cruel war but also a series of brutal ethnic cleansings, for which first and foremost the Serbs were responsible, but, as a reaction, Croats and Bosnians later on were also involved in these criminal actions against humanity and human rights.

The Yugoslav war demonstrated also the low profile of Western crisis management capacity. First, the Western powers wanted to preserve the unity of Yugoslavia at any price, not realizing the genuine will of these nations for independence. Later on the conflicting interests of the Western states impeded the elaboration of a common strategy and they could not stop the Serbian aggression against Slovenia, Croatia and Bosnia in which hundreds of thousands were killed and millions were forced to be refugees. When Yugoslavia eventually disintegrated and the independent states emerged, despite the former preponderance of the Serbian army, only then did Western crisis management became more active and assertive. The Dayton Peace Accord in November 1995 brought the end of civil war, with an agreement on Bosnia as a unified state and it produced the mutual recognition of the post-Yugoslav states, the first being Serbia and Croatia (see Luif, 1995: 268–9).

The disintegration of Yugoslavia brought about a new situation in East Central Europe and the Balkans. Yugoslavia had forcefully united within itself some Central European and some Balkan nations and cultures, which in the early 1990s became separated again. The two Central European states of Slovenia and Croatia have emerged and taken urgent steps to reintegrate into Central Europe through trade and cultural contacts and by joining regional organizations. The four new Balkan states – Serbia, Montenegro, Bosnia–Hercegovina and Macedonia – became involved in Balkan politics, for example, Macedonia has had to make arrangements with Greece and Bulgaria. Serbia and Montenegro, the two ethnic Serbian states, have formed a third Yugoslavia which has been labelled internationally as 'rump' or 'little Yugoslavia'. Despite the international recognition and the Dayton Peace Accords, the future of Bosnia is still unclear, whether it can be maintained as one unified state or breaks apart into the Serbian, Croatian and Bosnian–Muslim parts. But to a great extent the future of Serbia as a state is also unclear concerning its final borders, since there has as yet been no arrangement for the Kosovo province with its predominantly Albanian population. Still, in the second half of the 1990s the Yugoslav crisis is more or less over and we have to deal with separate political systems of the independent post-Yugoslav states.

Slovenia achieved its independence first and this event was followed shortly by political and economic consolidation. Slovenia is a small country in the Westernmost part of the former Yugoslavia with a very high level of socio-economic development. It declared its independence on 26 June 1991, together with Croatia, and after a week of war with the Federal Army it established its real independence. The Federal Army left Slovenia, since there was no sizeable Serbian minority there, and it turned against Croatia, with a large Serbian minority. Consequently, there was no substantial war damage in Slovenia and economic recovery could start shortly after the war under very favourable conditions.

The political transition to democracy began early in Slovenia in the spirit of the Central European negotiated transitions, influenced first of all by Hungarian developments (see Seroka, 1993: 105). The League of Slovenian Communists (LSC; ZKS) left the League of Yugoslav Communists in early 1990 and transformed itself into the Party of Democratic Revival (PDR; SDP).[3] This party and its leader, Milan Kucan, in fact played an initiatory role in the democratic transformation. In February 1990 the PDR began national roundtable talks with the opposition umbrella organization, Demos (Democratic Opposition of Slovenia), formed already in December 1989. The first free election in March 1990, as is usual in the ECE region, was won by the democratic opposition, Demos, but Milan Kucan was also elected President of Slovenia by popular vote. After the election a coalition government was formed by the Demos, headed by Lojze Peterle from the Slovenian Christian Democrats (SCD; SKD), but the reformed left as a parliamentary party (renamed before the 1992 election as the United List of Social Democrats, ULSD; ZLSD) has remained an important political force.

According to the new Constitution of December 1991, Slovenia has a bicameral parliament, a National Assembly with 90 seats and a National

Council with 40 seats. Independent Slovenia has always been ruled by centrist and moderate governments based on a broad coalition of parties. After the disintegration of the Demos umbrella organization, the Liberal Democratic Party (LDP; LDS) became the largest party and its leader, Janez Drnovsek, has headed the subsequent governments. There is a moderate fragmentation of the party system in Slovenia, with relatively middle-sized parties, within which the LDP and ULSD have a more Europeanizer and modernizer orientation, and the SCD and Slovenian Peoples Party (SPP; SLS) represent the traditionalist right. The results of both the December 1992 and November 1996 elections were rather balanced for these two forces, with a small advantage for the former parties. But Slovenia could not avoid the transition costs of a market economy either and the protest vote appeared in the 1996 election as well. As a result, it took a long time to form a new government and the second Drnovsek government includes also the more traditionalist and populist centre–right parties. It did not prevent the consolidation of Slovenian politics and the international situation of Slovenia has also consolidated. Slovenia has become a member of all major international organizations, and from January 1996 has also joined the East Central European regional organization, CEFTA.[4]

Independence for **Croatia** caused the biggest conflict in the Yugoslav crisis because of the traditional Croatian–Serbian animosities. Croatia is the second biggest and populous post-Yugoslav state which had a substantial Serbian minority in the *krajina*s, that is, in the military border zones organized in the sixteenth to seventeenth centuries by the Habsburg empire using Serbian refugees as soldiers to protect its borders against the Ottoman empire. When the war broke out in March 1991 between Serbia and Croatia through the attacks of the Federal Army against the Croatian police and militia, these *krajina*s declared their own independence, took up arms and fought against the Croatian state. Because of the supremacy in numbers of the Federal Army and the early weakness of the Croatian forces, Croatia was soon defeated and lost about one-third of its territory to Serbia. But Croatia established its own army very quickly and supplied it with modern arms, so that by August 1995 Croatia was in a position whereby it could liberate most of these territories, which caused a mass exodus of the Serbian minority to Bosnia and Serbia. With this victory the war ended in Croatia and, a year after this offensive, Croatia and Serbia established a diplomatic relationship.

Political transformation has been very troubled and distorted in war-damaged Croatia, which is still very far from its official programme of a return to Central Europe. Because of the supression of the 'Croatian Spring' in 1971 and massive purges of the reformist members of the Croatian League of Communists (CLC: SKH), the CLC had lost its vigour and initiative and it did not play a major role in the political transition either. The winner of the first multi-party election in Croatia in April 1990 was the newly formed Croatian Democratic Community

(CDC; HDZ), with 42 per cent of the popular vote and two-thirds of the seats. This traditionalist-nationalist umbrella organization still governs Croatia, led by Franjo Tudjman, who was also elected president in 1990. Tudjman had been one of Tito's generals but later on was imprisoned as a Croatian nationalist, so he had the 'charisma' to lead the country in the turbulent years of civil war.

War-damaged Croatia was not that successful in finding the path to democratization. The CDC, the new ruling party, created a system of 'tyrannical majority', and did not negotiate with the other parties about democratization. Moreover, it did not share power with them in the institutions of the newly independent Croatia. Croatia's attempt to build a modern polity died in the civil war. The nationalist rhetoric went back to the early twentieth century, civil society was oppressed on behalf of the state, and freedom of the press was drastically reduced (see Seroka, 1993: 112). Croatia in the first half of the 1990s created a facade democracy only and the slogan 'Back to Central Europe' remained empty rhetoric. It is an open question whether after the end of civil war and the economic reconstruction, Croatia can find the way to genuine democratization and its Central European traditions.

The new Croatian Constitution of December 1990 has established a bicameral parliament with a National Assembly and House of Provinces, but the actual power is in the hands of the president. Franjo Tudjman has been re-elected three times as president by popular vote (most recently in June 1997); so has his party, which has emerged as winner of both August 1992 and October 1995 parliamentary elections. The electoral law has been changed several times, rather arbitrarily, according to the current needs of the new ruling party, for example, the Bosnian Croats have also been invited to vote, although they cannot be considered as Croatian citizens. Both the historical, rightist-traditionalist parties – Croatian Party of Rights (CPR; HSP) and Croatian Peasant Party (CPP; HSS) – and the newly formed modernizer parties – the Croatian Social Liberal Party (CSLP; HSLS) and the Social Democratic Party of Croatia (SDPC; SPDH, the former CLC) – have tried to force the CDC to engage in some power sharing or to defeat it in the elections by forming coalitions, but it has so far been in vain. Thus, international recognition of Croatia as a democratic state has also been very controversial. In April 1996 it gained full membership in the Council of Europe which was suspended in July but regained in November 1996 in the hope of radical changes in the Croatian polity towards real democratization.

The biggest problem with democratization among the post-Yugoslav states has been in **Serbia**, or in the rump Yugoslavia. Serbia has not built up even a facade democracy, that is, even the formal-minimal requirements of democracy have been missing. The former ruling party and its leaders have kept full powers; the League of Serbian Communists (LSC; SKS) in July 1990 simply changed its name to the Serbian Socialist Party (SSP; SPS). It cannot be explained by the freezing effect of the war Serbia waged against the newly independent republics; on the contrary, the war waged by the Serbians for a Greater Serbia can be explained by the nationalistic orientation of the Serbian elite, including the SSP. Slobodan Milosevic came to power in May 1986 as the leader of the LSC with an extreme nationalist programme of keeping the Albanian inhabited Kosovo at any price and, in general, of ending 'the persecution of Serbs in Yugoslavia'. It was a slogan for creating a new federal system with clear Serbian hegemony in Yugoslavia. This claim of Serbs for hegemony was primarily responsible for the disintegration of Yugoslavia, since under the new international circumstances the Western republics were not ready to accept any further increase in Serbian dominance. With a more liberal Serbian leadership, Slovenia and Croatia might have considered a con-federal solution for Yugoslavia, but with the Milosevic regime ruling Serbia they had to face a confrontation with the Serbs anyway, and thus secession remained the only option for them.[5]

The civil war itself, as a Serbian reaction to the secession produced by the aggressive Serbian leadership, had, of course, a freezing effect on the domestic problems in Serbia and the nationalistic drive for a Greater Serbia pushed aside other political problems and considerations for some years. However, Milosevic has had a firm grip on Serbian politics – including the Federal Army – since 1986, and since 1990 he has repro-duced his personal powers through pseudo-democratic means. In the first multi-party election in December 1990 the SSP used many pre-election manipulations and intimidation of opponents, yet it managed to get only 40 per cent of the popular vote. This produced, however, a two-thirds majority for the SSP in the Serbian parliament. There were no negotiations in 1990 with the opposition parties, and the date of the election was announced just one month before, in order to prevent the opposition from proper preparation. Neither was there free access to the media.

After this victory at the first 'democratic' election, Milosevic took com-plete control of the residual federal organizations and in April 1992 estab-lished the Federal Republic of Yugoslavia with tiny Montenegro. Until 1993–4 the chances of creating a Greater Serbia looked good, but after a series of military defeats and after a long boycott by the international community against Serbia, Milosevic had no other choice but to sign the Dayton Peace Accord in November 1995, which meant the end of dreams about a Greater Serbia. This did not shake the powers of Milosevic, since in the first half of the 1990s he consolidated his personal rule and the hegemony of the SSP, legitimizing it through pseudo-democratic elec-tions in December 1992 and December 1993.

The consolidation of the Milosevic regime was also due to popular consent about a Greater Serbia, and as a result, most of the other parties wanted only to outcompete the SSP in nationalism. First and foremost, the Serbian Radical Party (SRP; SRS), led by Vojislav Seselj, but also the Serbian Renewal Movement (SRM; SPO), headed by Vuk Draskovic, at that time went in the nationalistic direction. Milosevic included the SRP several times in a governing coalition and used brutal measures to oppress the other opposition parties. Mass demonstrations were met with police violence and Draskovic was imprisoned. But after the 'Belgrade Spring' in March 1991, for some years the intensity of this 'internal war' was limited by the 'external war', the opposition was fragmented and democratic parties were weak.

After the war ended, and with the strengthening of democratic parties, the former practice of fake elections no longer worked in Serbia. The November 1996 parliamentary and municipal elections were won by the SSP again, but with rampant electoral fraud which was not tolerated by the three leading democratic parties (the SRM of Vuk Draskovic, the Democratic Party of Zoran Djindjic and the Serbian Civic Alliance of Vesna Pesic). Municipal elections were actually won by the opposition alliance of the three parties, Zajedno (Together) in the major Serbian cities, including Belgrade, but the authorities falsified the polls and ordered re-elections. This aggressive fraud launched a mass protest movement in Serbia from November 1996 to February 1997, and hundreds of thousands marched almost every day in the streets of Belgrade as a political protest. The international organizations of the Council of Europe and the OSCE condemned the Milosevic regime. Under domestic and international pressure, Milosevic had to accept the original results of the municipal elections in February 1997, with the effect, for example, that Zoran Djindjic became the Lord Mayor of Belgrade (see McCarthy, 1997).

This marked the beginning of some erosion of the Milosevic regime, and, in general, we see a second round of democratization in Romania and Bulgaria as well, after the failure in the first half of 1990s, and these Balkan transformations reinforce each other. However, at present, Milosevic has again consolidated his personal rule. On 17 July 1997 the Federal Parliament elected Milosevic president of Yugoslavia because, according to the constitutional arrangements, he could have not been re-elected as president of Serbia for a third time. Thus, despite some erosion of his personal power and the power of the ruling SSP, Spring 1997 did not see the start of a real democratization process in Yugoslavia.

The disintegration of Yugoslavia has produced a series of small states, including Bosnia and Macedonia. In **Bosnia–Hercegovina**, Bosnian Muslims were estimated to be the relative majority (39.6 per cent), Serbians were 32.0 per cent and Croats 18.4 per cent, and at the beginning of the war in 1991, (7.9 per cent of the population declared themselves Yugoslavs). The Bosnian Muslims formed their own party, the Party of Democratic Action (PDA; SDA) under the leadership of Alija Izetbegovic. Serbs and Croats also created their ethnic parties, and in the first multi-party election in November 1990 the population voted exclusively along ethnic lines. The Bosnian Muslims declared the independence of Bosnia as a unified republic with three ethnic groups in October 1990 but the Bosnian Serbs formed their own republic in Bosnia with a desire to join Greater Serbia. The Dayton Peace Accord in 1995 recreated the unified Bosnian state with a federal government in Sarajevo but provided for considerable autonomy to its three parts. Some stabilization has been felt in Bosnia in the late 1990s, but still it is an open question whether this country can be maintained as a unified state or will yet break apart.

Macedonia had to face similar difficulties in the first half of the 1990s, although it was not devastated by a civil war. The Macedonian issue has traditionally been the most divisive political tension in the Balkans, since all the neighbouring states have claimed the Macedonian territory for themselves. The Greeks consider Macedonia an ancient Greek territory, but according to the Bulgarians Macedonians are ethnic Bulgarians. The Serbs consider them Serbs, and finally, one-quarter of the population is Albanian. Macedonia declared its independence in January 1991 and for some years it was disputed by its neighbours, but with the assistance of international organizations Macedonia has consolidated its existence. By the mid-1990s Macedonia was recognized as an independent state by both international organizations and the neighbouring states and it has also stabilized its domestic structures.

Since the first multi-party election in November 1990, Kiro Gligorov, the former party chief, has led the country as President of Macedonia. He transformed his former ruling party, the League of Macedonian Communists (LMC; SKM) and re-organized it as the Social Democratic Union of Macedonia (SDUM; SDSM). Since the early 1990s this party has governed an independent Macedonia through various coalition governments, sometimes including the Albanian parties or at least making a viable compromise with them. The political future of independent Macedonia seems to be assured but a real stabilization of this new country can occur only by economic consolidation and through a durable solution of the ethnic problems in this multi-ethnic and multicultural state.

The disintegration of Yugoslavia has come to an end and the post-Yugoslav countries have begun their independent histories. Their divergencies come from the extreme heterogeneity of the former Yugoslavia, Slovenia being one of the most and Macedonia one of the least developed countries in Europe as a whole. The relationships among the post-Yugoslav states have been arranged by and large but the memories of the devastating war are still vivid and present an obstacle to meaningful cooperation. In December 1996 the United States suggested the establishment of an international organization called the South-East European Cooperation Initiative (SECI), involving the post-Yugoslav states and some neighbour states, in a post-war reconstruction programme. Slovenia and Croatia have so far been rather unimpressed by the SECI because they do not want to get involved in Balkan affairs. In general, however, the future of Balkan regional cooperation will certainly depend on the success of democratization in Serbia and in other post-Yugoslav countries.

Facade democracies in Bulgaria, Romania and Albania

The snowball effect of the ECE democratizations reached Bulgaria in November 1989, Romania in December 1989 and Albania in late 1990. Bulgaria as a state socialist country was the most loyal to the Soviet Union and became a political laggard under the long rule of Todor Zhivkov (1953–89). Romania, in turn, was the least loyal to the Soviet Union but had built up a more totalitarian domestic system under the personal, 'sultanistic' rule of Nicolae Ceausescu (1965–89). The fall of the state socialist regimes occurred accordingly: in Bulgaria Petar Mladenov removed Zhivkov from power by a palace coup on 10 November 1989 and set up a negotiating mechanism with the opposition which led to some kind of power-sharing; in Romania Ceausescu was removed only by a large-scale violent revolution but almost the same nomenklatura ruled the country for some more years. Albania's democratization is an even more complicated story with a late start and many setbacks, since the mature totalitarian system in Albania, and its isolation from the rest of world, has left a historical legacy which is very difficult to overcome.

In 1989 three political cleavage lines were formed in Bulgaria leading to independent political organizations fighting against the state socialist regime. First, the Bulgarian workers formed an autonomous trade union called Podkrepa (Support), the urban middle class and intellectuals created the Ecoglasnost (referring by its name to ecological issues and to the freedom of the press) and finally, the Turks organized their own party, the Movement for Rights and Freedoms (MRF; DPS). In Spring 1989 ethnic tensions in Bulgaria reached a high conflict level and in Summer about 300,000 ethnic Turks were forced to emigrate to Turkey. Although somewhat later they were allowed to come back because of an international protest, this ethnic crisis provoked a deep political crisis and exacerbated it. Reacting to these domestic conflicts and to the international snowball effect, the Mladenov leadership wanted to introduce changes from above in order to avoid the total collapse of the regime.[6]

This is the typical Balkan model of democratization. The ruling elites with a Byzantine tradition take the initiative and try to outmanoeuvre or manipulate the masses which do not have a tradition of organizing themselves and forming their own programmes to properly articulate their demands. Bulgaria provides the classic case of this Balkan model in the recent democratizations with elite initiatives and angry, spontaneous, that is 'anomic', responses by the masses. Yet, in the early 1990s, the Bulgarian case was the closest to the ECE type of negotiated transition. The Bulgarian opposition wanted a Spanish type of 'gentle revolution', they also followed carefully ECE developments and copied the institutions and procedures (see Bell, 1993: 88–9). There were, indeed, national roundtable negotiations in Bulgaria in early 1990 with some results, but they had to be repeated a year later to accomplish the political transition. Bulgaria was a front-runner in the Balkans and the negotiated transition smoothed the way to democratization. Nevertheless, mass violence could only be reduced and not completely avoided.

The Union of Democratic Forces (UDF; SDS) as a loose and heterogeneous umbrella organization was formed in December 1989 by Zheliu Zhelev, a social scientist of Sofia University, from 16 organizations, including Podkrepa and Ecoglasnost. In November and December 1989 there were some mass demonstrations in Sofia, which continued also in early 1990, indicating that people were not satisfied by the palace coup of Mladenov promising only minor changes. The national roundtable talks between the Bulgarian Communist Party (BCP; BKP) and the UDF between 16 January and 12 March 1990, which were televised and served as a substitute for free parliamentary discussions, concluded in some partial agreements and constitutional amendments, although no formal pact was signed. Based on these negotiations, the first free election was held in June 1990 for the Grand National Assembly with 400 seats, usually elected only for constitution-making. (Subsequently, 'regular' parliaments have been elected with only 240 seats.) This Grand National Assembly passed a new democratic constitution in July 1991, establishing a unicameral parliamentary system in Bulgaria.

As a typical Balkan democratization pattern, the BCP; BKP (renamed in April 1990 as the Bulgarian Socialist Party, BSP; BSP) easily won the first free election, with a relative majority of votes (47.15 per cent) and with an absolute majority of seats (211). Still, Bulgaria was a frontrunner in the Balkans because, unlike in other Balkan countries, the opposition umbrella organization was formed quite early, there were national roundtable talks and the opposition figured as a serious partner in these meaningful negotiations. The UDF received 36.20 per cent of popular vote with 36 per cent of seats (144) in the first free election and introduced itself as an important political force. The Bulgarian Agricultural National Union (BANU; BZNS), the great Bulgarian historical party, was third (8.03 and 4.0 per cent) and the Turkish ethnic party, the MRF, was the fourth (6.03 and 5.7 per cent, respectively).

The first free election was indeed free and fair in Bulgaria, which is again exceptional in the Balkans. It did not produce a political breakthrough at most it created a multi-party system which operated rather well in parliamentary power-sharing. Yet, the large urban masses were disappointed with the results of the first free election, hence in 1990 a 'hot summer' followed the June election. There were violent clashes between the police and the 'anomic' movements, burning down the headquarters of the BSP and taking the mummy of Georgi Dimitrov out of its mausoleum (Pundeff, 1992: 109–11). We see here a political dynamism similar to the 'moving walls' in Poland. In July 1990 Mladenov was forced to resign and Zhelev was elected President of Bulgaria. In November 1990 Andrei Lukanov, the BSP prime minister, also had to resign under popular pressure and in December 1990 Dimitar Popov, was elected prime minister in a BSP–UDF coalition government, the first non-communist leading politician. The second free election in October 1991 was won by the UDF with a relative margin, 34.36 versus 33.14 per cent of the popular vote and 45.8 versus 44.2 per cent of the seats. After the election Filip Dimitrov formed a UDF minority government but an ensuing split in the UDF already showed the new difficulties in democratic transition and crisis management.

The UDF as a 'blue-coloured' umbrella organization split somewhat before this electoral victory to 'light blue' and 'dark blue' tendencies, that is, to the liberal democratic and nationalist-conservative wings. It produced a polarized pluralism in Bulgaria between the BSP and the UDF for some years (see Karasimeonov, 1996a: 263). The 1991 election was won by the national-conservatives organized in the UDF-Movement, and the two post-UDF organizations of liberals (UDF-Centre and UDF-Liberals) did not get enough votes to reach the 4 per cent threshold. In 1991, therefore, a three-party parliament emerged – the UDF-Movement, the BSP and the MRF – in which the Filip Dimitrov minority government needed the support of the MRF. But, paradoxically, acting as a traditional-ist right party with its nationalist policy, the UDF completely alienated this Turkish ethnic party. The Dimitrov government also had a hysterical anti-communist campaign combined with a 'Return to the Past' pro-gramme, like the Olszewski government in Poland, which generated an angry reaction from liberals, again as in Poland. This UDF government became so unpopular with most Bulgarians that many former UDF member organizations (Podkrepa, Ecoglasnost and social democrats, etc.) joined the BSP in the December 1994 election. The BSP became again the winner and the UDF, at that time as a clearly nationalist-traditionalist party, was the loser. The BSP won 52 per cent of seats and the UDF only 28 per cent, so the BSP formed a government led by Videnov.

This can be treated as the 'return of the post-communist vote' in Bulgaria, but in this case the parallel with East Central Europe is sense-less. Certainly there was no return of the reformed left, as in the cases of the HSP in Hungary and the SDRP in Poland. The BSP dropping the 'communist' label made for neither institutional nor membership dis-continuity and after the October 1991 electoral defeat the party did not reform itself either. At the BSP congress, convened in November 1991, the only major change was that they elected a new young leader, a 32-year-old economist, Zhan Videnov. There was no substantial change in the economic policy of the BSP either, since after the dismissal of the Filip Dimitrov government the interim government of Luben Berov, supported by both the BSP and the UDF, did not start any real economic and political transformations. Even the electoral victory of the BSP did not mark a turning point in these transformations, because the hardly reformed BSP was not ready for genuine economic crisis management and this paralysis or inability to reform led to a new economic and political breakdown in 1996–7. This was a typical Balkan blind alley of development when both large parties as contenders for power proved to be, in fact, successor parties of the former regime and were unable to reform themselves and their country.

Romania had a much more difficult start for democratization. The beginnings were very violent, similar to the nineteenth century revolutions, with a large participation of urban masses and students, but also with a regular warfare between the Romanian army and the Securitate – the secret police, which was the private army of Ceausescu. In late December 1989, power was seized by the National Salvation Front (NSF; FSN) headed by Ion Iliescu, a leading member of the former nomenklatura. This organization, as later it turned out, was actually a nationalist party run by ex-communist apparatchiks refusing the adoption of Western economic and political models (see Gallagher, 1995: 2–3).

First NSF presented itself as a temporary organ preparing for a free election and initiating other procedures for democratization. In January 1990, however, the NSF announced that it would run at the election. In fact, in the last days of December and early January 1990 Iliescu and his associates succeeded in a silent *coup d'état*, when Iliescu authorized the local organs of the NSF to play the role of the state administration and to build up these local organs from the units of the former ruling party. Thus, the NSF and Iliescu monopolized political power from the first minute of the political takeover from Ceausescu. NSF did not engage in any negotiations with the other parties either, but used violence to deter the other political forces from using their democratic rights in this thinly veiled facade democracy. In the first half of 1990 a wave of terror swept through Romania against any kind of opposition or alternative political force. First, in January the headquarters of the newly organized parties were attacked in Bucharest, then in mid-March in Transylvania (above all in Tirgu–Mures) mass violence was used against the Hungarian minority to intimidate it. Finally, when a student protest against this new oppressive regime reached its peak in June 1990, the Iliescu leadership carried more than ten thousand miners to Bucharest who attacked the students with extreme brutality (see Gallagher, 1995: 86–9).[7]

After these violent events, severely damaging downtown Bucharest and the university area on 13–15 June 1990, the first period of the political transformation came to a close. The masses and students understood that Iliescu and the NSF had 'stolen' the revolution. They realized from the brutally oppressive actions that new democratic rights were but a facade for the new oppressive regime and could not be implemented. Thus, the first multi-party election in May 1990 was easily won by the NSF with 66.31 per cent of the popular vote and 67.9 per cent of the seats, and Ion Iliescu was elected president by a large majority of votes (85 per cent). Among the other parties only the Democratic Alliance of Hungarians in Romania (DAHR; RMDSZ), coming second, could command a substantial amount of public support, based exclusively on the ethnic vote (7.23 and 7.2 per cent respectively). This first multi-party election was very similar to that in Serbia, that is, very far from being free and fair, since intimidation and oppression were combined with electoral fraud. It shows that in the Balkan countries a real multi-party system has emerged with great difficulty. In these facade democracies the organization of parties and the mobilization of population needs a long time, until real political alternatives can be presented against the incumbent regimes.

The new–old Romanian political system proved to be a 'one-man-show', as in Serbia, following the same tradition of authoritarian populism (see Gallagher, 1995: 292–3). The personal rule of Iliescu was stabilized by the new constitution approved by a referendum in December 1991. This constitution has established a presidential system, concentrating all major powers in the hands of the president. The parliament has become quite weak, and, at that time, was completely controlled by the NSF. The September 1992 election indicated a quasi consolidation along these lines because the opposition remained weak and very fragmented. NSF disintegrated before the second election but its successor party, the Democratic National Salvation Front (DNSF; FSND) supported Iliescu. DNSF received enough seats to rule the country through a coalition government involving two extreme nationalist parties, the Party of Romanian National Unity (PRNU; PUNR) and the Greater Romania Party (GRP; PRM). Iliescu himself was re-elected president in September 1992, although with declining support (61 per cent) and only in the second round. The DNSF was re-organized after the 1992 election as the Party of Social Democracy in Romania (PSDR; PDSR), and remained basically the same party of the traditionalist, anti-West nomenklatura.[8]

This political model is quite similar to the Slovakian one with a 'strong man' in power and supported by a large umbrella organization in an alliance with the extremist parties which form together a coalition of traditionalist-nationalist forces. The Romanian opposition, in turn, was not weak and fragmented but it could not produce its own umbrella organization, unlike in Bulgaria. The two big historical parties – the Christian Democratic National Peasant Party (CDNPP; PNT-cd) and the National Liberal Party (NLP; PNL) – reorganized themselves in early 1990 but were unsuccessful in both elections. After the first election, about a dozen parties, including the above-mentioned historical parties, formed some kind of alliance for the second election. The Democratic Convention of Romania (DCR; CDR) came in second with 25 per cent of both the popular vote and parliamentary seats. The DCR was not an umbrella organization in the sense of a unified, although heterogeneous, party. It was only a loose and fragile alliance of different parties which were all the time leaving the DCR and joining it again. The leading personality of the DCR, Emil Constantinescu, the Rector of Bucharest University, however, competed well with Iliescu in the first round of the presidential election, and was defeated only in the second round. Through the mid-1990s, the PSDR was able to keep monopolized power and to intimidate people in order to deter them from real political participation.

In Albania the erosion of the very strong totalitarian system began when the Ceausescu system collapsed in Romania, which had a great impact on both the party elite and the population of Albania. The first mass demonstrations took place in Tirana in January 1990 and later they continued more or less violently during 1990 and 1991. The ruling party, the Albanian Workers Party (AWP; PPS) launched a cautious reform programme in April 1990, that is, its leader, Ramiz Alia tried to appease the population with minor changes from above, as Mladenov did in Bulgaria. In December 1990 the parliament approved a multi-party system and the Albanian Democratic Party (ADP; PDS) was immediately formed by Sali Berisha. After a series of violent demonstrations the first multi-party election took place in March–April 1991 and was easily won by the AWP with 56.17 per cent of the popular vote and 70.4 per cent of the seats. But the ADP also established itself as a major opposition force with 38.71 and 27.2 per cent respectively. A year after, in the March 1992 election, the ADP became the largest party (62.09 and 65.7 per cent), defeating the AWP renamed as the Albanian Socialist Party (ASP; PSS) having only 25.73 per cent of the popular support and 27.1 per cent of the seats.[9]

However, the Albanian Democratic Party and its leader, Sali Berisha, who was elected President of Albania in 1992 and re-elected twice since then, could not get rid of the totalitarian legacy. After having established itself as the new ruling party, the ADP took full powers in the state machinery and established the personal rule of Berisha. This takeover from the ASP by the ADP, therefore, was not a real beginning of democratization, for even its democratic facade was shaky. The ADP organized an authoritarian regime without any separation of powers and with no legitimacy for the opposition and minorities. It is very characteristic that at a referendum about the new constitution in November 1994, which was supposed to legitimize the personal rule of Berisha, the majority not only voted against, but demonstrated *en masse* against Berisha with the slogan: 'Yes for the Constitution, Yes for the Dictatorship!' All the problems that we have discussed in the Balkan countries as difficulties, bottlenecks and setbacks in the democratization process appeared in Albania in the strongest possible way. Thus, for Albania, as for the Balkans in general, a second round of democratization was urgently needed by the mid-1990s.

The second round: between old and new

After the collapse of the bipolar world system and under the impact of the snowball effect of the ECE redemocratizations, the Balkan countries reached the stage of the *pre-transition crisis* in the early 1990s but they hardly entered the next stage of *democratic transition*. No real systemic change began there, just facade – or at most, formalist – democracies were created in various ways and to a different extent. All Balkan countries were stuck half-way between the old and the new systems. There were a variety of forms of this facade democracy, with Serbia and Albania representing minimal development for the Balkans on one side, and Romania and Bulgaria showing the most progress on the other, with Macedonia and Bosnia as newly born countries somewhere in between. There was, openly and manifestly, no systemic change in Serbia in the first half of the 1990s and political changes in Albania so far produced only the resurrection or 'incarnation' of the totalitarian mind in a new form, provoking chaos and disaster. No doubt, there were many changes in Bulgaria, but in too many directions instead of a radical transformation in stepwise fashion towards democratization. Finally, there was a 'continuity in disguise' in Romania after the silent *coup d'état* of Iliescu and this political continuity seems to have been broken only in the second half of the decade. All in all, the real democratic transition has only just begun in the Balkans, and then only in a very controversial way. The first steps have been taken in Bulgaria and Romania, and Macedonia may follow suit. There is still a big question mark about the future of democracy in Serbia and about the existence of Bosnia as a state. Albania headed for disaster, and following the June 1997 election most needs consolidation as a country first of all.

After a protracted pre-transition crisis and many setbacks in democratic transition, a new effort for democratization is needed in the Balkan states. The first round of democratization in the Balkans led only to mixed results, but by the mid-1990s there were obvious signs a second round of democratization had begun. The reasons for the beginnings of this second round are complex. International factors, again, have played the dominant role, with the end of the Yugoslav war and pressure from international organizations and Western governments. There is an increasingly pressing need for structural adjusment to the globalizing world and to its European architecture in economic and political terms. Nevertheless, domestic factors are also very important, such as the devastating legacy of the Yugoslav war, and/or the missing accommodation to the competitive world or European market. The Balkan states have hardly engaged in a genuine transition to a market economy with mass privatization and economic (monetary and fiscal) crisis management. Hence, manifestly, by the mid-decade a new cycle of economic crisis appeared with a near-collapse situation in all Balkan countries, which forced Romania and Bulgaria to react in 1997 with strong shock therapy in their crisis management.

Finally, political developments have also reached a critical point of maturation. The emergence of representative democracy and competitive party systems with mass participation is, of necessity, a rather lengthy process which cannot be introduced formally and legally, overnight. Democratization in the early 1990s was not a case of returning to some kind of 'pre-communist' traditions either. Democratic traditions were very weak and, hence, the old authoritarian traditions prevailed with a return to history prior to state socialism. However, in the early 1990s the demonstration effect of the ECE countries, and the West in general, generated a fermentation process in these Balkan facade democracies. In all politically laggard countries the slogan 'return to normalcy' was echoed by both opposition leaders and the population, meaning that democratization, that is, free elections, legitimate opposition, a free press and human rights, is 'normal', and should be given to the populations of Romania, Serbia and Bulgaria as well (see, for example, Shafir, 1997: 154). It suggests a new snowball effect of the more mature democracies of East Central Europe, considering them as 'normal' countries because they have adjusted themselves to a great extent to the Western democracies. Under the impact of the ECE countries and the international organizations a quick political learning process has been going on in the Balkan countries concerning political participation, social mobilization, party formation and the organization of public relations and media activities. People have learnt better how to 'speak and act politically', that is, how to articulate and aggregate their interests and to organize themselves in civil society associations and parties. The period of violent 'anomic' movements is more or less over. As a result of this learning process, the latest mass demonstrations in Serbia, Bulgaria and in other countries were strikingly well disciplined and politically conscious instead of the former violent and erratic eruptions of mass discontent.

In Autumn 1996 the new period of democratization began almost simultaneously in all Balkan countries. The parliamentary elections were scheduled for November 1996 in Romania and Serbia, and so was the presidential election in Bulgaria. But by Autumn both the economic and the political situation had worsened so much in Albania that this country was also ready for change. The clearest and deepest turning point was in Romania. People were tired of economic mismanagement and political corruption, the continued rule of former apparatchiks and the nationalistic hysteria. Whereas the masses felt simply that 'enough was enough', the large circles of political and economic elite realized quite precisely that the Iliescu regime provoked Western alienation and made Romania a pariah of the international system. The 'age of normalcy' came, indeed, with the November 1996 parliamentary and presidential elections. For the first time, the DCR as an umbrella organization appeared unified and had an alternative political programme. It was joined by the Social Democratic Union of Petre Roman and by the DAHR, the Hungarian ethnic party, in a common desire to overthrow the Iliescu regime by peaceful means at the ballot box. The opposition was victorious at both the parliamentary and presidential elections, that is, this *de facto* three party alliance managed to elect Emil Constantinescu as president and formed a coalition government under the leadership of Victor Ciorbea with a near 60 per cent majority. The Ciorbea government began a 'good neighbour' policy in order to attain the desired NATO membership and initiated shock therapy to overcome the economic crisis and to prepare the country for EU membership (see Shafir, 1997). There has been a danger that popular protest as a reaction to the harsh measures would undermine the new government but, despite strikes and demonstrations, the social peace has been maintained and the Ciorbea government has a good chance for success. Although Romania was not invited to join NATO in July 1997 in the first round of enlargement as the Romanian leadership expected, the NATO declaration, issued at the Madrid summit, promising to take Romania into consideration in the second round has also been a great success for the new Romanian political elite.

The Bulgarian situation in 1996 seemed to be much more complicated, since the UDF, the opposition umbrella organization, had already seized power in 1991–2 but had proved unable to act properly in marketization and democratization. The real turning point came not only with the deepening economic crisis and the impotence of the Videnov government to cope with it, but more with the reform of the UDF, which was also indicated by its slightly changed new name: instead of United Democratic Forces, by regaining some of their former partners they took the name Alliance of Democratic Forces. Indeed, the ADF leaders, both Petar Stojanov, the new president elected in early November 1996, and Ivan Kostov, the new prime minister appointed in April 1997, seem to be reform-minded and decisively oriented for marketization and democratization. In December 1996 the Videnov government was forced to resign under the pressure of mass demonstrations and in the April 1997 election the ADF received a stable majority in the parliament also. Another positive development has been that the BSP split before the April election and the reform-oriented socialists formed a new party of the 'European left' which established itself as a parliamentary party (called Democratic Left) and which offers hope for the emergence of a strong centre–left party in Bulgaria. After this turning point, the results of crisis management have so far been less clear in Bulgaria than in Romania, both domestically and internationally. The year 1997 was crucial for the survival of these reform efforts. The international community has been very supportive and the Bulgarian population is also definitely for change.

Unlike in Romania and Bulgaria, the breakthrough toward democratization has not yet been reached in Serbia or rump Yugoslavia. The 'hot winter' in Serbia between November 1996 and February 1997 was, however, a very important political event for the Balkan region as a whole. In this case we witness a snowball effect within the Balkans, because this 'long march', as a three month peaceful demonstration against the Milosevic regime, certainly influenced the other Balkan developments – chiefly a similar hot winter in Bulgaria – with the model of disciplined, well-organized and regular mass demonstrations carefully avoiding any violence, despite the occasional police violence and provocation. What actually happened, was a fraudulent election in November 1996 which this time provoked a mass reaction. The federal parliamentary and municipal elections took place simultaneously on 3 November 1996 and with the usual tricks the SSP of Milosevic won the parliamentary election with ease. But on 17 November, in the second round of municipal elections, surprisingly, the electoral coalition of opposition, Zajedno (Together) was victorious in 14 larger Serbian cities out of 19. The Milosevic regime was not ready to accept the results of the municipal elections and ordered a third round. The popular anger erupted at this moment. On 19 November mass demonstrations were staged in Nis, the second largest Serbian city, where the opposition also won. The storm of protest reached Belgrade the next day and mass demonstrations went on until 4 February 1997 when Milosevic gave up and accepted the results of the municipal elections. Hundreds of thousands of Belgrade dwellers demonstrated peacefully day by day, with the students being the most active and innovative.

The partial victory of the opposition was mainly due to public pressure, but was also thanks to the intervention of international organizations (for example, the OSCE) and Western governments. Moreover, finally, the Orthodox Church turned against Milosevic too (see McCarthy, 1997). This was only a partial victory, however, because although one of the Zajedno leaders, Zoran Djindjic was elected mayor of Belgrade and the opposition controls most of the major cities, Zajedno disintegrated in June 1997 and in July 1997 Milosevic was elected as president of Yugoslavia. Consequently, Milosevic has kept the major power position and has only suffered some erosion of his regime. In general terms, however, the long hot winter in Serbia indicates the political learning process of the Serbian population and forecasts a new decisive turn towards democratization in the coming years – as a 'normalization' for Yugoslavia as well.

The most dubious case in the democratization process is Albania, with the heaviest burden of a former totalitarian regime. Sali Berisha and his party, the ADP, was an heir of Enver Hoxha in brutally suppressing the opposition and organizing the May 1996 election with rampant fraud and intimidation, and occasionally with open violence, against opposition candidates and their mass rallies. The situation exploded, however, when most of the population lost their small shares in 'pyramid' schemes, supported by government circles. This fraudulent enterprise collapsed in mid-February 1997 and a wave of popular protest shook the Berisha regime. The old North–South, that is, Geg and Tosk, tension came to the forefront, the Southener Tosks rioting against the Northener Gegs' rule, symbolized by Berisha. In late February a kind of civil war broke out; people stormed police and army stations and took up arms. The state power disintegrated and the local armed mobs ruled the cities and streets in complete anarchy. The Sunrise Manoeuvre, suggested by Italy as a multinational effort to restore law and order in Albania, began on 14 April and was relatively successful in preparing the minimal conditions for the next election.

The latest parliamentary election took place on 29 June 1997 and, not surprisingly, produced a total defeat of Berisha, who resigned after the election, and his party. The ASP had a landslide victory with a two-thirds majority, and so, on 5 July 1997, the parliament elected Rexhep Mejdani as president of Albania and he appointed Fatos Nano as prime minister, both from the ASP. The big question mark in the Albanian situation is, of course, whether this is just a change between the ruling parties of the same authoritarian style or a real turning point toward genuine democratization. First the unity of the country and public order must be restored in Albania, then reforms may be put in force. The international community tries to control the situation in Albania quite closely and directly, given the series of political setbacks, human rights violations, mass starvation and regular violence in the streets. A relative stabilization can be expected in the short term but for a serious transformation towards democratization and marketization one may have to wait many years to see a definite rupture with the totalitarian past in Albania.

To summarize this analysis of the Balkan developments, the first round of democratization can be characterized by three major features.

1 The violent character of political changes, such as the Yugoslav war, the Christmas revolution and suppression of dissent in Romania, and the 'hot summer' of 1990 in Bulgaria, or the Spring 1997 uprising in Albania.
2 The dominant character of nationalist efforts, both as the continuity of national-communism and the re-emergence of traditionalist, conservative right-wing nationalisms, due to delayed nation-building and to the still rampant ethnic tensions, for example in the Kosovo province.
3 The weakness of a modernization-Europeanization profile of political forces, or the underdog position of the political formations supporting this tendency in opposition to the provincialist-nationalist forces, with the result that left and right concerns are still secondary and the markedly centre–left or centre–right oriented parties are still conspicuously missing.

All three negative features were quite drastically changed in 1996–7. The new features of the second round of democratization can be summarized in the following points.

1 There has been a transformation from formalistic multi-party elections to real, free and fair elections. The Balkan countries have made a great stride to meet the minimal requirements of democracy. They have mostly eliminated electoral mismanagement, or at least the rampant electoral fraud that caused huge mass protests in Serbia and Albania. Free access to the media has been by and large assured in most Balkan countries, with the notorious exception of Serbia. People in the Balkans have been accustomed to genuine participation in the elections as

seeking peaceful political alternatives to the incumbent regimes, most prominently in Romania and Bulgaria.

2 The party formation process has reached a critical turning point. The successors of the former parties have undergone a deep crisis and made some efforts towards intra party reform. The original opposition umbrella organizations have been transformed into parties with a marked political profile (Bulgaria); or into more coordinated and durable organizations (Romania); or, at the least, a loose heterogeneous umbrella organization was finally born for a transitory period (Serbia); or, at the negative end of the process, both totalitarian successor parties have imploded (Albania).

3 More or less democratic constitutions have provided an institutional framework and political space for these positive changes. In general, political institutions have been democratized to some extent or democratic institution-building has reached the point where facade democracy has proved to be absurd and no longer tenable.

The major conclusion is that the Balkan countries may begin their real democratization in the late nineties. Events seen latterly in Romania and Bulgaria have been quite encouraging in this respect, and their impact may be felt sooner or later on the renewed democratization process of other Balkan countries as well.

Notes and further reading

1 In this short summary I cannot deal with the historical development of Yugoslavia, with the history of the war or with the peace efforts. I have focused on the emergence of the new states and their political structures.

2 The specificity of the Yugoslav political system among the state socialist countries has been analysed by many scholars, I refer only to the summary edited by Goati (1995). For recent developments in Yugoslavia see Carter and Norris (1996) and Dyker and Vejvoda (1997). On the more recent developments in the whole Balkan area see Dawisha and Parrott (1997b).

3 The reader is again referred to the Appendix to Chapter 5 for clarification of abbreviations.

4 There has been a great deal of literature produced about the independent Slovenia and Croatia. I refer only to the writings of Drago Zajc, Danica Fink-Hafner and Nenad Zakosek in Ágh (1994a), and Ágh and Ilonszki (1996).

5 Kosovo is a province in Serbia, predominantly (more than 90 per cent) populated by Albanians, and yet the Serbs claim it for themselves for historical and

emotional reasons. Thus, since 1986 Kosovo has also become the symbol of the Serbian nationalism.

6 There is limited literature on Bulgaria; see primarily Pundeff (1992), Bell (1993), Karasimeonov (1996a, 1996b) and Waller (1993).

7 Concerning Romania, the major works are Gallagher (1995), Gilberg (1992) and Almond (1988).

8 Petre Roman was one of the leaders of the NSF, who then, in 1991, turned against Iliescu. He carried on the name of the NSF in the September 1992 election in opposition to the DNSF of Iliescu, and later formed the Social Democratic Union, running successfully in the November 1996 election and becoming part of the new coalition.

9 The literature on Albania is very scarce; see Pano (1992) and Milojevic in Szajkowski (1991). Most writings are newspaper items.

Appendix: Summary of election results in the Balkans

Slovenia

Parties	Votes (%)		No. of seats		Seats (%)	
	1992	1996	1992	1996	1992	1996
LDP (LDS)	23.5	27.0	22	25	24.4	27.7
SPP (SLS)	8.7	19.3	10	19	11.1	21.1
SDPS (SDSS)	3.3	16.13	4	16	4.4	17.7
SCD (SKD)	14.5	9.6	15	10	16.7	11.1
ULSD (ZLSD)	13.6	9.03	14	9	15.6	10.0
SNP (SNS)	10.0	3.22	12	4	13.3	4.4

Croatia

Parties	Votes (%)		No. of seats		Seats (%)	
	1992	1995	1992	1995	1992	1995
CDC (HDZ)	43.7	45.2	85	75	70.8	59.0
CSLP (HSLS)	17.3	11.6	14	11	10.8	8.7
SDPC (SPDH)	5.4	8.9	11	9	8.0	7.1
CPR (HSP)	6.9	5.0	5	4	4.2	3.1
Coalition[a]	10.8	18.3	7	21	5.8	16.5
SNP (SNS)		1.0(-)	3	3	2.2	2.4

[a] The 1995 electoral Coalition consisted of PPC (HNS), CPP (HSS) and some smaller parties. I count here only the results of PPC and CPP in 1992.

Serbia

Parties	Votes (%)		No. of seats		Seats (%)	
	1992	1993	1992	1993	1992	1993
SSP (SPS)	28.8	36.7	101	123	40.4	49.2
Depos^a	16.9	16.6	50	45	20.0	18.0
SRP (SRS)	22.6	13.8	73	39	29.2	15.6
DP (DS)	4.2	11.6	6	29	2.4	11.6
DCHV (VMDK)	3.0	2.6	9	5	3.6	2.0

^a Depos was a coalition around the SRM (SPO).
The final results of the extremely fraudulent November 1996 election have not yet been published officially.

Bulgaria

Parties	Votes (%)			No. of seats			Seats (%)		
	1991	1994	1997	1991	1994	1997	1991	1994	1997
BSP (BSP)	33.1	43.5	22.2	106	125	57	4.2	52.0	21.6
UDF (SDS)	34.3	24.2	52.2	110	69	137	45.8	28.7	55.7
MRF (DPS)	7.6	5.4	7.5	24	15	20	10.0	6.2	12.5

Romania

Parties	Votes (%)		No. of seats		Seats (%)	
	1992	1996	1992	1996	1992	1996
DCR (CDR)	20.0	30.2	82	122	25.4	35.5
PSDR (PDSR)	27.7	22.2	117	91	35.5	26.5
SDU (USD)	10.1	13.7	43	53	13.2	15.4
DAHR (RMDSZ)	7.5	5.8	27	25	8.1	7.3
GRP (PRM)	3.9	4.1	16	19	5.1	5.5
PRNU (PUNR)	7.7	3.7	30	18	8.9	5.2

Albania

Parties	Votes (%)		No. of seats		Seats (%)	
	1992	1997	1992	1997	1992	1997
ASP (PSS)	25.7	53.4	38	118	27.1	76.1
ADP (PDS)	62.0	25.3	92	24	65.7	15.4

Parties	Votes (%)	No. of seats	Seats (%)
	1997	1997	1997
ASP (PSS)	53.4	118	76.1
ADP (PDS)	25.3	24	15.4
Others	21.3	13	8.5

Turnout 65.2 per cent, 155 seats

Chronologies

Transition in Yugoslavia

1 December 1918	The Kingdom of Serbs, Croats and Slovenes
6 January 1929	The name changed to Yugoslavia by the royal dictatorship
29 November 1945	Proclamation of the Federal Republic of Yugoslavia
28 June 1948	Expulsion of Yugoslavia from the pro-Soviet Cominform
4 May 1980	Tito dies
15 March 1989	Ante Markovic as the last prime minister of Yugoslavia
11 November 1989	Slobodan Milosevic re-elected as president of Serbia
20–23 January 1990	The last congress of the League of Yugoslav Communists
8 April 1990	The first multi-party elections in Slovenia
22 April, 6–7 May 1990	The first elections in Croatia
1 October 1990	Knin Republic of Serbs organized in Croatia
11, 18 November 1990	Elections in Macedonia
18, 25 November 1990	Elections in Bosnia
9, 23 December 1990	Elections in Montenegro and Serbia

1–2 March 1991	In Pakrac (Western Slavonia) start of war between Croatian police and Serbian–Yugoslav army
26 June 1991	Slovenia and Croatia declare their independence
27–30 June 1991	The short war in Slovenia
22–31 July 1991	The extended war begins in Croatia, in both Eastern Slavonia and the Knin region
15 January 1992	The EU member states recognize Slovenia and Croatia
6 March 1992	The start of war in Bosnia
30 May 1992	The UN Security Council declares a boycott against Serbia
26 May 1993	The Security Council establishes a court in The Hague to investigate war crimes in the Yugoslav war
4–7 August 1995	Croatia liberates the Knin region and the whole of Western Slavonia
7 August 1995	Tudjman's map on partitioning Bosnia published in *The Times*
21 November 1995	Dayton Peace Accords
23 August 1996	Croatia and the small Yugoslavia establish diplomatic relations

Transition in Slovenia

7 December 1989	Demos as an umbrella organization of opposition
4 February 1990	Slovenian Communist Party turned to Party for Democratic Rebirth
8 April 1990	The first free parliamentary elections
23 December 1991	The new democratic constitution and referendum on independence
6 December 1992	Second parliamentary elections
14 May 1993	Full membership of Council of Europe
1 January 1996	Membership of CEFTA
10 November 1996	Third parliamentary elections
17 February 1997	Janez Drnovsek's new coalition government

Transition in Croatia

17 June 1989	The Croatian Democratic Community founded
17 February 1990	The Serbian Democratic Party formed
22 April, 6–7 May 1990	The first free elections
19 May 1991	Referendum on independence
19 December 1991	Krajina Serbian Republic declares independence
2 August 1992	Second parliamentary elections
1 May 1995	Operation Blitz in Western Slavonia
4–7 August 1995	Operation Storm in Krajina

29 October 1995	Third parliamentary elections
24 April 1996	Full membership of Council of Europe offered
6 November 1996	Full membership of Council of Europe finally confirmed
16 June 1997	Tudjman re-elected president

Transition in Serbia

March 1986	Declaration of the Serbian Academy of Sciences and Arts on the 'discrimination' of Serbs in Yugoslavia by the Titoist regime
May 1986	Milosevic elected president of the League of Serbian Communists
1988	The 'anti-bureaucratic revolution' as a start for national populism
March 1989	The autonomy of Kosovo and Vojvodina dissolved in Serbia
2 December 1989	The Albanian Democratic League of Kosovo (LDK)
2 July 1990	The Kosovo parliament declares independence from Yugoslavia
16 July 1990	The Serbian Socialist Party (SPS) renamed
9 December 1990	The first multi-party elections in Serbia
9 March 1991	Mass demonstration in Belgrade against the personal rule of Milosevic dissolved by fierce police attacks (two people killed)
27 April 1992	The Declaration and Constitution of the 'Third Yugoslavia'
24 May 1992	Ibrahim Rugova elected president of 'Kosovo Republic'
31 May 1992	Federal elections, boycotted by the opposition and the Albanians
2 July 1992	Milan Panic prime minister of Federal Yugoslavia
20 December 1992	Second multi-party parliamentary elections in Serbia and presidential elections; Milosevic re-elected against Panic
19 December 1993	Third parliamentary elections in Serbia
14 March 1994	The Mirko Marjanovic government in Serbia
22 November 1995	UN suspends the international sanctions against Serbia
1 October 1996	UN lifts international sanctions against Serbia
3 November 1996	Federal parliamentary elections in small Yugoslavia
17 November 1996	Municipal elections followed by widespread mass demonstrations
November 1996–February 1997	'Hot winter' of mass demonstrations
21 March 1997	Zoran Djindjic, opposition leader, elected Mayor of Belgrade
23 June 1997	Zajedno, opposition alliance, disintegrated

| 17 July 1997 | Milosevic elected president of Yugoslavia |
| 21 September 1997 | Parliamentary and presidential elections in Serbia |

Transition in Macedonia

17 June 1990	IMRO reorganized in Macedonia
11, 18 November 1990	The first multi-party elections in Macedonia
25 January 1991	Declaration of Independence
28 January 1991	Kiro Gligorov elected president by the parliament
17 November 1991	Constitution of independent Macedonia adopted
8 September 1991	Referendum on independence
6 January 1992	Bulgaria is the first country to recognize Macedonia
8 April 1993	Membership of the UN
16 October 1994	Second multi-party and presidential elections
3 October 1995	Failed attempt to kill president Gligorov
12 October 1995	Membership of OSCE
9 November 1995	Full membership of the Council of Europe

Transition in Bosnia–Hercegovina

1463	The medieval Bosnian state occupied by the Turks
1908	Bosnia annexed by the Austrian empire
1918	Bosnia becomes part of Yugoslavia
18, 25 November 1990	The first multi-party elections in Bosnia
15 October 1991	Declaration of Independence by Bosnia
10 January 1992	Declaration of Independence by Serbian Republic in Bosnia
29 February 1992	Referendum on independence
6 March 1992	The start of civil war in Bosnia
6 April 1992	Recognition of the Bosnian state by the EU and USA
5 July 1992	Hercegbosna as a Croatian state in Bosnia emerges
9 November 1993	The destruction of the historic Mostar bridge at the height of the Muslim–Croat war in Bosnia
14 December 1995	Paris Peace Treaty signed
14 June 1996	Local self-government elections in Mostar
14 September 1996	IFOR controlled elections in Bosnia
6 October 1996	Bosnia and small Yugoslavia establish diplomatic relations
September 1997	Internationally monitored municipal elections in Bosnia

Transition in Bulgaria

1878	San Stefano Peace Treaty defines the borders of Greater Bulgaria
1879	Constitution of Trnovo
1913	The end of the Balkan wars
1923	Mass terror against Agrarians; Stamboliyski killed
16 April 1925	150 politicians killed in the Cathedral of Sofia as a revenge
January 1935	Royal dictatorship by King Boris
August 1943	King Boris dies unexpectedly
9 September 1944	Second World War ends in Bulgaria
17 November 1946	Georgi Dimitrov becomes prime minister
23 September 1947	Nikola Petkov, the Agrarian leader, executed after a show trial
2 July 1949	Georgi Dimitrov dies
14 March 1954	Todor Zhivkov becomes first secretary
8 February 1989	Podkrepa formed as independent trade union
13 April 1989	Ecoglasnost emerges as an oppositional movement
2 June, 22 August 1989	About 300,000 ethnic Turks expelled to Turkey
10 November 1989	Zhivkov forced to resign, Petar Mladenov follows
18 November 1989	The first mass demonstration in Sofia with 150,000 participants
7 December 1989	Zheliu Zhelev forms the Union of Democratic Forces
8, 15 January 1990	Demonstrations for the restoration of Turkish minority rights
16 January–12 March 1990	National roundtable talks
8 February 1990	Andrei Lukanov government
25 February 1990	The biggest opposition rally in Sofia (200,000)
3 April 1990	Bulgarian Communist Party renamed Socialist
10, 17 June 1990	The first multi-party elections
June–September 1990	'Hot summer' of mass demonstrations
6 July 1990	Mladenov forced to resign as president by mass demonstrations
24 July 1990	Mass strike (1,000,000 participants)
1 August 1990	Zhelev elected president by the parliament
26 August 1990	Street riots in Sofia, burning BSP headquarters
20 September 1990	Lukanov (BSP) re-elected as prime minister
23 November 1990	Opposition boycotts parliament
29 November 1990	Lukanov resigns after a mass demonstration and a general strike
7 December 1990	Dimitar Popov becomes the first non-communist prime minister
3 January 1991	Renewed roundtable talks for the peaceful transition
12 July 1991	New constitution adopted by the BSP dominated parliament
13 October 1991	UDF wins elections against BSP by a narrow margin
8 November 1991	Filip Dimitrov minority government without BSP

14–19 December 1991	BSP congress elects Zhan Videnov party president
12 January 1992	Zhelev elected president by a popular vote (52.85 per cent)
20 November 1992	Filip Dimitrov resigns; hangover parliament
22 December 1992	Luben Berov government
8 September 1994	Berov resigns
18 December 1994	BSP wins the third election
25 January 1995	Zhan Videnov BSP coalition government
27 October, 3 November 1996	Presidential elections, Petar Stojanov (UDF) wins
21 December 1996	Videnov resigns because of the economic crisis
January–February 1997	Mass demonstrations with some violent clashes
19 April 1997	Parliamentary elections, ADF wins
29 April 1997	Ivan Kostov ADF government with crisis management

Transition in Romania

1862, 1878	Gradual independence of Romanian duchies from the Ottoman Empire
1 December 1918	The 'unification' of Romanian territories
December 1933	The temporary liquidation of the Iron Guard (fascist organization)
February 1938	Royal dictatorship by King Charles
6 March 1945	Petru Groza government
30 December 1947	King Michael forced to abdicate
July 1958	Soviet troops leave Romania
19 March 1965	Gheorghiu-Dej dies, Nicolae Ceausescu follows
1968	The Hungarian Autonomous Region completely abolished
15 November 1987	Mass demonstration in Brassow
2 March 1988	Ceausescu Plan to destroy 8,000 villages
3 July 1988	US refuses the most favoured nation clause
7 July 1988	European Parliament condemns human rights violations
15–17 December 1989	Demonstrations in Timisoara
21 December 1989	Ceausescu addresses a mass rally which turns against him
22 December 1989	Popular uprising, Ceausescu escapes
22 December 1989	National Salvation Front formed
25 December 1989	Ceausescu captured and executed
25 December 1989	The NSF Declaration to the Nation
26 December 1989	Ion Iliescu, the NSF leader, controls the situation
26 December 1989	Petre Roman interim government
January 1990	Decrees of NSF as transformations from above
8 January 1990	National Peasant Party reorganized
10 January 1990	National Liberal Party reorganized
12, 28 January 1990	Mass demonstrations against the NSF

23 January 1990	The NSF declares it will run at the elections
28–29 January 1990	Miners attack the opposition brutally in Bucharest
6 February 1990	The NSF formed as a party
6 February 1990	Vatra Romaneasca formed as a cultural association
18–19 February 1990	Attacks on the headquaters of opposition parties; miners attack opposition in Bucharest
11 March 1990	The Timisoara Declaration
15 March 1990	The Party of Romanian National Unity formed
16–19 March 1990	Ethnic clashes in Tirgu Mures
5 April 1990	Bilateral Friendship Treaty with the Soviet Union
20 May 1990	Parliamentary and presidential elections, the NSF and Iliescu wins
13–15 June 1990	Student riot in Bucharest, miners oppress it with great brutality
28 June 1990	Petre Roman elected as prime minister
16 December 1990	National Convention for the Restoration of Democracy
16–17 March 1991	Split in NSF between Iliescu and Roman
15 June 1991	Greater Romania Party
26–27 September 1991	Miners attack opposition in Bucharest
27 September 1991	Petre Roman resigns as prime minister
October 1991	Theodor Stolojan government (non-party technocrat)
21 November 1991	New constitution passed by parliament
9 February 1992	The first local elections
27 September 1992	Second parliamentary elections
27 September, 11 October 1992	Presidential elections, Iliescu wins
17 November 1992	The EU and Romania initial an association agreement
18 November 1992	Nicolae Vacaroiu government
May, August 1993	Strike waves
15 July 1993	The Party of Social Democracy in Romania (PSDR, earlier DNSF)
7 October 1993	Romania becomes a full member of the Council of Europe
November, December 1993	Strikers demand the resignation of the government
14 September 1994	Romania joins the Partnership for Peace programme
20 January 1995	The GRP and the PRNU enter the government
2 June 1996	Local government elections
8 September 1996	Roman's SDU becomes a member of the Socialist International
16 September 1996	The bilateral basic treaty is signed with Hungary
3 November 1996	Third parliamentary elections
3, 17 November 1996	Presidential elections, Constantinescu wins
11 December 1996	Victor Ciorbea government

Transition in Albania

28 November 1912	Albania is declared independent
29 July 1913	The great powers recognize the Albanian state
21 January 1925	Albania is proclaimed a republic
1 September 1928	Ahmed Zogu becomes king of Albania
November 1941	The Albanian Communist Party formed
29 November 1944	Declaration of Independence
Late 1944	The communist-led National Liberation Movement takes power
11 January 1946	Proclamation of Republic of Albania with Enver Hoxha as president
28 June 1948	Break with Yugoslavia and purges of 'Titoists'
10 December 1961	Break with the Soviet Union and alliance with China
July 1978	The full termination of Chinese assistance
11 April 1985	Hoxha dies, Ramiz Alia follows
11 January 1990	The first mass demonstration in Tirana
10 April 1990	The AWP launches a cautious reform programme
18 December 1990	The parliament approves a multi-party system
19 December 1990	Albanian Democratic Party (ADP) formed by Sali Berisha
3–5 January 1991	Mass demonstrations in Albania
February 1991	Violent demonstrations continue ('Hoxha = Hitler')
31 March, 14 April 1991	The first multi-party elections
2 April 1991	Violent clashes in Shkodra and elsewhere
22 April 1991	The 'reform communist' government of Fatos Nano
11 June 1991	Ylli Bufi's national stabilization government as a coalition between the AWP and ADP, and other parties
19 June 1991	End of isolation, Albania joins CSCE
June 1991	The AWP changes its name to ASP
25 November 1991	Special guest status in the Council of Europe
16 December 1991	Vilson Ahmeti 'expert' government
1, 22 March 1992	The second multi-party elections, ADP wins
6 April 1992	Sali Berisha elected president
20 April 1992	The Aleksander Meksi ADP government
13 July 1995	Full membership of the Council of Europe (36th state)
26 May, 2, 16 June 1996	Third multi-party elections, the ADP wins amidst electoral fraud and intimidation
26 July 1996	The new Aleksander Meksi government
20 October 1996	Municipal elections
March–April 1997	Civil war in Albania
11 March 1997	Baskim Fino of ASP forms caretaker government
14 April 1997	Sunrise Manoeuvre of Western crisis management
29 June 1997	Parliamentary elections under chaotic conditions
24 July 1997	Fatos Nano government (ASP)

PART FOUR

CONCLUSIONS AND PERSPECTIVES FOR THE FUTURE

8

The Future of Democracy in East Central Europe and the Balkans

Summarizing the key turning points of transition

The short period of time since the miraculous year of 1989 has produced a Great Transformation in the East Central European and Balkan regions. The main turning points within this short time span were very marked – deep ups and downs breaking the monotony of the evolutionary process. These major changes can be briefly summarized thus:

1 There was a fierce 'decommunization' period with a turning point from communism to traditionalism which was overcome in ECE countries around 1993 and some steps have been taken to create a consensual democracy in these conflict-ridden societies.
2 In the mid-1990s a transition began in socio-economic developments from a vicious circle to a virtuous circle in the ECE countries which gives them a chance to reach a democratic consolidation in the next decade. Democratic institution-building has come to an end in ECE

countries and the new regimes in the Balkan countries have achieved some political stability. For the ECE countries this has meant a transition from 'democratization' to 'modernization'.

3 Democratic transition first produced a regional disintegration in the new democracies and only vague relationships with the EU. By the mid-1990s a transition had occurred in East Central Europe from regional competition to cooperation and some regional cooperation was visible even in the Balkan region. The associated countries have entered a pre-accession period, with some countries beginning negotiations about full membership in early 1998.

4 In late 1996 a new struggle for democracy was launched in the Balkan countries, partly as a reaction to the lack of democratization, partly as a result of the faulty economic crisis management. This turning point was the most marked in Romania, with a new president and a new government in the latest election, most spectacular and least successful in Serbia, with many months of long mass demonstrations in late 1996 and early 1997, and also clearly marked in Bulgaria after the Spring 1997 election and the immediate economic austerity measures of the new government. All these events give hope for further democratization of the Balkans, while Albania is still a political laggard.

Ethnic issues have played a very important role in these multi-ethnic, multi-cultural societies, so here we begin our summary. We then continue with the problems of political modernization and regional cooperation, and close our conclusions with the prospects for Europeanization.

Issues of ethnicity

We have discussed the transition from communism to traditionalism in greater detail as an authoritarian renewal, which was overcome in the ECE countries in 1993–4. This feature separates East Central Europe from the Balkan countries, which, even currently, suffer considerably from the problems of 'national communism'. It has been combined in the Balkans with a kind of traditional conservatism which has proved so far to be a major obstacle, if not a blind alley, in their democratization process. After the enthusiastic period of liberation from the Soviet external empire, as Michnik argues, 'the central political cleavage in Eastern Europe was no longer between left and right, but between those – primarily urban-based, secular, liberal progressive groups – who spoke of a "European potential" and who favoured an outward-looking and liberal approach, and proponents of an inward-looking and parochial obscurantism who emphasized the need for a revival of pre-communist, national traditions and cultures (often linked to the more conservative trends in Catholicism' (quoted in Hyde-Price, 1996: 62). The first group advocates a more

Westward-looking and Western-oriented policy and stresses a rapid transition to a market economy. The second group, in turn, seeks to protect the nation from the contamination of Western influence, and tends to pursue a populist policy which is suspicious of radical economic reform.

Western public opinion usually missed this new turning point towards 'traditionalism' to a great extent and maintained the old divide between the former ruling party and its opposition for many years afterwards. Hence, the West mostly failed to notice the danger connected with the authoritarian renewal and later, in 1993–4, mobilized against the 'return of post-communists', although in East Central Europe they belonged to the camp of Westernizers. Criticizing the Western common wisdom, Gabriel Partos wrote in 1995 that:

> The initial record of the post-communist Governments suggest that the once sharp distinction between ex-communists and the rest of the political establishment is becoming increasingly irrelevant. There has been considerable cooperation across the old divide. The main division that cuts across East-Central Europe's new political landscape is between parties that support radical or extreme forms of nationalism, intolerance and authoritarian rule as against those that espouse broadly liberal and pluralistic values. (quoted in Hyde-Price, 1996: 63)

The return of traditionalism-nationalism with its populist movements and parochial views, although it was overcome rather quickly in East Central Europe, still indicated a deep problem, that of ethnic minorities in the new democracies, and this problem has to be dealt with much more carefully in the Balkans. The importance of ethnic minority issues has also been realized by the European organizations, but with some hesitation and delay. In 1990 the Council of Europe organized a special commission to assist Central and East European countries in drafting new constitutions. This is the European Commission for Democracy through Law (often called simply the Venice Commission), which has drawn up its own 'Draft Proposal for a European Convention for the Protection of Minorities'. The European authorities have understood that the protection of national minorities has become a key constitutional and political issue in Central and Eastern Europe. In addition to the Venice Commission's proposals, the Parliamentary Assembly of the Council of Europe adopted an Additional Protocol to the European Convention on Human Rights 'Concerning National Minorities and Their Members' in February 1993. The Organization of Security and Cooperation in Europe (OSCE) has also established a post of High Commissioner for National Minorities, and has devoted considerable time and energy to the thorny issue of minority rights. Thus, there is a growing consensus in Europe today that effective legal protection of minorities' rights must be followed in order to defuse ethnic conflicts and lay a lasting foundation for peace on the European continent (see Hyde-Price, 1996: 192–3).

The situation of ethnically divided countries is not hopeless, with the cases of many West European countries having proved that there are a large number of legal-political devices for regional conflict resolution. The major difference between the two parts of Europe is not so much in the existence of the ethnic conflicts themselves, but in the application of constitutional, legal-political devices for political conflict resolution. The West European countries are also multi-cultural and multi-ethnic societies, but during the long decades of democratization most of them have successfully developed through these issues some constitutional and/or institutional solutions for conflict resolution and management. These legal-political devices have been almost completely missing in the 'other Europe', albeit there have been some efforts in Central Europe to implement them, but only the first steps have been taken so far. In the Balkans and Eastern Europe militant nationalisms have been confronting each other without meaningful constitutional restrictions which reflects the general backwardness of democratization also in the form of an ethnic 'tyrannical majority' forcing the minorities to the only escape road of separatism. Without democratization, however, national self-determination has also proved to be a blind alley, since in the newly independent countries of Central Europe and the Balkans – or elsewhere – the new majorities oppress the new minorities, sometimes even the former majorities, and this goes on and on.

Consequently, democratization and collective rights for all kinds of minorities are inseparable. The methods for conflict resolution in multi-cultural and multi-ethnic societies are too well known to neglect them, but in most cases the political will is missing to implement them. As the extreme cases have shown, in some countries ethnic cleansing has been used to 'solve' the problems of multi-ethnic societies in an effort to create a homogeneous nation-state. This suggests for political scientists that the narrow meaning of democracy – with only free and fair elections and democratically elected governments, based on a simple parliamentary majority – is not just theoretically insufficient, but also politically dangerous, since it legitimizes some regimes elected 'democratically' which otherwise softly or brutally oppress many kinds of minorities in the spirit of a 'tyrannical majority'. Originally, the assumption was that democracy was possible only in societies that are culturally and ethnically more or less homogeneous, like supposedly the British one. Therefore, the majoritarian model or Westminster type of democracy was taken not simply as the ideal case but also the only case for real democracy. The 'segmented' or 'plural', that is multi-cultural and multi-ethnic, societies were considered much less suitable for democracy, if suitable at all. This tradition glorifying majority rule as the only means for democracy – which, incidentally, has been counterbalanced in political practice by the British democratic political culture anyway – was discontinued in the 1960s and 1970s. It became clear that segmented and plural societies of smaller West European countries, with many ethnic and cultural cleavages, successfully developed a stable and efficient democracy as a new type of consensus democracy opposed to the Westminster model of majoritarian rule. The French model of the overcentralized and homogenized national state still haunts the ECE and the Balkan countries. The nationalizing and centralizing states in these regions, in fact, have been unsuitable for a genuine democratization, not only for their ethnic or cultural minorities but also for the citizens belonging to the ethnic-national majority.

The initiative to generalize the features of a consensus democracy into a coherent theoretical model came from Arend Lijphart in the 1980s, so the model was ready before the breakdown of authoritarian systems in East Central Europe and the Balkans, but insufficient attention has been paid to it so far by the policy-makers in these regions. We have already seen the contrast of the two – majoritarian and consensual – democracy models in general terms, clearly summarized by Lijphart. Now we have to draw some conclusions from his theory for the legal-political devices applicable to ethnic conflict resolution. Lijphart asserts quite clearly that in plural societies – that is, in the societies that are sharply divided along religious, ideological, linguistic, cultural, ethnic, or racial lines, so that they form virtually separate sub-societies with their own political parties, interest groups, and media of communication – the flexibility necessary for majoritarian democracy is absent.

> Under these conditions, majority rule is not only undemocratic but also dangerous, because minorities that are continually denied access to power will feel excluded and discriminated against and will lose allegiance to the regime.... In plural societies, therefore, majority rule spells majority dictatorship and civil strife rather than democracy. (Lijphart, 1984: 23)

The major legal-political devices in Western Europe for the democratic institutionalization of segmented or plural societies, in order to ensure the stability of democracy and to avoid minority conflicts, are the following.

Executive power-sharing: grand coalitions   The principle of a consensus democracy is to involve all the important parties – or most of them, even with a rotation – into executive power as a broad coalition of different minorities. The illustrative cases here are from Switzerland or Belgium. The Swiss seven-member Federal Council has the participation of four large parties and, at the same time, the linguistic groups in rough proportion to their sizes: four or five German speakers, one or two French speakers and one Italian speaker. The Belgian constitution rules that the government has to have an equal number of Flemish and Walloon ministers, with the possible exception of the prime minister, and this provision does not apply, of course, to the partisan composition of the cabinet. This executive power-sharing provides access for minorities to the real decision-making process and, therefore, strengthens both their interest representation and the political cohesion of the given country.

Balanced bicameralism and minority representation   The basic justification for the bicameral parliament is to give special representation to certain minorities in the second chamber. This model has a political function only if the second chamber or upper house has real power and senators, representing ethnic-national minorities or regional interests, can have a real say in the parliamentary decision-making process, as it is in Spain, Switzerland or Belgium. In all West European countries, cultural and ethnic cleavages have become more and the socio-economic ones less important in the past decades, therefore the organizations and representatives of the various minorities have also become much more significant (see Dogan, 1995).

'Multi-dimensional' party system with ethnic parties   In most West European countries not only large parties exist which represent the major socio-economic cleavages but – as parts of a 'multi-dimensional' party system – also middle-sized or even small ethnicity-based parties represent the interests of particular national minorities. (Actually, for example in Belgium and the Netherlands, the whole party system has been organized along ethnic-linguistic lines.) These ethnic-linguistic parties may have seats in the parliament or not, but they can formulate the vital interests of the given national, religious and ethnic minority in public life. If they have some access to the media they can express these interests clearly, hence, the rationalization of interests and their conflict resolution – so characteristic for the democratic polity – takes place in an institutionalized way.

Proportional representation in public institutions   The basic aim of proportional representation in a general election is to divide parliamentary seats among the parties in proportion to the votes they receive which also enables the smaller ethnic parties to gain parliamentary representation. But beyond this, the principle of proportional representation may be applied to all other public bodies, primarily in regional and local self-government, which facilitates communication and conflict resolution in a given region between or among different ethnicities.

Federalization and decentralization of powers   In multi-cultural and multi-ethnic societies, the federal structure of the state seems to be a better organizational principle of political life than the unitary state. Federalization, in fact, in smaller as well as larger countries like Austria and Germany, offers a possibility for further democratization by decentralization of state powers and gives more rights and duties to local–regional authorities. In the case of acute contradiction between or among ethnic minorities, only federalization with provincial governments can produce a stable and efficient democracy, as the Spanish case has shown where the alienation of regions and their populations from the central state has been solved by a meaningful federalization. Territorial autonomy for the ethnic minorities helps greatly to diffuse the conflict and separatism, as the case of South Tirol shows in Italy and Åland island in Finland.

Written constitutions and minority veto   Constitutions can usually be amended only by a qualified – two-thirds or more – majority, indicating the need for a large consensus concerning the basic rules of governance. This can involve the principle of a 'concurrent majority', that is, a majority emerging from the consent of different political minorities or parliamentary parties, but in the case of multi-cultural and multi-ethnic societies it can also include a *minority veto* by those ethnic minorities. A constitutional amendment in its major outlines can thus presuppose the support of the important ethnic minorities, or at the least, their power of veto if it hurts their fundamental collective and individual rights. This provision can be applied, of course, only to the vital issues for those minorities, which have to be clearly defined in order to avoid the abuse of these veto rights. However, the application of this device prevents not only the alienation of that minority in general, but also keeps confrontation from becoming total with armed fights or terrorism, which is the *ultima ratio* for minorities if their vital interests are hurt or they are excluded from a system of institutionalized interest representation.

These six cases – described following the criteria of Lijphart for consensus democracies (see Lijphart, 1984: 23–30) – comprise the most important constitutional and institutional devices used to contain cultural-ethnic tensions and solve minority conflicts in the Western world. These methods are very efficient in both already consolidated and in young democracies if the political will is there to implement them. Yet, even in the Western world there have been acute cases, like the Northern Ireland tragedy which has continued for many years as a failure of conflict management with a 'Yugoslav' scenario; and also the Basque or South Tirolian conflicts have shown some 'East European' features in former decades, before their successful crisis management. Again, the Western and Eastern parts of Europe in this respect differ, first of all in the application of legal-political devices for the resolution of ethnic, and/or religious and cultural conflicts, and not so much in the presence of multi-cultural and multi-ethnic societies. It is an optimistic presumption for East Central Europe and the Balkans, since it means that through the application of the West European constitutional provisions the democratization process can first ease, then solve the existing ethnic strife in this region as well.

   In the political practice of the ECE countries that are close to using the rational mechanism of conflict resolution, in fact, two other legal-political devices have been invented and applied which facilitate the integration of national minorities through their increased socio-political interest representation and democratic institutionalization.

Transborder regional integration   The transparency of borders and transborder activities are part of general democratic practice. In this case, however, a special region as a territorial unit has been formed to integrate all kinds of activities in the given multi-country region. The integration of transportation and communication systems, common efforts for environment protection and cooperation in trade and education, etc., etc. facilitate the contacts among the members of the national minorities separated by the borders. It relieves the burden of being separated and belonging to different national states and, by promoting civic activities and associations on both sides of the border, it solves the conflicts of dual loyalty. These regional integrations as the Alps–Adria region (from Bavaria across Austria to Hungary, including some parts of Italy) or the Carpathian Euro-region (embracing some districts of Ukraine, Poland, Slovakia, Hungary and Romania) accelerate local socio-economic development and make the national borders transparent for different kinds of minorities without changing the national borders and creating new frustrated minorities.

Minority representation in parliaments and local governments   Some ECE and Balkan countries have introduced a special system of parliamentary representation for ethnic minorities, granting them extra seats beyond the normal electoral competition. This system has been introduced in Poland and Slovenia with a genuine effort to open up the political space for minorities, and in a much more symbolic and less effective way in Croatia, Romania and Yugoslavia. Yet, even fake representation matters a lot as a point of departure to extend this system and give a real opportunity for smaller and larger minorities to have meaningful political representation in order to combine popular sovereignty with ethnic diversity (see Flores Juberias, in Longley and Zajc, 1997).

National minorities live sometimes in bigger enclaves, and sometimes in a dispersed way in distant communities. They exercise most of their collective and individual rights and duties, however, in both cases in their local communities and they need interest representation there. These organizations may be the base for the further institutionalization of minority rights at provincial and national levels. The Act LXXVII of 1993 in Hungary on the Rights of National and Ethnic Minorities seems to provide a good initiative for the solution of local government representation of minorities. There are two major types: first, settlement minority self-governments for the whole settlement where the majority of the population belongs to the same national-ethnic minority, and secondly, local minority self-governments for minority groups in a given settlement which take part in the workings of the local council, representing the interests of the minorities concerned. In the December 1994 local government elections these minority self-governments were elected in relatively large numbers and after these elections the 12 most relevant ethnic minorities in Hungary have formed self-governing bodies at the national level as well.

It is clear that democratization in the ECE and Balkan regions has also to include the solution of ethnic conflicts by granting rights to the national and cultural minorities. Furthermore, there are substantial connections between the inner nature of transition and the external, environmental factors which should be taken into consideration when we analyse the nature of the new regimes. Philippe Schmitter has put forward the suggestion that the way in which the new systems have emerged has determined the particular type of democracy in those given countries, that is, there is a correlation between modes of transition and types of democracy in the Central European and Balkan countries. The correlation between modes of transition (transitional problems) and types of democracy (systemic problems) can be grasped through the classification of various transitions. In other words, the genuine nature of different transitions appears through the concretization of the particular conditions that prevailed when the previous regime was overthrown.

Schmitter distinguishes transitions according to actors (elite or masses) and ways of change (peaceful or violent). These can result in four types: *pact* (by elite compromise), *reform* (by the peaceful pressure of masses), *imposition* (a constitution brought into force by the pressure of an elite, as a form of 'octroi' forced upon all from above) and *revolution* (by mass violence). These categories are very helpful for a classification of the Central European and Balkan transitions, although it is evident that in all cases the individual transitions were mixed, albeit with a dominant type. Pact and reform accompanied each other in Hungary, imposition and revolution in Romania, etc.

In Schmitter's model, pact leads to *corporative* democracy (where the state is active in interest concertation), reform to *consociational* democracy (where the heterogenous groups retain their relative autonomy and special activity versus the state), imposition to '*populist*' democracy (or rather, an *elitist* democracy, where elites dominate and the masses are passive) and revolution to *electoralist* democracy (where the masses keep some basic political activity and the state is not too active and strong). It is not too difficult to discover behind this model Schmitter's efforts to react to the debates in democracy theory and to summarize their results (see Schmitter and Karl, 1992: 67).

Participation and competition are the basic, 'primary' democratic values, involving the active *participation* of the population in the whole political process and free *competition* of (party) political elites. These basic values appear in the particular forms of 'secondary' or derivative values. In fact, the two axes of Schmitter represent them: the state–society relationships in political activities and the peaceful or violent forms of political competition (or those of seizing power). In his transition typology this leads to a vertical axis according to the levels of participation in transition (elite versus mass actions), or to a horizontal axis according to the forms of transition (compromise versus violence). In the democracy typology the same axes represent the structural elements of mature or stable democracies and this leads to four models in which participation and competition are combined in different ways.

1 **Corporative** democracy, in which (group) participation is high and the competition is reduced by the active and strong state (it is a functional democracy which dominates in this well-organized and well-articulated society).

2 **Consociational** democracy, in which competition is stronger (although restricted and regulated for the groups), and the state is weaker (all kinds of organized minorities take part in the socio-political life, all strata have representation and there are only concurrent majorities).

3 **'Populist'** (or elitist) democracy, in which competition is high among the elite groups but mass participation is very low (it is still a 'liberal', permissive state, but it is rather centralized).

4 **Electoralist** democracy, in which competition is also high but the political participation has been ritualized to some extent in general elections. Consequently, actual participation has been reduced to lower levels, to grassroots activities of the population.

These four types indicate four models of existing democracies:

1 socio-political articulation of particular interests (Austria, Sweden);
2 strong minority representation with veto power (Belgium, Switzerland);
3 dominant administrative state (France);
4 base or grassroot democracy in a 'weak', decentralized state (USA).

It is clear that all these versions are, in principle, only equal varieties of *mature* democracies. The different modes of transition to democracy or the types of *new* democracies, however, are not equal at all as far as their chances for consolidation are concerned. Schmitter himself points out that violent transitions are less likely to produce a stable and genuine democracy than negotiated transitions. Indeed, it is obvious that there has been a marked dividing line between the peaceful ECE transitions and the violent Balkan ones. Thus, violence itself reflects the immature character of the political actors and their interactions. It shows that the preconditions for democracy are missing because of the lack of strong parliamentary and party traditions in the Balkan countries.

As Schmitter indicates, the turn towards consensus and corporative types of democracy (for ethnic conflict resolution and for building partial regimes) is essential for both domestic democratic consolidation and for Europeanization, since unlike in Southern Europe the systemic change in the ECE and Balkan regions has altered the external circumstances as

well: 'Unlike in Southern Europe and Latin America, where democratization did not substantially alter longstanding commercial relations or
international alliances, regime changes in Eastern Europe triggered a
major collapse in intraregional trade and the dissolution of the Warsaw
Pact' (Schmitter and Karl, 1992: 49).

From democratization to modernization

In mid- to late 1990s we witness a return to economic growth in the ECE
countries under the conditions of newly emerging market economies. At
the same time, a new economic recession has entered the Balkan and East
European countries, hence the diverging nature of these three sub-regions
has become more marked. This has led to different political problems in
the two regions. In East Central Europe the emphasis has shifted from the
creation of new institutions to their effective workings and to the 'invention of democratic traditions' as a resurgence of civil society; and in the
Balkan countries to the partial destabilization of the new political order.
Economic growth has opened a positive, virtuous circle in East Central
Europe, that is, it has had a 'spillover' effect to social systemic change
which has run parallel with political-administrative modernization, and
with Europeanization.

In the literature of international political science democratization has
been a key word in describing systemic change, and rightly so. During the
initial period of systemic change quick and abrupt changes dominate,
which are reflected in terms of high-level abstraction such as 'democracy'
and 'systemic change'. We now find ourselves at a turning point and we
have to describe the changes we see more and more in terms of 'modernization', which is only a middle-level abstraction, indicating slow and
evolutionary changes following the 'great transformation'. Modernization as evolutionary change means continuous adaptation and innovation within the given polity, whereas systemic change means
transforming that polity fundamentally: democratization embraces the
political dimension and modernization the *policy* dimension of social
change. Modernization is much more practice-oriented, 'earth-bound'
and closely connected to the concrete social sciences, unlike the theories
of systemic change which are conceived and perceived in the spirit of an
ideological discourse. Administrative-institutional modernization is especially high on the political agenda for all ECE countries in the 1990s.

The modernization approach was significant in the ECE reform countries, Poland and Hungary, until the late 1980s, since it had two advantages at that time. First, it was oriented toward practical issues and
concrete social sciences instead of abstract ideological formulas, and secondly, although it did not necessitate a direct ideological confrontation
with the former regime, it could still argue for evolutionary changes.

From the late 1980s on these advantages turned more and more into disadvantages and the modernization approach was pushed into the background. Its role and place has been taken by a more ideologically oriented democratization approach with its exclusive practice in basic macro-political changes, which has itself produced a new disadvantage by neglecting complex socio-technical changes. By the mid-1990s a new turning point can be seen, namely the return of the modernization approach in East Central Europe. The major issues of institution-building are more or less over, and – although democratic institutionalization has not yet been completely finished – there is now an increasing need to deal with the all-embracing modernization process.

The structural adjustment to the EU, above all, also demands a modernization approach, since the ECE countries need a well-working democracy for full membership which is able to implement the 'key policies' of the EU efficiently. This transition to a modernization approach has been facilitated by the results of the democratization process itself. The legitimacy of the democratic regimes in the West is based on two pillars: the democratic procedures of the given polity and the efficiency of democratic rule which presupposes a constant political modernization and innovation process. The ECE countries have been democratized to a great extent so far, but they have hardly been modernized, therefore the new democratic regimes – parliaments, parties and governments – have worked at very low efficiency and have shown some kind of 'crisis of governability'.

This contrast between the rather well advanced democratization and the sluggish political modernization lagging very much behind, appears in a different way in the various parts of the ECE polities, and this contrast can be felt to some extent also in the Balkan countries. Democratization has been arranged in a more or less satisfactory manner in the Big Power Triangle, in the relationships of parliament – government – president of the republic as power centres. Here the contrast is very large indeed to the low efficiency of the workings of the new democratic polity, that is, between democratization and modernization. As far as the Small Power Triangle is concerned – that is the intergovernmental relations between central government, functional (or 'private') governments and local (or territorial) self-governments – the situation is even worse, since both democratization and modernization are lagging behind the Big Power Triangle. Democratization is still half-made, neither functional nor territorial interest organizations are developed and integrated enough, but their modernization is even more lagging behind. Hence, the need for transition from the great transformation to modernization can be felt here in a most marked way (Hesse, 1993: 219).

The extension of democratization within the Big Power Triangle to complete it, and even more to the Small Power Triangle to accomplish it, has two motivations which are equally important. One can argue about social justice and representativeness in the case of the organized interests, that is, they need and deserve the same treatment as political parties in democratic institutionalization to gain constitutionally regulated rights and duties as parts of the wider policy-making process, and so do the civil society associations. But we can also make a different argument, referring to the low efficiency of the present workings of the decision-making processes. Obviously, a major bottleneck in the decision-making process has been created by the system overload. This is not just because of systemic change, which necessitates many decisions being made to effect transformations in all social sub-systems. It is mainly due to the overconcentrated power structure which overburdens the central government, and also the parties and the parliament, but it does not leave any elbow room in the policy-making process for the social actors in their own sphere of action to participate in decision-making.

Democratization is, indeed, a prelude as well as a precondition for modernization, but a 'partyist' or 'partocratic' elite-democracy can also be an obstacle to modernization, even at the level of macro-politics. A multi-actor democracy involving meso-politics in the policy-making process, however, is not only more democratic than a 'partyist' or 'partocratic' democracy, but it is at the same time more efficient, since most of the problems and conflicts are solved on the spot and do not overload the macro-political system. In modern societies meso-politics (even more so the micro-politics at the level of the civil society associations) play a tremendous role in conflict management and it facilitates the workings of very complex social systems, already unmanageable by the state or government itself. Therefore, one has to look at the functions of the organized interests from the angle of their 'governing' or 'administering' roles. Without involving the interest associations in the decision-making process, whole political systems remain in danger of a permanent overload with issues, of being insufficiently informed and of lacking adequate support of social groups. Interest groups perform the functions of social integration that neither state nor market can serve. They organize membership and provide an aggregation of their interests, and this interest-creating role rationalizes the interaction between state and society. This *rationalization* hugely increases the efficiency of modern societies and a structured pattern of interest representation protects state or government from fluctuating and overwhelming demands from society. Democracy needs a set of social preconditions, and therefore rationalization of social conflicts is the core of democracy in its efficient workings.

Consequently, there is no further democratization without modernization as 'interest rationalization' and institutionalization of interest groups, play a self-regulating role in their own fields. This statement can be extended to all sorts of interest representations, not only to the functional, but also to the territorial 'self-governments', given the contrast between the limited 'regulatory capacity' of states and the increasing 'social complexity' in democratic transition. Moreover, this effort to create a multi-actor democracy coincides with those to establish a consensual democracy for the various minorities, and they reinforce each other. The real question for the ECE states and societies is not whether they need this interest rationalization and 'administrative modernization', but how it can be arranged. It has been coupled with a 'participatory revolution' in the ECE countries, not in political parties but in social organizations and civil associations in the 1990s. Tens of thousands of civil associations have been organized in each country from the early 1990s onwards, which have been very active at the level of civil society and have faciliated its efficient workings. These associations have also contributed to the 'invention of a democratic tradition', and with their increasing activity and the resurrection of civil society democratic consolidation gets closer, too.

We have described the initial period of systemic change in terms of overpoliticization ('politics running amok' we called it). In the analysis of political and socio-economic systemic change this period can be taken as a point of departure. No doubt, initially, political systemic change is the most important, and in some fundamental aspects it can be done quickly and demonstratively, with constitutional changes, founding elections and the emergence of new parties and parliaments etc. The phenomenon of politics running amok was based on this temporary priority of political change over socio-economic change and on the efforts of politics to retain this monopoly in the long run. Politics as a sub-system of society is meant to regulate and coordinate all the other sub-systems in that society, and yet still politics in this first period of democratic transition neglects socio-economic crisis management to a great extent and concentrates upon itself. This 'degenerate' and 'selfish' politics is a characteristic phenomenon in all ECE countries (and even more so in the Balkan countries), and has been reflected in the disillusionment of the populations and a turning away from politics after a very short period of euphoria and enthusiasm. It is not an exaggeration to say that politics even in East Central Europe has performed its role very much below expectation, although it has to be taken into account that the task has been too heavy and the expectations were too high. But a moralistic approach, the feeling of a national and/or a humanistic mission, pervaded the new political elite immediately after the power transfer and this intellectual 'fundamentalism' and voluntarism was a major reason for the failure by the new elite, which itself proved to be only transitory and has more or less completely disappeared from the political scene. The transitory elite was to some extent suitable for launching the democratization process, albeit with many contradictions because of its shortsightedness and historical arrogance, but this elite was completely ill equipped and intellectually unfit for the modernization process. The launching of a modernization process presupposes the clearing of both institutional and cultural deficits, that is, the completion of democratic institutionalization and the *professionalization* of the new elite, the political top elite as well as the policy sub-elites (organized usually in the ministries), and beyond, in meso- and micro-politics.

The professionalization of a new, extended elite and the rationalization of interests should go hand in hand. The political and policy lines (political or administrative institutions and decision-making processes) have to be clearly separated. Even in the same institutions, step by step a shift of emphasis is needed from the large ideologico-political considerations to the policy-making processes, from the political institutions to policy-making bodies, starting with the parliament as the 'mother institution'. This shift of emphasis would mean an introduction of the service function of politics in social and economic systemic change, a real 'triple revolution' (democratization, 'marketization' and nation-building as a combined process of reorganizing the society within a national framework), which is a precondition of the fourth process – Europeanization. Conversely, pressure for structural adjustment in the European integration process necessitates that such a triple revolution be fully carried out.

In the early 1990s most Western authors were, and some of them still are, rather pessimistic concerning social systemic change in East Central Europe and usually drew up negative scenarios only, with a 'breakdown of democracy' provoked by a deepening economic crisis and increasing populism. A 'vicious circle' theory has been elaborated in international political science regarding the Central European region. The theory of 'virtuous circles', that is a positive spiral between political, social and economic changes, has been elaborated to a much lesser extent so far, while obviously it has happened to Southern Europe, but has been thought to be a prerogative of this region only. This view produces not only an undue and unsubstantiated political pessimism, but is also a theoretical mistake. It neglects the opposite time sequences in the interaction of parallel processes of systemic change in East Central Europe. Namely, this view neglects those economic, social and political transformations which can be seen *first* in the vicious circle model but as we witness now, there comes a point where the virtuous circle model comes in, that is, there is positive rather than negative feedback among the different transformations.

The analyses of shortcomings and bottlenecks of social systemic change usually do not take into consideration the perspectives of positive feedback between the newly emerging social strata and their reorganized interest organizations in a new post-industrial society. They rather see the present (actually, the former) social strata in deep crisis and in an open contradiction with their existing interest organizations in an obsolete industrial society (see Slomczynski and Shabad, 1997). The real question is not whether the existing social actors can represent better the interest of the present social strata during the crisis of the industrial society (although in the short run this issue is also important, but has no solution in itself); the real question is how the ECE societies actually move toward a new social stratification, leading to the emergence of new social actors and identities that fit together in a new model, that is, how the logic and time sequence of mutually re-inforcing transformations, as positive feedback loops or virtuous circles, work in an emerging post-industrial society. At the present time politics is still changing the former social actors, but soon the newly emerging social strata organized as new actors, will change politics.

Nation-building, therefore, is not just a political process – organizing the national polity with its institutions – but also a social process where three questions will be decided:

1 Who are the citizens of the given country?
2 What are they entitled to as social rights?
3 How are they to be incorporated into a new social structure, within their social stratum and with their social identity?

Everything started in this respect with a social crisis which, in fact, had already ruined the 'old' society, not just the state socialist polity but also its oversized industrial society which was beyond repair. The failures of the ECE governments to consolidate the old industrial society (like the Lenin shipyard in Gdansk) prove that a point of no return has been reached. There is no society of 'peasant and working classes' any longer in East Central Europe. State socialism eliminated its class pillars by overprotecting them with state subsidies, without which they cannot survive at all. The ensuing social crisis catapulted social transformations forward and with them the emergence of a new social structure. Finally, the new social actors were to come not from the internal reforms of the present organizations directly, but above all from the demands and pressures of the newly emerging social strata, looking for 'interest creation and rationalization'. In the ECE countries the 'transformation recession' is over; some kind of 'cooperative modernization' might have been noticed in these countries as a combination of relative low wages with a developmental strategy, still preserving the social peace by some corporatist-type measures and through institution transfers from the West in the field of social conflict management. The social costs of transformation have been very high but it has paid off, not only in the regained economic growth but also through the implementation of Western methods and strategies in meso-politics, that is, in the relationships of social actors or organized interests.

This short summary of social systemic change – coupled with nation-building – has tried to prove that the social preconditions for democracy, going beyond the formal-procedural meaning of democracy, are essential for an efficient democracy (see also Comisso, 1997). The emerging new social strata and their new actors are about to create a multi-actor democracy where all the 'partial regimes' (Philippe Schmitter, 1995) are made ready for an efficiently working democracy, and these actors and partial regimes are, at the same time, the preconditions for the next stage of democratic consolidation. It is true that the rapidity and profundity with which the transformation is accomplished varies a great deal and diverse roads of development can be identified even in within East Central Europe, yet still the common features of the social and political systemic changes have dominated in the development of these countries. We have discussed so far the domestic developments in the period of mature democratic transition from the point of view of the preparation for democratic consolidation. We have to summarize now the international factors that facilitate this consolidation.

Regional cooperation and the prospects for Europeanization

In the early 1990s all ECE and Balkan countries desired to become integrated with Europe in general and with the EU in particular only in the form of a rather nebulous slogan: 'Return to Europe'. By the mid-1990s, however, the associated countries of the EU had designed ever more concretely their association strategies for the end of the decade. We can identify three periods so far in the intraregional relationships of the ECE, and to some extent the Balkan, countries. The first period was immediately before and during the collapse of the state socialist systems, the second in the first half of the 1990s and the countries have now entered the third period. The first period, in 1989–90, can be characterized by positive mutual feedbacks (usually called demonstration effects), through which Polish and Hungarian developments influenced those in Czechoslovakia and in the other countries (and later on vice versa). The cumulated result of all this can be referred to as the domino or snowball effect. It was a virtuous spiral, indeed, with euphoria and high expectations concerning the drastic improvements in the bilateral and multilateral relationships between the ECE countries. This naive hope was soon dissipated and in the second period the intraregional relationships worsened after 1992 and soon began moving in a vicious spiral. The counter-productive character of these actions turned out to be so clear that it has lately unleashed some opposite efforts, and these new endeavours point in the direction of a third period in the second half of the 1990s.

A negative-sum game between the ECE countries has appeared in and resulted from the following processes.

1 With the collapse of the former regime, which had involved close ECE cooperation in the framework of institutions (WTO, CMEA) that had been imposed on the area, the new elites turned away from ECE cooperation completely. In their search for legitimation they sought Western contacts exclusively (even in a naive effort to copy the West). There was also a naive hope of being embraced by the West individually, as when competing with each other for the title of 'best pupil' or engaging in a 'beauty contest' (see above all the Czech case).

2 The disintegration of the Eastern markets led to panic reactions on the part of the ruling circles and, as a result, to a further destabilization of each other's economies and currencies. This proved to be a self-fulfilling prophecy, because these ECE economies and national currencies were weakened by a drastic decrease in commercial contacts between neighbours and by a mutual refusal to accept each other's currencies.

3 The new transitory elites turned to the use of nationalist rhetoric, and to slogans and styles that were arrogant even by the standards of the ECE countries, that is, to the arrogance of 'we are different, we are much better than the others'. In this way the new ECE leaderships hoped to legitimize and stabilize themselves. The re-establishment of national sovereignty and the actual tasks of nation-building were overexaggerated, and the rising nationalisms, along with their official rhetoric, irritated their neighbours and provoked even more outraged answers. Thus, a vicious circle of mutual non-confidence was once again set in motion.

4 The transitory elites, in general, were inexperienced, awkward and ideologically oriented. They made many simple mistakes before being selected out, but carried on in this way until being humbled by dropping out of politics or losing at elections, or being removed by other political actors. This inexperience itself created numerous misunderstandings between the new states and their elites, and normal methods of conflict resolution have only recently begun to function. Western leaders themselves were also annoyed by the mutual accusations of the ECE governments against each other in bilateral talks or in international fora.

5 Regionalization itself, with an emergence of regional organizations, also showed similar 'infantile disorders'. These regional organizations were caught between processes that involved widening and deepening at the same time. The original Pentagonale has been extended to the Central European Initiative and has lost all the pragmatic functions of the Pentagonale, since it became a loose group of 16 states with an uncertain future. Therefore, a much smaller organization, the Visegrád group (VG), has emerged, with first three and later four members (Poland, the Czech Republic, Slovakia and Hungary), and this organization has been fighting with the problems of deepening, yet has been constantly threatened with the demands of too much widening. The CEFTA (Central European Free Trade Area) perspective has been quite promising for deepening even after a proper widening (in 1996 Slovenia joined as a fifth member) but the character and the priorities of this organization are still not yet clear enough. They became even more blurred after the Velvet Divorce in Czechoslovakia, albeit they may become clearer after the Spring 1997 'velvet crisis' in the Czech Republic.

The assessments of the Visegrád group or CEFTA vary a lot. Some consider VG a mere euphemism, or a form imposed upon ECE cooperation from outside (by the EU), which will collapse immediately if the EU gives up this 'team approach'. This EU approach, supposedly with common criteria for the whole group with regard to entry to the Union, might have been important in the emergence of the VG, but it was not the only reason. The EU hesitates even now between the team and the invididual approaches, but the VG as a waiting room of the EU has been a rather constant part of EU strategy, in which this regional *cooperation* is seen as a preparation for European *integration*. The prospects for political cooperation, however, look good again after the May 1996 parliamentary elections in the Czech Republic, and even more after the 'velvet crisis,' which proved the failure of the policies of Klaus in going alone and securing a Western priority through marketing rhetoric.

The increase of intraregional trade and other forms of regional cooperation in the mid- to late 1990s are good signs, and they point to the beginning of a third stage in VG interrelationships. However, the negative-sum game in linkage politics is still the biggest bottleneck for the ECE countries in their Europeanization process. There are different forms of overcompetition in the 'who is ahead of whom' game. Linkage politics includes both neighbourhood policies of the ECE states and mutual relationships between Western and Central Europe. The ECE region has been theoreticized from the very beginning in the spirit of the conflicting principles of competition and cooperation – or rather, as a contrast between easily observable overcompetition and the abstract goals of regional cooperation. The experts (and some outsiders) have argued for years whether the ECE countries *should* cooperate meaningfully. However, leading politicians have not listened to any 'rational', 'scientific' or Euro-centric argument and have followed their separate roads in a shortsighted way. The five CEFTA countries have had at least three major common interests.

1 Achieving full membership in the EU, since in this process they could harmonize their interests and develop a common negotiating strategy in order to enhance their bargaining power.
2 Promoting regional cooperation in trade, transport, health regulation, customs etc. by preserving existing contacts as neighbouring countries, as well as grasping the opportunities emerging from the new situation.
3 Preventing the spillover of the harmful effects coming from the collapse of the Soviet Union and Yugoslavia, and from the continued instability of the new Balkan and East European states (migration, internationalized crime, epidemics, smuggling etc.).

These three major objectives or common interests were subjected for some years to the dominant particularistic interests of each ECE country following the logic of the negative-sum game. Obviously no rational argument can convince national political elites to change their minds to switch from competition to cooperation, but two new factors can be brought forward in the real processes which will force them to change their political course.

First is the EU pressure in the sphere of 'high politics', meaning the continued exhortations of the EU authorities for regional cooperation in state-to-state relations or multilaterally, in the international fora. It is true that the EU authorities have not yet decided which strategy to follow: sometimes they argue that the ECE states can reach full membership more or less at the same time as a team, sometimes they suggest the elaboration of individual criteria for membership (EU capacity) and emphasize separate roads to maturation.

Second is the internal spillover coming from 'low politics', which refers to the dozens of practical issues (migration, travel, transport, health regulations, etc.) which demand a concertation of policies having common measures. However, these 'technical' spillovers have not yet reached a level of awareness which enables the coordination of policies as political packages between governments. In other words, they have been addressed on the *ad hoc* level, or only separate policies have been coordinated.

Elite (or party) competition and cooperation in conflict resolution is, of course, fundamentally different within one country or among different countries. Yet, this argument is instructive in two ways. First, competition and cooperation are not totally exclusive, that is, they belong together. If competition does not degenerate completely into a negative-sum game, then cooperation can offer a positive-sum game. Secondly, to some extent the transition to democracy can still be described as a political learning process of the ruling elites, nationally as well as internationally. The present stage of bargaining and compromise in East Central Europe has indeed been a real learning process for their elites in 'democracy studies', as a preparation for both competition and cooperation.

In the Old World Order (OWO) security was the magic word in international relations in its reduced, almost exclusively military meaning. According to this logic, Pentagonale had a 'security' function as a confidence-building organization between NATO, WTO and the neutral countries. In their present form the regional organizations, although the security dimension is still a major issue in and for East Central Europe, have less in the way of security functions than before. The ECE and some Balkan countries want full NATO membership and are very much concerned to achieve EU membership as well. The re-interpretation of this key word 'security' for Europe began in the early 1990s under the conditions of the New World Order (NWO). In the Eastern part of Europe, the NATO bodies were no longer facing direct military threat but an increasing economic destabilization and rising nationalism. It has been formulated by NATO that the major sources of security threat in the New World Order are the chronic and acute socio-economic instability and the conflicts involving national minorities. Otherwise, the military security dimension can only be provided for East Central Europe and some

Balkan countries by a multilayered system comprising pan-European (that is, OSCE), (at least partial) NATO, regional and bilateral organizations, assuming that there is no major military security threat from the East. If it were to emerge, the Turkization scenario would come in with a heavy emphasis on military security and conflict resolution and it would again, in this respect, take the form of 'command and imposition', this time by the Western powers.

EU integration and ECE regional organization do not exclude but presuppose each other. In general, globalization and regionalization are the two sides of the same coin: increased globalization means that different levels of regionalization have been strengthened. In a great effort to create a new philosophy for the New World Order, Börn Hettne describes the major features of the new regionalism, and this is very instructive for the ECE region as well. According to him the 'new' regionalism differs from the 'old' regionalism in the following respects. First, whereas the old regionalism was formed in a bipolar Cold War context, the new is taking shape in a more multipolar world order. Secondly, whereas the old regionalism was created from outside and 'from above' (that is, by the superpowers), the new one is a more spontaneous process from within and 'from below', in the sense that the constituent states themselves are the main actors. (see Hettne, 1994: 2–3). Hettne adds to these two features a third, namely whereas the old regionalism was specific with regard to objectives, the new is a more comprehensive, multidimensional process. The process of regionalization can be compared with the historical formation of nation-states with the important difference that a coercive centre is lacking in the process of regionalization which presuppose a shared intention among the potential members. The new regionalism also presupposes the growth of a regional civil society opting for regional solutions to local and national problems. The implication of this, emphasized by Hettne, is that not only economic, but also social and cultural networks are developing more quickly than the formal political cooperation at the regional level.

In the spirit of the new regionalism we have to investigate the chances the ECE and Balkan countries have to develop good neighbour relations, to enhance regional trade contacts and to elaborate common policies. The hope is that these actions in 'low' politics can be elevated to the ranks of 'high' politics as coordinated steps by the ECE states in Europeanization-cum-regionalization with the main impulse being to concert their strategies *vis-à-vis* the EU to reach full membership. Linkage politics suggests that the beginnings of internal consolidation and change in regional politics towards more effective cooperation should go hand in hand. As the South European transition shows, democratic transition takes usually 8–10 years, leading to a consolidation period. After this some more years are needed before the countries can create fully consolidated, advanced democracies. Obviously, for the ECE countries democratic transition would overlap more or less with the association period and later democratic consolidation with the accession period to the EU.

It is usual to discuss the relative backwardness of the ECE countries in EU terms and the tasks ahead of them to reach the Euro-capacity. It is right to do so, but the other side of the coin, the obstacles to their EU integration placed by the EU itself, has often been neglected. Some analysts, however, have made it clear that the EU has raised obstacles to integration of the ECE countries and needs to elaborate a new policy for accelerating this process of accession: 'Sadly, the enthusiasm and commitment in the Visegrád countries has not been matched by the West Europeans. On the contrary, the EU member states have responded to the historic challenge of reuniting a divided continent with a lack of imagination and a meanness in spirit which beggars belief' (Hyde-Price, 1996: 201–2). Hyde-Price points out that the EU has consistently failed to open up its markets in the areas where the East Central Europeans are most competitive, for example, in agricultural products, steel and textiles. Quite understandably, this has caused tremendous resentment in the Visegrád countries, who argue that they have largely eliminated trade barriers against Western goods, but are not only being denied free access to the markets they could best compete in, but are also being asked to open their service and financial sectors to competition from stronger Western firms. The result has been a growth in the EU's trade surplus with the former Warsaw Pact countries, from £2.50 billion in 1989 to around £4 billion at the end of 1993. Hyde-Price quotes here in his analysis the Report of the Vienna Institute for Comparative Economics, which has noted that, 'The widening trade and current account deficits are widely regarded as the major obstacles to the sustained economic recovery for the east Europeans.' One can observe, indeed, that in the late 1990s, 'The EU therefore faces a real test of commitment: is it prepared to support the reform process in Eastern Europe with more than rhetoric and statements of good intention?' (Hyde-Price, 1996: 202).

This is the other side of the argument which has to be taken into consideration when the chances of the ECE countries for both EU integration and democratic consolidation are investigated. In fact, the latest systemic change has proved to be global, it has shaken both 'East' and 'West', hence, its consequences cannot be limited to the ECE, Balkan and EE regions, they have also been extended to Western Europe as well. This can be seen in the present tensions within the EU in its post-Maastricht period, including the uncertainties in its policy towards the Eastern extension. These uncertainties could have also been seen at the June 1997 Amsterdam summit of the EU which, however, gave a green light to the start of negotiations about full membership in early 1998 for four ECE states (Poland, Czech Republic, Hungary and Slovenia). The ECE countries have returned to economic growth more or less on their own, so it can be realistically expected that the EU would provide for them that marginal plus which would accelerate this growth and facilitate its 'spillover' to socio-political developments in order to reach democratic consolidation. Altogether, these chances are very good, despite the above-mentioned obstacles of continuing benign neglect or unsatisfactory attention by the EU. As a result, in the political science literature dealing with East Central Europe there has been a definite turn from 'transitology' to 'consolidology', that is, a shift of attention from the problems of democratic transition to the preconditions of democratic consolidation (see, for example, Linz et al., 1995; Linz and Stepan, 1996).

In 1996 Larry Diamond rightly raised the issue 'Is the Third Wave Over?' He answers this question positively and argues that after the third wave the democratic states have a paramount interest to prevent the reverse wave, that is, the breakdown of still vague and fragile new democracies. The third wave has produced so far three kinds of democracies, according to Diamond:

1 pseudo-democracies, where there are legal opposition parties and some other constitutional features of democracy but this system fails to meet one of the crucial requirements of democracy, that is, to provide a fair arena of contestation to allow for the ruling party to be turned out of power;
2 semi-democracies, as an extension of the above type with more constitutional rights, but the hegemonic party system is still able to reproduce itself through a series of elections, also minority rights are not sufficiently protected;
3 liberal democracies, with party alternation in government and, what is especially important for the ECE and the Balkan regions, 'Cultural, ethnic, religious and other minority groups, as well as traditionally disadvantaged or unempowered majorities, are not prohibited (legally or in practice) from expressing their interests in the political process, and from using their language and culture' (Diamond, 1996: 23).

These two major criteria, i.e. a real chance of alternating power between government and opposition on one side and the free political expression of minority rights on the other, have proved to be the crucial issues in the ECE and Balkan regions as well. We have described these three types of democracies: the liberal democracy in Poland, the Czech Republic, Hungary and Slovenia; the semidemocracy in Slovakia, Croatia, Macedonia, Romania and Bulgaria; and the pseudo-democracy in Serbia and Albania — although after the November 1996 elections a real democratization process began in Romania and after the April 1997 elections in Bulgaria. Actually, it is very difficult to make a distinction between the second and third groups because some countries are in-between, and/or moving in different directions; in the last years, for example, Slovakia has become more authoritarian and Romania more democratic. The stabilization of these kinds of liberal and semi-democracies, at least in the present form, is a basic interest of the leading democratic powers, which means also some opportunities for each type to develop, including the progress from the lower types to the higher ones. Larry Diamond predicts a fourth wave of democratization in the first two decades of the twenty-first century which will bring, obviously, not only a further extension of democratization to new regions, but also the upgrading of new democracies in the ECE, Balkan and EE regions. It means a stage of democratic consolidation for the countries of East Central Europe and a further step towards liberal democracy for the Balkan and East European states.

Bibliography

Ágh, Attila (ed.) (1994a) *The Emergence of East Central European Parliaments: The First Steps*, Budapest: Hungarian Centre for Democracy Studies.

Ágh, Attila (1994b) 'The Hungarian Party System and Party Theory in the Transition of Central Europe', *Journal of Theoretical Politics*, vol. 6, no. 2, April.

Ágh, Attila (1995a) 'The Transition to Democracy in Central Europe: A Comparative View', in G. Pridham (ed.), *Transitions to Democracy*, Aldershot: Dartmouth.

Ágh, Attila (1995b) 'The "Comparative Revolution" and the Transition in Central and Southern Europe', in. G. Pridham (ed.), *Transitions to Democracy*, Aldershot: Dartmouth.

Ágh, Attila and Gabriella Ilonszki (eds) (1996) *Parliaments and Organized Interests in Central Europe: The Second Steps*, Budapest: Hungarian Centre for Democracy Studies.

Ágh, Attila and Sándor Kurtán (eds) (1995) *Democratization and Europeanization in Hungary: The First Parliament, 1990–1994*, Budapest: Hungarian Centre for Democracy Studies.

Ágh, Attila, László Szarvas and László Vass (1995) 'The Europeanization of Hungarian Polity', in Attila Ágh and Sándor Kurtán (eds), *Democratization and Europeanization in Hungary: The First Parliament, 1990–1994*, Budapest: Hungarian Centre for Democracy Studies.

Almond, Mark (1988) *Decline without Fall: Romania under Ceausescu*, London: Institute for European Defence and Strategic Studies.

Ash, Timothy Garton (1990) *We The People: The Revolutions of '89 Witnessed in Warsaw, Budapest, Berlin and Prague*, Cambridge: Granta Books.

Bartlett, David (1996) 'Democracy, Institutional Change, and Stabilisation Policy in Hungary', *Europe-Asia Studies*, vol. 48, no. 1.

Bartolini, Stefano and Peter Mair (eds) (1984) *Party Politics in Contemporary Western Europe*, London: Frank Cass.

Batt, Judy (1991) *East Central Europe from Reform to Transformation*, London: Pinter Publishers.

Bell, John (1993) 'Bulgaria', in Stephen White, Judy Batt and Paul Lewis (eds), *Developments in East European Politics*, Durham: Duke University Press.

Bermeo, Nancy (ed.) (1992) *Liberalization and Democratization: Change in the Soviet Union and Eastern Europe*, Baltimore, MD and London: Johns Hopkins University Press.

Bielasiak, Jack (1997) 'Substance and Process in the Development of Party Systems in East Central Europe', *Communist and Post-Communist Studies*, vol. 30, no. 1.

Blackburn, Robin (ed.) (1991) *After the Fall: The Failure of Communism and the Future of Socialism*, London and New York: Verso.

Bonime-Blanc, Andrea (1987) *Spain's Transition to Democracy: The Politics of Constitution-Making*, Boulder, CO: Westview Press.

Bozóki, András, András Körösényi and George Schöpflin (eds) (1992) *Post-Communist Transition: Emerging Pluralism in Hungary*, London: Pinter Publishers.

Brokl, Vladimir and Zdenka Mansfeldová (1993, 1994, 1995) 'Czechoslovakia' and 'Czech Republic', *European Journal of Political Research*, vol. 24, no. 4; vol. 26, nos 3–4; vol. 28, nos. 3–4. *Political Data Yearbook: 1993, 1994, 1995*.

Brown, James (1994) *Hopes and Shadows: Eastern Europe after Communism*, Durham, NC: Duke University Press.

Brubaker, Rogers (1995) 'National Minorities, Nationalizing States, and External National Homelands in the New Europe', *Daedalus*, vol. 124, no. 2.

Bryant, Christopher and Edmund Mokrzyczki (eds) (1994) *The Great Transformation? Change and Continuity in East-Central Europe*, London and New York: Routledge.

Budge, Ian and David McKay (eds) (1994) *Developing Democracy*, London: Sage.

Budge, Ian, Kenneth Newton and R.D. McKinley (eds) (1997) *The Politics of the New Europe*, London and New York: Longman.

Bugajski, Janusz (1995a) *Ethnic Politics in Eastern Europe: A Guide to Nationality Policies, Organizations, and Parties*, Armonk, NY: M.E. Sharpe.

Bugajski, Janusz (1995b) *Nations in Turmoil: Conflict and Cooperation in Eastern Europe*, Boulder, CO: Westview Press.

Bútora, Martin and Zora Bútorová (1993) 'Slovakia after the Split', *Journal of Democracy*, vol. 4, no. 2.

Carpenter, Michael (1997) 'Slovakia and the Triumph of Nationalist Populism', *Communist and Post-Communist Studies*, vol. 30, no. 2.

Carter, F.W. and H.T. Norris (eds) (1996) *Changing Shape of the Balkans*, London: University College of London.

Chirot, Daniel (ed.) (1991) *The Crisis of Leninism and the Decline of the Left: The Revolutions of 1989*, Seattle, WA and London: University of Washington Press.

Cichy, Michal (1996) 'Requiem for the Moderate Revisionist' (with a 'Letter to the Editor' written by Andrzej Tymowski), *East European Politics and Societies*, vol. 10, no. 1.

Collier, David and Steven Levitsky (1996) *Democracy 'with Adjectives': Conceptual Innovation in Comparative Research*, Working Paper, The Kellogg Institute, Southbend, IN: University of Notre Dame.

Comisso, Ellen (1991) 'Political Coalitions, Economic Choices', *Journal of International Affairs*, vol. 45, no. 1.

Comisso, Ellen (1997) 'Is the Glass Half Full or Half Empty? Reflections on Five Years of Competitive Politics in Eastern Europe', *Communist and Post-Communist Studies*, vol. 30, no. 1.

Cox, Terry and Andy Furlong (eds) (1995) *Hungary: The Politics of Transition*, London: Frank Cass.

Crampton, Richard and Ben Crampton (1996) *Atlas of Eastern Europe in the Twentieth Century*, London and New York: Routledge.

Dahl, Robert (1971) *Polyarchy, Participation and Oppression*, New Haven and London: Yale University Press.

Dahl, Robert (1989) *Democracy and Its Critics*, New Haven and London: Yale University Press.

Dahrendorf, Ralf (1990) *Reflections on the Revolution in Europe*, London: Chatto and Windus.

Dawisha, Karen (1990) *Eastern Europe, Gorbachev and Reform*, Cambridge: Cambridge University Press.

Dawisha, Karen and Bruce Parrott (eds) (1997a) *The Consolidation of Democracy in East-Central Europe*, Cambridge: Cambridge University Press.

Dawisha, Karen and Bruce Parrott (eds) (1997b) *Politics, Power, and the Struggle for Democracy in South-East Europe*, Cambridge: Cambridge University Press.

Diamond, Larry (1996) 'Is the Third Wave Over?', *Journal of Democracy*, vol. 7, no. 3.

Diamond, Larry and Marc Plattner (eds) (1993) *The Global Resurgence of Democracy*, Baltimore, MD and London: Johns Hopkins University Press.

Di Palma, Giuseppe (1990) *To Craft Democracies: An Essay on Democratic Transitions*, Berkeley, CA: University of California Press.

Dix, Robert (1994) 'History and Democracy Revisited', *Comparative Politics*, vol. 27, no. 1, October.

Djordjevic, Dimitrije (1992) 'The Yugoslav Phenomenon', in Joseph Held (ed.) *The Columbia History of Eastern Europe in the Twentieth Century*, New York: Columbia University Press.

Dogan, Mattei (1995) 'Erosion of Class Voting and of the Religious Vote in Western Europe', *International Social Science Journal*, no. 146 (December).

Dyker, D.A. and I. Vejvoda (eds) (1997) *Yugoslavia and After: A Study in Fragmentation, Despair and Rebirth*, London and New York: Longman.

East, Roger (1992) *Revolutions in Eastern Europe*, London and New York: Pinter Publishers.

The Economist (1993) 'Looking Back from 2992: The Disastrous 21st Century', 26 December 1992–8 January 1993, pp. 17–19.

Evans, Geoffrey and Stephen Whitefield (1995) 'The Economic Ideology and Political Success: Communist-Successor Parties in the Czech Republic, Slovakia and Hungary Compared', *Party Politics*, vol. 1, no. 4.

Flores Juberias, Carlos (1995) 'The Transformation of Electoral Systems in Eastern Europe and its Political Consequences', *Journal of Constitutional Law in Eastern and Central Europe*, vol. 2, no. 1.

Flores Juberias, Carlos (1997) 'The Parliamentary Representation of Ethnic Minorities in Eastern Europe', in Lawrence Longley and Drago Zajc (eds), *The Parliaments of Young Democracies*, Appleton, WI: IPSA Research Committee of Legislative Specialists.

Gallagher, Tom (1995) *Romania after Ceausescu: The Politics of Intolerance*, Edinburgh: Edinburgh University Press.

Gilberg, Trond (1992) 'The Multiple Legacies of History: Romania in the Year 1990', in Joseph Held (ed.), *The Columbia History of Eastern Europe in the Twentieth Century*, New York: Columbia University Press.

Giordan, Henri (1994) *Multicultural and Multiethnic Societies*, Discussion paper series No. 1, Management of Social Transformations (MOST), Paris: Unesco.

Glenny, Misha (1990) *The Rebirth of History: Eastern Europe in the Age of Democracy*, London: Penguin Books.

Goati, Vladimir (ed.) (1995), *Challenges of Parliamentarism: The Case of Serbia in the Early Nineties*, Belgrade: Institute of Social Sciences.

Goldfarb, Jeffrey (1992) *After the Fall: The Pursuit of Democracy in Central Europe*, New York: Basic Books.

González Enríquez, Carmen (1995a) 'Electoral Systems and Political Stability in Central and Eastern Europe', *Budapest Papers on Democratic Transition*, no. 132.

González Enríquez, Carmen (1995b) 'Electoral Behaviour in Central and Eastern Europe', *Budapest Papers on Democratic Transition*, no. 148.

Gray, Victor (1996) 'Identity and Democracy in the Baltics', *Democratization*, vol. 3, no. 2, Summer 1996.

Griffith, William (ed.) (1989) *Central and Eastern Europe: The Opening Curtain?*, Boulder, CO: Westview Press.

Gunther, Richard, Nikiforos Diamandouros and Hans-Jürgen Puhle (eds) (1995) *The Politics of Democratic Consolidation: Southern Europe in Comparative Perspective*, Baltimore, MD and London: Johns Hopkins University Press.

Haggard, Stephan and Robert Kaufmann (1994) 'The Challenges of Consolidation', *Journal of Democracy*, vol. 5, no. 4.

Hankiss, Elemér (1990) *East European Alternatives*, Oxford: Clarendon Press.

Held, Joseph (ed.) (1992) *The Columbia History of Eastern Europe in the Twentieth Century*, New York: Columbia University Press.

Hesse, Joachim Jens (ed.) (1993) *Administrative Transformations in Central and Eastern Europe: Towards Public Sector Reform in Post-Communist Societies*, Oxford: Blackwell.

Hesse, Joachim Jens and Nevil Johnson (eds) (1995) *Constitutional Policy and Change in Europe*, Oxford and New York: Oxford University Press.

Hettne, Björn (1994) *The New Regionalism*, Tokyo: The United Nations University.

Hill, Ronald (1994) 'Democracy in Eastern Europe' in Ian Budge and David McKay (eds), *Developing Democracy*, London: Sage.

Hockenos, Paul (1993) *Free to Hate: The Rise of the Right in Post-Communist Eastern Europe*, New York and London: Routledge.

Holmes, Leslie (1997) *Post-Communism: An Introduction*, Cambridge: Polity Press.

Howard, Dick (ed.) (1993) *Constitution Making in Eastern Europe*, Washington, DC: The Woodrow Wilson Center Press.

Hudecek, Jaroslav, Zdenka Mansfeldová and Lubomir Brokl Mansfeldová (1992) 'Czechoslovakia', *European Journal of Political Research*, vol. 22, No. 4 (*Political Data Yearbook: 1992*) vol. 22, no. 4.

Huntington, Samuel (1991) *The Third Wave: Democratization in the Late Twentieth Century*, Norman, OK and London: University of Oklahoma Press.

Huntington, Samuel (1996) *The Clash of Civilizations and the Remaking of World Order*, New York: Simon and Schuster.

Hyde-Price, Adrian (1996) *The International Politics of East Central Europe*, Manchester and New York: Manchester University Press.

Ilonszki, Gabriella and Sándor Kurtán (1992, 1993, 1994, 1995) 'Hungary', *European Journal of Political Research*, vol. 22, no. 4; vol. 24, no. 4; vol. 26, nos 3–4; vol. 28, nos 3–4 (*Political Data Yearbook: 1992, 1993, 1994, 1995*).

Janos, Andrew (1982) *The Politics of Backwardness, 1825–1945*, Princeton, NJ: Princeton University Press.

Jasiewicz, Krzysztow (1992, 1993a, 1994, 1995) 'Poland', *European Journal of Political Research*, vol. 22, no. 4; vol. 24, no. 4; vol. 26, nos 3–4; vol. 28, nos 3–4 (*Political Data Yearbook 1992, 1993, 1994, 1995*).

Jasiewicz, Krzystow (1993b) 'Structures of Representation', in Stephen White, Judy Batt and Paul Lewis (eds), *Developments in East European Politics*, Durham, NC: Duke University Press.

Jowitt, Ken (1992) *New World Disorder: The Leninist Extinction*, Berkeley, CA: The University of California Press.

Kaminski, Bartlomiej (1991) *The Collapse of State Socialism: The Case of Poland*, Princeton, NJ: Princeton University Press.

Karasimeonov, Georgi (1996a) 'Bulgaria's New Party System', in G. Pridham and Paul Lewis (eds), *Stabilising Fragile Democracies*, London and New York: Routledge.

Karasimeonov, Georgi (1996b) 'The Legislature in Post-Communist Bulgaria', in David Olson and Philip Norton (eds), *The New Parliaments of Central and Eastern Europe*, London, Frank Cass.

Katz, Richard and Peter Mair (eds) (1994) *How Parties Organize*, London: Sage.

Katz, Richard and Peter Mair (1995) 'Changing Models of Party Organization and Party Democracy: The Emergence of the Cartel Party', *Party Politics*, vol. 1, no. 4.

Király, Béla (ed.) (1995) *Lawful Revolution in Hungary, 1989–94*, Boulder, CO: Atlantic Publications (distributed by Columbia University Press, New York).

Kitschelt, Herbert (1992) 'The Formation of Party Systems in East Central Europe', *Politics and Society*, vol. 20, no. 1.

Kitschelt, Herbert (1995) 'Formation of Party Cleavages in Post-Communist Democracies: Theoretical Propositions', *Party Politics*, vol. 1, no. 4.

Kopecky, Petr (1995) 'Developing Party Organizations in East-Central Europe', *Party Politics*, vol. 1, no. 4.

Kornai, János (1989) *The Road to a Free Economy, Shifting from a Socialist System: The Example of Hungary*, New York: Norton and Company.

Kornai, János (1992) *The Socialist System: The Political Economy of Communism*, Princeton: Princeton University Press.

Kornai, János (1993) *Transformational Recession*, Discussion Paper no. 1, Budapest: Collegium Budapest.

Kramer, Mark (1995) 'Polish Workers and the Post-Communist Transition, 1989–1993', *Communist and Post-Communist Studies*, vol. 28, no. 1.

Lane, Jan-Erik and Svante Ersson (1987) *Politics and Society in Western Europe*, London: Sage.

Lane, Jan-Erik and Svante Ersson (1996) *European Politics*, London: Sage.

Leska, Dushan and Viera Koganová (1995) 'The Elections 1994 and Crystallization of Political Parties and Movements in Slovakia', in Sonja Szomolányi and Grigorij Meseznikov (eds), *Slovakia: Parliamentary Elections 1994*, Bratislava: Slovak Political Science Association.

Lewis, Paul (1994a) *Central Europe since 1945*, London and New York: Longman.

Lewis, Paul (1994b) 'Political Institutionalisation and Party Development in Post-Communist Poland', *Europe-Asia Studies*, vol. 46, no. 5.

Liebert, Ulrike and Maurizio Cotta (eds) (1990) *Parliament and Democratic Consolidation in Southern Europe*, London and New York: Pinter Publishers.

Lijphart, Arend (1984) *Democracies: Patterns of Majoritarian and Consensus Government in Twenty-One Countries*, New Haven, CT and London: Yale University Press.

Linz, Juan (1978) *The Breakdown of Democratic Regimes*, Baltimore, MD and London: Johns Hopkins University Press.

Linz, Juan and Alfred Stepan (1996) *Problems of Democratic Transition and Consolidation*, Baltimore, MD and London: Johns Hopkins University Press.

Linz, Juan and Arturo Valenzuela (eds) (1994) *The Failure of Presidential Democracy: Comparative Perspectives*, vol. 1, Baltimore, MD and London: Johns Hopkins University Press.

Linz, Juan, Alfred Stepan and Richard Gunther (1995) 'Democratic Transition and Consolidation in Southern Europe, with Reflections on Latin America and

Eastern Europe', in Richard Gunther, Nikiforos Diamandouros and Hans-Jürgen Puhle (eds), *The Politics of Democratic Consolidation: Southern Europe in Comparative Perspective*, Baltimore, MD and London: Johns Hopkins University Press.

Longley, Lawrence and Attila Ágh (eds) (1997) *The Changing Role of Parliamentary Committees* (Working Papers on Comparative Legislative Studies II), Appleton, WI: IPSA Research Committee of Legislative Specialists.

Longley, Lawrence and Drago Zajc (eds) (1997) *The Parliaments of Young Democracies* (Working Papers on Comparative Legislative Studies III), Appleton, WI: IPSA Research Committee of Legislative Specialists.

Luif, Paul (1995) *On the Road to Brussels: The Political Dimension of Austria's, Finland's and Sweden's Accession to the European Union*, Vienna, Braumüller (for the Austrian Institute for International Affairs).

Magocsi, Paul Robert (1995) *Historical Atlas of East Central Europe* (*A History of East Central Europe*, vol. I), Seattle, WA and London: University of Washington Press.

Mair, Peter (ed.) (1990) *The West European Party System*, Oxford: Oxford University Press.

Malova, Darina (1994, 1995) 'Slovakia', *European Journal of Political Research*, vol. 26, nos 3–4; vol. 28, nos 3–4. (*Political Data Yearbook 1994, 1995*).

Mansfeldová, Zdenka (1996) 'The Pluralistic System of Interest Representation in Czech Society', in Szabó, Máté (ed.), *The Challenge of Europeanization in the Region: East Central Europe*, Budapest: Hungarian Political Science Association.

Mansfeldová, Zdenka (1997) 'The First Czech Parliament in the View of the Members of Parliament', in Lawrence Longley and Drago Zajc (eds), *The Parliaments of Young Democracies*, Appleton, WI: IPSA Research Committee of Legislative Specialists.

Mason, David (1993) 'Poland', in Stephen White, Judy Batt and Paul Lewis (eds), *Developments in East European Politics*, Durham, NC: Duke University Press.

McCarthy, Paul (1997) 'Serbia's Opposition Speaks', *Journal of Democracy*, vol. 8, no. 3.

Meseznikov, Grigorij (1995) 'The Parliamentary Elections 1994: A Confirmation of the Split of the Party System in Slovakia', in Sonja Szomolányi and Grigorij Meseznikov (eds), *Slovakia: Parliamentary Elections 1994*, Bratislava: Slovak Political Science Association.

Michnik, Adam (1994) 'A lengyel krétakör' (The Polish Chalkcircle), *Mozgó Világ* (Budapest), vol. 15, no. 3.

Musil, Jiri (ed.) (1996) *The End of Czechoslovakia*, Budapest, London and New York: Central European University Press.

O'Donnell, Guillermo, Philippe Schmitter and Laurence Whitehead (eds) (1986) *Transitions from Authoritarian Rule* (4 vols), Baltimore, MD and London: Johns Hopkins University Press.

Offe, Claus (1991) 'Capitalism by Democratic Design? Democratic Theory Facing the Triple Transition in East Central Europe', *Social Research*, vol. 58, no. 4.

Olson, David (1993) 'Political Parties and Party Systems in Regime Transformation: Inner Transition in the New Democracies of Central Europe', *American Review of Politics*, vol. 14, (Winter).

Olson, David (1994) 'The New Parliaments of New Democracies: The Experience of the Federal Assembly of the Czech and Slovak Federal Republic' in Attila

Ágh (ed.), *The Emergence of East Central European Parliaments: The First Steps*, Budapest, Hungarian Centre for Democracy Studies.

Olson, David and Philip Norton (eds) (1996) *The New Parliaments of Central and Eastern Europe*, (with their Introduction, 'Legislatures in Democratic Transition'), London: Frank Cass.

OMRI (1996) *Building Democracy: The OMRI National Survey of Eastern Europe and the Former Soviet Union 1995*, London and New York: M.E. Sharpe.

O'Neil, Patrick (1996) 'Revolution from Within: Institutional Analysis, Transition from Authoritarianism, and the Case of Hungary', *World Politics* vol. 48, no. 4.

Pano, Nicholas (1992) 'Albania', in Joseph Held (ed.), *The Columbia History of Eastern Europe in the Twentieth Century*, New York: Columbia University Press.

Pestoff, Victor (1995) *Reforming Social Services in Central and Eastern Europe: An Eleven Nation Overview*, Cracow: Cracow Academy of Economics.

Plasser, Fritz and Andreas Pribersky (eds) (1996) *Political Culture in East Central Europe*, Aldershot: Avebury.

Plasser, Fritz and Peter Ulram (1996) 'Measuring Political Culture in East Central Europe. Political Trust and System Support', in Fritz Plasser and Andreas Pribersky (eds), *Political Culture in East Central Europe*, Aldershot: Avebury.

Potter, David, David Goldblatt, Margaret Kiloh and Paul Lewis (eds) (1997) *Democratization*, Cambridge: Polity Press.

Poznanski, Kazimierz (ed.) (1992) *Constructing Capitalism: The Reemergence of Civil Society and Liberal Economy in the Post-Communist World*, Boulder, CO: Westview Press.

Pridham, Geoffrey (ed.) (1990) *Securing Democracy: Political Parties and Democratic Consolidation in Southern Europe*, London and New York: Routledge.

Pridham, Geoffrey (ed.) (1991) *Encouraging Democracy: The International Context of Regime Transition in Southern Europe*, Leicester and London: Leicester University Press.

Pridham, Geoffrey (ed.) (1995) *Transitions to Democracy*, Aldershot: Dartmouth.

Pridham, Geoffrey and Paul Lewis (eds) (1996) *Stabilising Fragile Democracies*, London and New York: Routledge.

Pridham, Geoffrey and Tatu Vanhanen (eds) (1994a) *Democratization in Eastern Europe: Domestic and International Perspectives*, London and New York: Routledge.

Pridham, Geoffrey, Eric Herring and George Sanford (eds) (1994b) *Building Democracy? The International Dimension of Democratization in Eastern Europe*, London: Leicester University Press.

Przeworski, Adam (1991) *Democracy and the Market: Political and Economic Reforms in Eastern Europe and Latin America*, Cambridge: Cambridge University Press.

Pundeff, Marin (1992) 'Bulgaria', in Joseph Held (ed.), *The Columbia History of Eastern Europe in the Twentieth Century*, New York: Columbia University Press.

Pusic, Vesna (1994) 'Dictatorship with Democratic Legitimacy: Democracy versus Nation', *East European Politics and Society*, vol. 8, no. 3.

Ramet, Sabrina Petra (1995) *Social Currents in Eastern Europe: The Sources and Consequences of the Great Transformation*, Durham, NC and London: Duke University Press.

Remington, Thomas (ed.) (1994) 'Introduction' and 'Conclusion' in *Parliaments in Transition*, Boulder, CO: Westview Press.

Rose, Richard (1996) *What is Europe? A Dynamic Perspective*, New York: Harper Collins College Publishers.

Roskin, Michael (1994) *The Rebirth of East Europe*, Englewood Cliffs, NJ: Prentice-Hall.

Rothschild, Joseph (1974) *East Central Europe between the Two World Wars*, Seattle, WA and London: University of Washington Press.

Rupnik, Jacques (1989) *The Other Europe*, London: Weidenfeld and Nicolson.

Rustow, Dankwart (1970) 'Transitions to Democracy: Toward a Dynamic Model', *Comparative Politics*, vol. 3 (April).

Sartori, Giovanni (1976) 'A Typology of Party Systems', in Peter Mair (ed.) (1990) *The West European Party System*, Oxford: Oxford University Press.

Schmitter, Philippe (1995) 'The Consolidation of Political Democracies' in G. Pridham (ed.), *Transitions to Democracy*, Aldershot: Dartmouth.

Schmitter, Philippe and Terry Karl (1992) 'The Types of Democracy Emerging in Southern and Eastern Europe and South and Central America', in Peter Volten (ed.), *Bound to Change: Consolidating Democracy in East Central Europe*, New York and Prague: Institute for East West Studies.

Schöpflin, George (1993) *Politics in Eastern Europe, 1945–1992*, Oxford: Blackwell.

Selbourne, David (1990) *Death of the Dark Hero: Eastern Europe, 1987–90*, London: Jonathan Cape.

Seroka, Jim (1993) 'Yugoslavia and its Successor States', in Stephen White, Judy Batt and Paul Lewis (eds), *Developments in East European Politics*, Durham: Duke University Press.

Seton-Watson, Hugh (1982) *Eastern Europe Between the Wars, 1918–1941*, Boulder, CO and London: Westview Press.

Shafir, Michael (1997) 'Romania's Road to ' "Normalcy" ', *Journal of Democracy*, vol. 8, no. 2.

Slomczynski, Kazimierz and Goldie Shabad (1997) 'Systemic Transformation and the Salience of Class Structure in East Central Europe', *East European Politics and Societies*, vol. 11, no. 1.

Smith, Gordon (1983) *Politics in Western Europe*, London: Heinemann.

Staniszkis, Jadwiga (1991) *The Dynamics of the Breakthrough in Eastern Europe: The Polish Experience*, Berkeley, CA: University of California Press.

Swain, Nigel (1993) 'Hungary', in Stephen White, Judy Batt and Paul Lewis (eds), *Developments in East European Politics*, Durham, NC: Duke University Press.

Szajkowski, Bogdan (ed.) (1991) *New Political Parties of Eastern Europe and the Soviet Union*, Harlow: Longman.

Szelényi, Iván (1995) *The Rise of Managerialism: The 'New Class' After the Fall of Communism*, Collegium Budapest Discussion Paper Series, Paper No. 16 (November).

Szomolányi, Sonja and Grigorij Meseznikov (eds) (1995) *Slovakia: Parliamentary Elections 1994*, Bratislava: Slovak Political Science Association.

Tôkés, Rudolf (1996) *Hungary's Negotiated Revolution: Economic Reform, Social Change and Political Succession*, Cambridge: Cambridge University Press.

Tymowski, Andrzej (1993) 'The Unwanted Social Revolution', *East European Politics and Societies*, vol. 7, no. 2.

Van Ham, Peter (1995) *The EC, Eastern Europe and European Unity: Discord, Collaboration and Integration since 1947*, London and New York: Pinter Publishers.

Verney, Susannah (1990) 'To Be or Not to Be within the European Community', in G. Pridham (ed.), *Securing Democracy: Political Parties and Democratic Consolidation in Southern Europe*, London and New York: Routledge.

Volten, Peter (ed.) (1992) *Bound to Change: Consolidating Democracy in East Central Europe*, New York and Prague: Institute for East West Studies.

Vuylsteke, Richard (1995) 'Third Wave Democracies: Building Democratic Staying Power', *Free China Review* (Taipei), vol. 20, no. 11, November.

Waller, Michael (1993) *The End of the Communist Power Monopoly*, Manchester and New York: Manchester University Press.

Waller, Michael (ed.) (1995) *Party Politics in Eastern Europe* (a special issue of *Party Politics*), vol. 1, no. 4.

Waller, Michael, Bruno Coppieters and Kris Deschouwer (eds) (1994) *Social Democracy in a Post-Communist Europe*, London: Frank Cass.

White, Stephen, Judy Batt and Paul Lewis (eds) (1993) *Developments in East European Politics*, Durham, NC: Duke University Press.

Wiarda, Howard (1989) *The Transition to Democracy in Spain and Portugal*, Washington, DC: American Enterprise Institute for Public Policy Research.

Wightman, Gordon (1993) 'The Czech and Slovak Republics', in Stephen White, Judy Batt and Paul Lewis (eds), *Developments in East European Politics*, Durham, NC: Duke University Press.

Wightman, Gordon (ed.) (1995) *Party Formation in East-Central Europe: Post-Communist Politics in Czechoslovakia, Hungary, Poland and Bulgaria*, Aldershot: Edward Elgar.

Wightman, Gordon and Sonja Szomolányi (1995) 'Parties and Society in Slovakia', *Party Politics*, vol. 1, no. 4.

Wolchik, Sharon (1992), 'Czechoslovakia', in Joseph Held (ed.), *The Columbia History of Eastern Europe in the Twentieth Century*, New York: Columbia University Press.

Woo-Cumings, Meredith and Michael Loriaux (eds) (1993) *Past as Prelude: History in the Making of a New World Order*, Boulder, CO: Westview Press.

Wyman, Matthew, Stephen White, Bill Miller and Paul Heywood (1995) 'The Place of "Party" in Post-Communist Europe', *Party Politics*, vol. 1, no. 4.

Zajc, Drago (1994) 'The Foundations of Parliamentary Coalitions in Slovenia', in Attila Ágh (ed.), *The Emergence of East Central European Parliaments: The First Steps*, Budapest, Hungarian Centre for Democracy Studies.

Zakosek, Nenad (1994) 'The Croatian Parliament during the Period of Democratic Transition' in Attila Ágh (ed.), *The Emergence of East Central European Parliaments: The First Steps*, Budapest, Hungarian Centre for Democracy Studies.

Zubek, Voytek (1994) 'The Reassertion of the Left in Post-communist Poland', *Europe-Asia Studies*, vol. 46, no. 5.

Zubek, Voytek (1995) 'The Phoenix out of Ashes: The Rise to Power of Poland's Post-Communist SdRP', *Communist and Post-Communist Studies*, vol. 28, no. 3.

Yanov, Alexander (1987) *The Russian Challenge and the Year 2000*, Oxford: Blackwell.

Index